Dorothy Arzner: Interviews

Conversations with Filmmakers Series
Gerald Peary, General Editor

DOROTHY ARZNER
INTERVIEWS

Edited by Martin F. Norden

University Press of Mississippi / Jackson

The University Press of Mississippi is the scholarly publishing agency of
the Mississippi Institutions of Higher Learning: Alcorn State University,
Delta State University, Jackson State University, Mississippi State University,
Mississippi University for Women, Mississippi Valley State University,
University of Mississippi, and University of Southern Mississippi.

www.upress.state.ms.us

The University Press of Mississippi is a member
of the Association of University Presses.

Copyright © 2024 by University Press of Mississippi
All rights reserved

∞

Library of Congress Cataloging-in-Publication Data

Names: Norden, Martin F., 1951–2023 editor.
Title: Dorothy Arzner : interviews / Martin F. Norden.
Other titles: Conversations with filmmakers series.
Description: Jackson : University Press of Mississippi, 2024. | Series: Conversations
    with filmmakers series | Includes bibliographical references and index.
Identifiers: LCCN 2023028680 (print) | LCCN 2023028681 (ebook) |
    ISBN 9781496848253 (hardback) | ISBN 9781496848260 (trade paperback) |
    ISBN 9781496848277 (epub) | ISBN 9781496848284 (epub) | ISBN 9781496848291 (pdf) |
    ISBN 9781496848307 (pdf)
Subjects: LCSH: Arzner, Dorothy, 1900–1979—Interviews. | Women motion picture producers
    and directors—United States—Interviews. | Women in the motion picture industry—
    United States—20th century. | Motion picture producers and directors—United States—
    Interviews. | Motion pictures—Production and direction—United States.
Classification: LCC PN1998.3.A763 A5 2024 (print) | LCC PN1998.3.A763 (ebook) |
    DDC 791.4302/33092 [B]—dc23/eng/20230831
LC record available at https://lccn.loc.gov/2023028680
LC ebook record available at https://lccn.loc.gov/2023028681

British Library Cataloging-in-Publication Data available

For Kevin Brownlow

Contents

Introduction   xi

Chronology   xxv

Filmography   xxxv

Leave Sex Out, Says Director   3
 Grace Kingsley / 1927

Camera!   7
 Enid Griffis / 1928

Do Ladies Prefer Brunettes?   11
 Frederick Isaac / 1928

Only Woman Director   14
 Mayme Ober Peake / 1928

"Dot" Arzner Proves Talker Ability   21
 Howard Hall / 1929

Hollywood's One Woman Director   23
 Washington (DC) *Evening Star* / 1929

Directed by Dorothy Arzner!   28
 Julie Lang / 1929

Custom Restricts Women   32
 Elena Boland / 1930

Hard for Girl to Become Film Director, Dorothy Arzner Says   34
 Jessie Henderson / 1930

Woman Movie Picture Director   36
     Eileen Creelman / 1930

Meeting Miss Dorothy Arzner, Screen's Only Woman Director   39
     Marguerite Tazelaar / 1930

She Thanks Her Lucky Stars   42
     Dora Albert / 1931

The Secret of Personality   46
     Dorothy Arzner / 1931

Do You Want a Studio Job?   48
     Mabel Duke / 1931

Clara Bow to Recover Fame, Director Says   51
     Duane Hennessy / 1931

How to Become a Woman Director   53
     Dorothy Arzner / 1932

"Get Me Dorothy Arzner!"—Samuel Goldwyn   56
     Adela Rogers St. Johns / 1933

Clothes Do Not Make the Stars   63
     Alice Tildesley / 1933

Silk Underwear Feelings and Nail Polish Effects   66
     Philadelphia Inquirer / 1934

Women Directors Are the Outlook, Says the Only One   68
     Marguerite Tazelaar / 1936

Woman among the Mighty   70
     New York World-Telegram / 1936

The Screen's Only Woman Director   73
     Marky Dowling / 1936

Would You Be Master of Your Fate?   75
    Alice Tildesley / 1937

Hilltop Tenant: Dorothy Arzner Thus Looks at Films with a Clear Eye   79
    Grace Wilcox / 1937

Woman Film Director Needs Tact   83
    Alma Whitaker / 1937

A Woman's Touch   85
    Pauline Gale / 1937

Woman Director!   88
    Jackie Martin / 1937

Starlight   93
    Dorothy Arzner / ca. 1965

Dorothy Arzner 1970 Interview   96
    Kevin Brownlow / 1970

Approaching the Art of Arzner   115
    Francine Parker / 1973

The Best Love Story on the Screen   121
    Charles Higham / 1974

Dorothy Arzner Interview   123
    Gerald Peary and Karyn Kay, with Joseph McBride / 1974

Film Director Dorothy Arzner: Tribute to an Unsung Pioneer   135
    Mary Murphy / 1975

Famous Filmmaker Is No Feminist   138
    John Hussar / 1975

Interview with Director Dorothy Arzner   141
    Kevin Brownlow / 1977

Dorothy Arzner   157
    Boze Hadleigh / 1978

Appendix: The Unfinished Autobiography of Dorothy Arzner   169
    Dorothy Arzner / 1955

Index   203

Introduction

One of the widespread beliefs about film director Dorothy Arzner (1897–1979) is that she disliked talking with reporters and seldom gave interviews. As readers of this book will discover, though, this general assumption is only partially true. Arzner did refuse to discuss her private life, perhaps believing that any public acknowledgment of her long-term relationship with choreographer Marion Morgan would lead to discriminatory repercussions in LGBTQ+-phobic Hollywood. However, Arzner was usually willing to discuss other aspects of her life, such as her childhood in Los Angeles, early years in the film business, and status as one of the very few women to direct feature films during Hollywood's Golden Age. She granted more than thirty interviews during her career and in retirement, and they form the core of this book.

The bulk of Arzner's published conversations took place during the late 1920s and 1930s, her prime years as a director. Prior to that time, she had labored in relative obscurity as a script typist, script continuity supervisor (a script clerk, in the language of the day), editor, and screenwriter. Reporters occasionally noted this ambitious young woman's accomplishments, such as her masterful editing of *The Covered Wagon* (1923) and *Old Ironsides* (1926), but did not take the next step and actually interview her.

The situation changed dramatically after Arzner signed a contract in late 1926 to direct films for Famous Players-Lasky, later known as Paramount Pictures. Soon thereafter, and much to her chagrin, she attracted the attention of numerous interview-seeking reporters. Many were women eager to highlight the successes of Arzner, the first woman to direct a string of Hollywood films since Lois Weber. The interviews steadily increased as Arzner took her place alongside such directorial peers as Cecil B. DeMille, John Ford, Frank Capra, George Cukor, Ernst Lubitsch, and Josef von Sternberg during the studio era. The number of interviews dropped precipitously during and immediately after the final stages of her Hollywood career, but they surged again in the 1970s after she had been rediscovered by film historians, feminists, and others interested in this rare woman director who had prospered in the American film industry. Though the 1970s interviews are fewer than the ones from the 1920s and '30s, they are much longer, more in-depth, and, of course, highly retrospective.

Arzner often proved a challenge for interviewers wishing to spread the word about her work. During her active studio years, she showed hardly any interest in discussing her previous films and their potential legacy. "As far as I am concerned, they are ancient history," she told Marky Dowling in 1936. Speaking with Alice Tildesley on the same topic the following year, Arzner used one of her most successful films as a case in point: "The latest picture of mine—*Craig's Wife*—happens to be a hit, but why should I talk about it and think about it now? It's finished. I'm through with it. There is nothing more I can do about it, so why should I dwell on it?"

She was even less interested in talking about herself. She took self-effacement to extraordinary levels in Hollywood, a place where modesty and demureness are as rare as snowstorms in Death Valley. "What am I going to do with you? You're not giving me anything to write about!" complained interviewer Jackie Martin, to whom a bemused Arzner replied, "Well, just say: 'There is nothing to say about Dorothy Arzner.'" Martin's lament echoed previously expressed sentiments in the press. In a photo caption for her 1931 interview with Arzner, for example, Dora Albert wrote that "she won't talk about herself but she'll rave about the stars she has guided to success." Simply put, Arzner saw no need for self-promotion.

Arzner's reticence peaked in December 1936 following an interview experience that went strangely awry. Chatting with a *Los Angeles Times* reporter about her early studio experiences, she mentioned a special Christmas present she had received after joining Famous Players-Lasky as a typist in 1919. Her supervisor had given her a pair of elegant gold cufflinks that bore her initials, and Arzner was so taken with the unexpected gift that she wore the cufflinks every day on the job for years. According to the published story, however, she collected unusual cufflinks and had more than a hundred pairs. This gaffe greatly upset Arzner, concerned that the public and her colleagues might see her as extravagant, eccentric, or both. She told Kevin Brownlow that she did not "want to have anything to do with people who interviewed me anymore" after this bit of slipshod reportage. Though she did speak with several reporters the following year, the number of interviews went into a steep decline soon thereafter.

Arzner's reluctance to discuss her film career extended well into her retirement years. "It is a life that I have rather closed the book on," she informed Brownlow in 1967. "I do not deal in the past except as it applies to the present. So, I find it hard to talk about my beginnings." She told him that "many people have tried to persuade me to write [a memoir], but I haven't the time or patience to go into my past. It's an ordeal for me to call it up. I'm just not interested in doing it. It bores me to talk about myself."[1] As revealed in Francine Parker's interview, Arzner maintained this perspective into the final decade of her life. She was having lunch with Parker at a restaurant in La Quinta, California, in 1973 when a waiter whom Arzner knew asked when she was going to write her life story. Her terse reply: "Never."

Arzner had actually started writing an autobiography in 1955 and gotten as far as discussing her childhood and young adulthood before abandoning the project. A family with whom she had become close, the Sumners, inherited the unfinished manuscript upon her death in 1979. It sat in their files for decades until they gave it to University of Arizona professor David Soren, who published it in 2010. The autobiographical fragment is a richly detailed account of Arzner's early life in San Francisco and Los Angeles and her relationships, mostly familial, during those years. It does not mention her youthful thespian experiences or the time she nearly fell into an active volcano,[2] but it covers many other pivotal moments in her young life—such as her family's escape from the San Francisco earthquake—and concludes with a discussion of her job as a script typist for Famous Players-Lasky. This major first-person account is included in *Dorothy Arzner: Interviews* as an appendix.

Though Arzner never revisited her autobiographical project, she changed her mind about interviewers after film historians, students, and feminists rediscovered her in the 1970s. She sounded dismissive of all the new attention ("I've gotten more calls since this women's lib stuff began," she told Gerald Peary in 1974),[3] but she did grant at least ten in-person, telephone, or correspondence-based interviews during the 1970s. Most are included in this book.

Throughout the years, Arzner's interviewers provided fascinating observations about this lone woman director. For example, Mayme Ober Peak, an early interlocutor, wrote, "If you could have seen her the day I interviewed her at Paramount Studios swinging down the concrete walk of the big lot, planting her tan oxfords firmly with each step, shoulders and head up, cool gray eyes alert, you would have recognized the surefire qualities that make for success." Julie Lang offered a more subdued verbal sketch, finding her a "quiet-voiced, dreamy-eyed girl . . . gracious without any studied effects with which to impress new acquaintances." Jessie Henderson enthused that Arzner "packs more ideas into five minutes' chat than the average author puts into a book." Adela Rogers St. Johns observed "an air of quiet and control about her that suggests complete command of herself and of everything about her, but it is never a passive quiet. And, in spite of it, you feel a strong emotional force and one of the keenest intellects you had ever encountered."

Arzner's latter-day interviewers had similarly strong impressions. Kevin Brownlow, who corresponded with her in the 1960s and interviewed her twice in the 1970s, wrote, "I was in awe of her. She had the kind of reserve and dignity that one might associate with a distinguished Oxford historian—certainly not with a Hollywood film director. She was hard to relax with, as a result, and she made you very aware that you could not treat her as a casual acquaintance." Francine Parker characterized her as "small, vibrant, gentle, devilish, very pretty, her eyes a sparkly blue and gleefully electric, her voice soft and slow and warm, no put-on, very much unremote, though perhaps too modest for a one time 'Top Ten' Hollywood director." Charles Higham, who interviewed Arzner in 1974 for his Katharine Hepburn biography, found her "Gertrude Steinish, sweet-natured, living in a coolly elegant house in the middle of a desert." Boze Hadleigh, who conducted a telephone interview with Arzner in 1978, wrote that she was "soft-spoken and seemed careful and pensive" and "sounded more like the confident but unassuming college instructor she became after the celluloid disintegrated."[4]

Arzner carefully controlled the topics she was willing to discuss. The tale she told most often by far was her introduction to the movie business. Variations on this narrative, which centered on a crucial if somewhat humbling meeting with William de Mille in 1919, appear in the Kingsley, Peak, Lang, Duke, and Wilcox interviews, and many others, and it figures prominently in the autobiographical fragment. As readers will discover, the details of this story change significantly over time.

A narrative that reaches back even further into her personal history centers on The Hoffman, a Los Angeles café run by her father Ludwig "Louis" Arzner during the early twentieth century. The Hoffman, famed for its German and Hungarian dishes, was a favorite hangout for movie pioneers such as Charles Chaplin, Tom Moore, and William S. Hart. Arzner, a child at the time, was not especially impressed with the clientele. "D. W. Griffith, Mary Pickford, Mabel Normand, Mack Sennett, and all the rest of them used to eat at my dad's restaurant, and seeing actors was not particularly interesting to me," she wrote in her unfinished autobiography. She mentioned her childhood experiences at the café in the Peak, Parker, Peary/Kay, and second Brownlow pieces, and numerous other interviewers highlighted them as well.

A Hoffman regular was producer-director James Cruze, for whom Arzner later worked as an editor and screenwriter. She discussed Cruze's profound influence on her in the Kingsley, Peak, Lang, and Peary/Kay interviews, both Brownlow conversations, and others. "I owe him a tremendous lot," Arzner told Kingsley. "He always treated me as though I were his son, without any frills but with a sort of comradely friendship."

Cruze encouraged his protégée to become a director, but the specific circumstances that led to her promotion are somewhat murky. Arzner told Eileen Creelman that the process was simple; after she announced her plans to leave Famous Players to pursue directing opportunities at another studio, *Old Ironsides* colleague Laurence Stallings convinced an unnamed FP executive to hire her as a director. In 1928, Arzner informed Lillian Genn that the executive was Jesse Lasky and even recalled what she supposedly said to him: "There are some women who are suited for men's jobs and others who are not. I am one who is. And if you don't believe me, give me a trial." The following year, however, she told Julie Lang that the Famous Players' bigwig was B. P. Schulberg, not Lasky. Adding to the confusion, Enid Griffis reported that Stallings and Cruze, not Stallings alone, approached Lasky about hiring Arzner, and neither she nor Lang acknowledged Arzner's announced plan to bolt the studio. Schulberg is nowhere to be found in Griffis's rendering of the critical meeting, but his children, Budd and Sonya, claimed years later that their mother Adeline had urged him to award Arzner a directing contract.[5]

Arzner had mixed feelings about reaching the top of the moviemaking hierarchy. When Griffis asked her in 1928 how it felt to be a director, she replied, "It was hardly a thrill to me when I reached that point. The long, gradual, slow process of seven years of hard work was too continuous in struggles for me to feel that I had been suddenly projected into a realization of my dreams." However, she struck a different note in a *Sound Waves* interview the following year: "When Jesse L. Lasky gave me the chance to direct Clara Bow in a talking production [*The Wild Party*], I believe I was even more thrilled than the day when, several years ago, he gave me a contract to direct *Fashions for Women*." The state of being thrilled, it seems, is relative.

Most interviewers mentioned *Fashions for Women*, her 1927 breakthrough film as a director, and she offered brief comments on it in the Griffis, Hall, Peary/Kay, Hussar, Brownlow, and *Washington Evening Star* interviews. Things did not go as smoothly as she had hoped on this first project. She told a reporter that "I took the assignment and found out promptly what the word 'headache' really meant. Every night, after we finished the day's shooting, I was ready to quit." In addition, Arzner found herself in the awkward position of having to defend the intelligence of the young women who played mannequins in the film. "Anyone who thinks obtuseness goes with beauty like ham with eggs is all moist," she declared shortly after the film opened. "In fact, I think beauty is a companion of mental cleverness. The fifteen girls finally selected are unusually bright. Several of them are college graduates. And none of the fifteen could come under the 'dumb' classification. They're all mentally alert, well read, well bred, and a type that might fit into any society group." Despite the various challenges that went with her initial film, or perhaps because of them, Arzner took great pride in its eventual success. "It was a best seller," she told Brownlow. "There was a board just as you entered the Paramount lot, and opposite the name of the picture, there was a gold star placed every week [to indicate] that the picture was top box office. Well, *Fashions for Women* seemed to stay there for some time."[6]

Arzner relished the opportunity to discuss specific actors and did so in the Albert, Duke, Hennessy, Higham, Wilcox, Tildesley, Martin, Peary/Kay, and Hadleigh interviews, among others. She occasionally mentioned performers with whom she wanted to have worked but never did, such as Greta Garbo, Marlene Dietrich, and Maurice Chevalier, but she was most interested in chatting about players with whom she collaborated multiple times. High on her list were Ruth Chatterton, Fredric March, and Clara Bow. Arzner treated Bow as a special case, if only because of the performer's difficulties during the early days of sync-sound film. In 1976, forty-five years after expressing her concerns about Bow to Duane Hennessy, she expanded on them to Guy Flatley. Bow, she said, "was a darling child, and she was thrown to the wolves. She was a vivacious, hair-trigger silent actress with a marvelous variety of expressions, but when the talkies came in, they just threw her right in, and the poor child stuttered all the way through *The Wild Party*. Oh, you wouldn't believe what the studios did to young people in those days."[7]

Arzner's interest in actors extended to such considerations as their costuming and the symbolic value of their hair color, topics that arose in talks with Isaac, Gale, Tildesley, and Brownlow. She asserted to Tildesley that costuming mattered little for certain charismatic performers, yet she clearly understood its importance. As Sylvia Sidney, star of Arzner's *Merrily We Go to Hell* (1932), said: "Dorothy doesn't care about clothes for herself, but she has a great appreciation of their dramatic values."[8]

Arzner saw filmmaking as a highly collaborative enterprise that depended on the contributions of actors, screenwriters, costume designers, and other production personnel. For example, she told a *New York World-Telegram* reporter that, unlike most directors, she preferred to have screenwriters with her on the set. Not surprisingly, a few interviews contain what could be construed as anti-*auteurist* perspectives. For instance, she told Alma Whitaker that "I always feel that the writer is the real creator, far more important than actors or directors, and I regard myself as just a translator."

Arzner's strong belief in collaboration extended to the way she comported herself on the set. Unlike many directors who bellowed orders during a shoot, she never raised her voice to cast and crew; instead, she preferred to talk things over quietly with them in the manner of Frank Capra, an important role model. Arzner was quite aware of her low-key demeanor and occasionally regretted it. As she told Whitaker, "I wish I could cultivate a more authoritative manner and wasn't afraid of hurting people's feelings. I'd love to be able to snap 'Out!' without being tactful when something displeases me."

It would be a mistake to assume, however, that Arzner was willing to minimize or relinquish her executive role as director. Her comments on filmmakerly authority, control, and independence, offered in her autobiography and interviews with Brownlow, Hadleigh, Hussar, and others, make her position clear. She summed up her views to reporter George Gent, noting that if "you know your business and know you have authority, you *have* the authority."[9] She had put this observation to the test in 1936 while negotiating with the famously abrasive president of Columbia Pictures, Harry Cohn. In a 1976 talk with Molly Haskell, Arzner vividly characterized her back-and-forth with Cohn over *Craig's Wife*:

> I had to fight to do it. I got my way because I was independent. I had a father who stood behind me and said I could leave the picture business anytime I wanted to. This gave me a security. This, and the box office—always the box office—gave me the security I needed. I had it, I had confidence, and I needed every ounce of it. Harry Cohn was always testing you. "This stinks," he would say. "No, it doesn't, Harry," you would answer, "and you better star Rosalind Russell in this." He thought she was awful. "Then I guess you don't want me to direct," you say. So he gives in. Then he says, "OK, I'm not coming on the set." "That's just fine," you answer. That kind of independence convinces them, because they're dependent on the director.[10]

Arzner revealed a far different side to her thinking while discussing the intertwined topics of philosophy, religion, and spirituality with Peak, Henderson, Boland, Martin, and others. She informed Marguerite Tazelaar that she was reading Plato, a point that may have prompted a *Vanity Fair* writer to conclude that Arzner was an authority on platonic philosophy. In the early 1970s, Arzner told Marjorie Rosen that she was "led by the grace of God to the movies," a view that echoed thoughts expressed in earlier interviews. She suggested to Peak in 1928 that film would become "the most spiritual medium" that we have, and she opined to Henderson two years later that "all roads lead to God." It is probably no coincidence that Arzner showed high interest in directing films with overtly religious themes—*The Great Commandment, Day of Grace, Mrs. Eddy*—late in her Hollywood years, though she ultimately made none of them.[11]

"Starlight," which Arzner wrote while a filmmaking instructor at the University of California Los Angeles, is an intriguing addition to this cluster of interviews. For it, she drew upon what is now known as chaos theory to support an argument about the influence of movies on people's lives. She concluded the essay by suggesting that filmmakers "consider whether the film picture we are making carries in it some element which could make for greater love, consideration, and understanding between human beings. Have we the will, the understanding, the love to do it?" The "Starlight" essay shares a kinship with her 1937 interview with Jackie Martin, who wrote that Arzner described "her own calm philosophy, which is based on no particular religion or creed. A philosophy, the essence of which is kindness, gentleness, and a forgiving down to its very depths." Ever the pragmatist, Arzner had suggested how to put that philosophy into practice in her "Secret of Personality" piece published in *La Opinión* six years earlier.

A relatively rare topic, and rare only because it occurred years after Arzner's Hollywood retirement, is her experience as a filmmaking educator. With her teaching appointments at the Pasadena Playhouse College of Theatre Arts and UCLA in the 1950s and 1960s, she was at the forefront of industry professionals who changed the way that newcomers learned how to make movies. She discussed her pedagogical work at length with Brownlow in 1970 and briefly with Parker, Hussar, and Hadleigh.[12]

Arzner's most contentious statements are on gender-related issues. During her years as a director, she frequently claimed she did not experience any discrimination due to her gender. Her comments to Marguerite Tazelaar in 1930 are typical: "I have found no obstacles in my own progress made by men. I have had their entire cooperation, their willing assistance. I have been treated on equal terms with other directors." Perhaps believing that such utterances would help her stay in the good graces of the all-powerful studio heads, she seldom acknowledged anything resembling what we now call institutional sexism. As she told Tazelaar, "the things that hinder you in anything are within yourself, not in the world about you."

Arzner's related commentary on the shortage of women directors is just as problematic. When asked why so few women were directing films, she often suggested the women themselves were to blame. She opined that most lacked sufficient motivation, physical endurance, and analytical reasoning to succeed as directors. In a 1928 interview, for example, she was blunt in her assessment: "Women don't want to be directors. They would rather do something else, such as write or act. I always wanted to be a director and just worked along those lines." She told Jessie Henderson that "the single thing which holds women back at this stage from full opportunity with men is a matter of physical strength," adding that "just as, generally, they have not developed the habit of analytical thinking." She elaborated on this latter point in 1932: "Most men think analytically. Women rely on what they call intuition and emotion in the crisis, but those qualities do not help anyone at directing. A director must be able to reason things out in logical sequence." With a nod to her androgyny, she suggested in 1936 that most women did not possess the dispassionate qualities that she felt were necessary to thrive as film directors. "Directing calls for an impersonal handling of people and situations that most women can't achieve," she said. "Women, after all, are essentially emotional creatures. To the average woman, everything is personal. Directing pictures demands what are primarily masculine traits. I happen to have at least some of them."[13]

Despite Arzner's pointed criticisms of women, she did expect—and want—to see more of them as directors. "There's a great place for women in motion pictures," she said. "There should be more of us directing. Try as man may, he will never be able to get the woman's viewpoint in directing certain pictures. Many of these demand treatment at the hands of a woman." Though she was extremely reluctant to consider herself a role model and often said she did not think of herself as a woman when she directed, she stated that women bring a different and highly welcome set of perspectives and experiences to the filmmaking process. "There is no doubt that for certain subjects, a woman is better equipped to direct than a man," she said. "She has a depth of feeling which comes through on the screen." She elaborated on these and other gender-related issues in conversations with Peak, Boland, Henderson, and Hennessy, among others.[14]

Arzner was inconsistent in her public statements on certain topics, and her views on gender-based discrimination are a major case in point. As late as 1937, she continued to assert that gender prejudice did not exist in Hollywood. "A woman is given equal opportunity with men," she said. "It has been my experience that the industry is constantly searching for capable people and women alike are given the same consideration." By the 1950s and 1960s, however, when she was neither employed in Hollywood nor pursued by journalists, she may have felt she could speak more candidly on those rare occasions when she did meet with members of the press. Her comments to Bob Thomas in 1965 are telling: "I knew every picture had to be a good one or I would be through. Nobody really wanted a woman director. I had to prove myself with each picture."[15]

Lest readers think this simple acknowledgment represented Arzner's final say on the matter, she astonishingly reverted to her earlier position several years later. Once again at the center of not-especially-welcome attention, Arzner fell back on the argument that she had not encountered prejudice due to her gender. As she told George Gent in 1972, "I can't say I had any difficulties, certainly no more difficulties than the men had."[16]

Arzner's shifting perspective on gender discrimination is only one of several instances that suggest that she, like so many other celebrities, was not a particularly reliable narrator of her own history. Consider her retrospective views on the following topics and what we now know about them:

* In 1975, she told Mary Murphy that no studio ever let her walk away, yet Paramount did just that in 1932 after she refused to take a salary cut.
* While discussing *Fashions for Women*, Arzner mentioned to several 1970s interviewers that she had never told anyone how to do anything before. Before *Fashions*, though, she had trained a staff of film editors at Paramount's Realart subsidiary and directed Rudolph Valentino in several *Blood and Sand* retakes.

* She seemed to enjoy telling interviewers that playwright George Kelly had strongly objected to her sympathetic treatment of Harriet Craig in her adaptation of *Craig's Wife*. In a 1936 interview, however, Kelly offered solid praise for Arzner's film. He said it hewed closely and accurately to his Pulitzer Prize–winning play, telling Marguerite Tazelaar that "Dorothy Arzner did a very good job" with the adaptation.[17]
* She told the Peary-Kay team that she rejected an offer to become a major in the Women's Army Auxiliary Corps in 1943, saying she "never wanted to be in the Army." However, Colonel Jerome Sears wrote a long and enthusiastic letter about her to WAAC director Oveta Hobby in May 1943, noting that Arzner "is extremely interested in the possibility of becoming associated as a commissioned officer with the Women's Army Auxiliary Corps."[18]
* She informed Marjorie Rosen in 1972 that "I don't believe I ever asked for a job," yet, as a 1944 employment-seeking letter she wrote to Preston Sturges makes clear, she did.[19]

Such revisionism, while hardly unusual, is part of a larger Arzner-related concern; despite the sheer number of interviews, there is much we do not know about her. Among the significant gaps in her life story are her views on Hollywood folk other than actors. She often mentioned James Cruze and William de Mille while discussing her early career, but she had surprisingly little to say about such important collaborators as screenwriters Zoë Akins and Paul Gangelin, directors Donald Crisp and Robert Milton, and cinematographers Gregg Toland and George Folsey. She appreciated the value of costuming but did not utter a single word about Travis Banton, who designed the costumes for at least eight of her films. Despite her professed belief in the importance of screenwriters, she had nothing to say about such wordsmiths as Doris Anderson, Ethel Doherty, Edwin Justus Mayer, and Tess Slesinger, each of whom wrote or cowrote several scripts for her; indeed, Slesinger's son, Peter Davis, said he was unsure if his mother had even met Arzner.[20] In addition, Arzner often expressed her appreciation for Agnes Brand "Mike" Leahy's kindness when she broke in as a studio typist in 1919, yet she said nothing about Leahy's contributions to the *Get Your Man* screenplay in 1927.

Another informational lacuna is her reaction to the numerous false starts in her career. As revealed in this book's chronology, studios—principally Paramount—would often line her up to direct a certain film only to replace her with another director or cancel the film outright. Arzner likely found these actions disruptive, particularly regarding projects in which she was heavily invested, such as *Glorifying the American Girl* (1929) and *Stepdaughters of War* (1931). However, she rarely said anything to the press about being buffeted around so much. Her silence while employed in Hollywood is understandable—she was not about to provoke studio executives with publicly aired grievances—but she seldom touched on the issue, even in her retirement years. The following comment to Guy Flatley in 1976 is a rare instance: "I used to tell myself, 'I'm the only woman director, so I'd better not complain.'" Arzner had developed a simple workplace philosophy to cope with the uncertainties: approach each film one day at a time. "I make no plans for the future," she told a reporter in 1932. "I do not know today what I shall be doing tomorrow. And certainly, I have no time for regrets about yesterday. I believe in living for today, in doing the best I can today, and I know that that will prepare me for tomorrow."[21]

It is also unclear why Arzner stopped directing while in her mid-forties. During the making of *First Comes Courage* (1943), she contracted a case of pleurisy so severe that Columbia executive Harry Cohn had to replace her with another director, and she did not work in Hollywood again after that experience. When interviewers asked why she did not resume directing after her yearlong recovery, she typically gave rather vague answers. She told Bob Thomas that "after twenty-five years, I felt I wanted to be myself again. But also, the industry left me." She informed John Hussar that she left Hollywood because "I had had enough. Twenty years of directing is, I think, about enough." She told Mary Murphy that MGM president Louis Mayer's blackballing of her was the reason she left, but a few years later, she tantalized Boze Hadleigh by suggesting that "the true reason I retired from Hollywood may forever remain a secret, and I'd rather it does." She was in no hurry to clarify the circumstances surrounding her exit from the studios or even when that exit occurred. Most historians suggest that she retired after *First Comes Courage*, but as the chronology shows, she continued to look for directorial work throughout the 1940s. In 1951, Arzner and her partner Marion Morgan moved from their Hollywood home to La Quinta, a desert community more than 130 miles away, and it is reasonable to assume that their relocation marked the true beginning of Arzner's Hollywood retirement.

Arzner's life with Morgan represents the biggest void in our knowledge of her. Arzner and Morgan were in a committed relationship for about fifty years, but Arzner never publicly discussed it and remained guarded on the subject for the rest of her life. In the dozens of interviews examined for this book, she mentioned her partner only once, in passing and in a professional context; she told Kevin Brownlow in 1977 that "Marion Morgan, who was Marion Morgan, the dancer," loaned her dance troupe to Arzner for *Get Your Man*. Arzner and her interviewers apparently had an understanding that the details of her adult personal life were off-limits as topics. With one notable exception—Hadleigh, who tried to get her to say she was a lesbian—her interviewers seemed respectful of her privacy. However, some reporters occasionally tried to sidestep Arzner's informational embargo by employing phrases that strongly hinted at her sexuality. For instance, Alma Whitaker wrote that "Dorothy is the boyish type, wears her hair in a mannish cut, and favors men-tailored suits and low-heeled shoes." Tempering this verbal portrait, however, she added that Arzner "remains judiciously feminine." Whitaker's brand of journalistic equivocation was not unusual for the time.

As should be clear from the foregoing discussions, Arzner was a formidable gatekeeper of her life narrative; she freely shared some bits of information but kept an exceptionally tight grip on others. Nevertheless, a complex and fascinating portrait begins to emerge from her interviews, essays, and unfinished autobiography. By studying Arzner's public utterances—and reading between the lines of these utterances—we should be in a better position to understand and appreciate this remarkable filmmaker and her legacy.

Dorothy Arzner: Interviews was conceived during the depths of the COVID-19 pandemic, and I am grateful that so many people helped me during this trying time. My interlibrary loan colleagues at the University of Massachusetts Amherst's Du Bois Library deserve commendation, as do their counterparts at the Wilson Library, University of Minnesota-Twin Cities. Archivists and special-collection librarians to whom I am indebted include Genevieve Maxwell of the Margaret Herrick Library; Simon Elliott, Amy Wong, and Neil Hodge of the Special Collections staff at UCLA's Young Research Library; Jenny Romero, AMPAS Reference & Public Services Head; and Rebecca Baker, Susan Fitch, and Nicolette Bromberg of the University of Washington Libraries Special Collections. For helping me navigate through various electronic resources, I thank Mattie Sanseverino of UCLA's *Daily Bruin*, Susan Kimball of Amherst College's Frost Library, and Angela Watercutter of *Wired*.

For their assistance in acquiring reprint rights, I thank David Soren of the University of Arizona; Sally Sumner of Firehouse Pictures; Susan Svehla of Midnight Marquee Press; Ralph Drew of the *Los Angeles Times*; Terry McCarthy, CEO of the American Society of Cinematographers; Jovita Dominguez and Morgan Rumpf of the Directors Guild of America; Demetri Xistris and Lorraine Perkins of Riverdale Avenue Books; and independent scholar/filmmaker Gerald Peary, who serendipitously is also the general editor of UPM's Conversations with Filmmakers Series. I also wish to thank Judith Mayne, Shelley Stamp, Jane Gaines, Kiki Loveday, and Emily Bandy for their encouragement and support.

I would be criminally remiss if I did not acknowledge my indebtedness to Kevin Brownlow, film preservationist nonpareil and dean of silent era Hollywood historians. This remarkable colleague readily granted me permission to reprint two interviews he conducted with Arzner in the 1970s and shared everything he had in his extensive Arzner file, which included copies of his correspondence with her, an MGM director's file she had sent him, and an audio recording of her. It was as if an archive had come to me instead of the other way around. Words cannot express my deep and sincere gratitude for the help, generosity, and kindness shown to me by this giant among silent-era film chroniclers. I humbly stand on his shoulders.

MFN

Notes

Quotations taken from interviews reproduced in this book are not endnoted below.

1. Arzner, letter to Kevin Brownlow, April 25, 1967, Brownlow Collection, London.
2. As a teenager, Arzner played principal roles in stage productions of *Cinderella in Flowerland* and *Endymion*. See "School Children Prepare Parent-Teacher Playlet," *Los Angeles Herald*, April 19, 1911; and "Gaily Gowned Girls to Give *Endymion* at Hospital Benefit," *Los Angeles Herald*, December 14, 1914. For an account of her near-fatal fall into Kilauea while trying to take snapshots, see "Their Trip to Volcano Was Near Tragedy," *Rockford* (IL) *Star*, May 14, 1916.
3. Arzner quoted in Gerald Peary, "Dorothy Arzner: Reluctant Celebrity," *Boston Globe*, March 24, 1974.
4. Kevin Brownlow, letter to Evelyn Scott, May 21, 1980, Brownlow Collection; Charles Higham, *Kate: The Life of Katharine Hepburn* (New York: Norton, 1975), x; Boze Hadleigh, *Hollywood Lesbians: From Garbo to Foster* (Riverdale, NY: Riverdale Avenue Books, 2016), 97.
5. Arzner quoted in Lillian Genn, "Women Who've Won: Dorothy Arzner," *Brooklyn Daily Eagle*, August 17, 1928; Budd Schulberg, *Moving Pictures: Memories of a Hollywood Prince* (New York: Stein & Day, 1981), 319; Sonya O'Sullivan, "Producer as Auteur," *New York Times*, March 5, 2000.
6. Arzner quoted in "Dorothy Arzner Proves It's Not Entirely a Man's World," *Washington* (DC) *Sunday Star*, August 18, 1940, and in "Beauty Doesn't Mean 'Dumbness,'" *Brooklyn Daily Star*, May 25, 1927; Arzner, letter to Brownlow.
7. Arzner quoted in Guy Flatley, "At the Movies," *New York Times*, August 20, 1976.
8. Sidney quoted in Eileen Creelman, "Picture Plays and Players," *New York Sun*, June 9, 1932.
9. Arzner quoted in George Gent, "Women Filmmakers," *New York Times*, June 15, 1972.
10. Arzner quoted in Molly Haskell, "Women Directors," *American Film*, June 1976, 21.
11. "We Nominate for the Hall of Fame," *Vanity Fair*, October 1931, 73; Arzner quoted in Marjorie Rosen, *Popcorn Venus: Women, Movies & the American Dream* (New York: Coward, McCann & Geoghegan, 1973), 377.
12. For more on Arzner's post-Hollywood career as an educator, see Martin F. Norden, "Exploring the Work of Dorothy Arzner as a Film-Making Teacher in Southern California," *Film Education Journal* 5.2 (Fall 2022): 68–79.

13. Arzner quoted in Stanley Bailey, "Hollywood Film Shop," *Twin Falls* (ID) *Daily Times*, September 11, 1928; in "Feminine Director Depends on Reason, Discards Intuition," *New York Herald Tribune*, June 26, 1932; and in Jesse Spiro, "Woman Director," *Screen & Radio Weekly*, July 26, 1936.
14. Arzner quoted in "Other Gossip and Oddments of the Film Studios," *Brooklyn Daily Eagle*, May 29, 1932, and in "Miss Arzner on Women Directors," *Daily Argus* (Mount Vernon, NY), August 15, 1931.
15. Arzner quoted in "Arzner Gives Success Tips for Women," *Metro-Goldwyn-Mayer Studio News*, September 28, 1937, and in Bob Thomas, "In the Entertainment Circle," *Findlay* (OH) *Republican Courier*, June 26, 1965.
16. Arzner quoted in Gent.
17. Kelly quoted in Marguerite Tazelaar, "George Kelly, Who Knows Both, Talks of Stage and Film Craft," *New York Herald Tribune*, October 4, 1936.
18. Jerome Sears, letter to Oveta Hobby, May 29, 1943, "Women in the U.S. Military: Correspondence of the Director of the Women's Army Corps, 1942–1946, Part I: General and Financial Correspondence," Folder 095, Record Group 165, National Archives, College Park, MD.
19. Arzner quoted in Marjorie Rosen, "Women, Their Films, and Their Festival," *Saturday Review*, August 12, 1972, 34. Arzner's letter to Sturges is reproduced in *Letters from Hollywood: Inside the Private World of Classic American Filmmaking*, ed. Rocky Lang and Barbara Hall (New York: Abrams, 2019), 127.
20. Patrick McGilligan, "Frank Davis and Tess Slesinger—the Lives They Led: An Interview with Peter Davis," *Film International* 18, no. 3 (September 2020): 120.
21. Arzner quoted in Flatley and in "Woman Director Is Keen for Work," *Washington* (DC) *Evening Star*, May 24, 1932.

Chronology

In an effort to foster a better understanding of the ups and downs in Arzner's career, this chronology goes beyond a listing of her major life events and films to include her many announced film projects that were ultimately assigned to other directors or abandoned. Though these instances do not represent films she actually made, their sheer number says something about the vicissitudes of the Hollywood industry and the high levels of stress they doubtless caused.

1897   Born Dorothy Emma Arzner in San Francisco on January 3. She is the second of two children born to Ludwig Adolph "Louis" Arzner and Janet "Jennie" Young Arzner. Her father is a native of Karlsruhe, Baden-Württemberg, Germany, her mother of Glasgow, Lanarkshire, Scotland.

1902   Arzner's parents divorce. Her father wins custody of the children, and she never sees her mother again. Her father sets up a series of living arrangements for Arzner in San Francisco while he pursues work in Los Angeles.

1905   Her father marries Mabel Mills, who becomes stepmother to Arzner and her brother David.

1906   Living with Mills's mother, Arzner survives the San Francisco earthquake. Several weeks after the quake, her father brings her and other relatives back with him to Southern California. She is reunited with her brother and her stepmother in LA. For the next few years, she spends considerable time at her father's restaurant, the Hoffman Café. The Hoffman is a favorite among members of the fledgling film industry, and she begins learning about the business through their conversations.

1909   Her mother, who had remarried and been living in San Francisco, dies in November at age forty-seven.

1911   At age fourteen, she plays the quarrelsome character "Hollyhock" in a stage production of Marion Loder's operetta *Cinderella in Flowerland* at the Cambria St. School in LA.

1912   Her stepmother arranges for her to attend the Westlake School for Girls in LA.

1914	On December 15, she and about two dozen Westlake "society girls" perform in a stage production of the Greek play *Endymion*, held at LA's Gamut Club to benefit a local children's hospital.
1915	On June 9, she graduates from Westlake. She works briefly as a secretary for a friend of her father and then as a physician's assistant. In the fall, she enters the University of Southern California as a pre-med student and joins the USC rowing club as an extracurricular activity.
1916	In April, she visits Hawaii with two friends. She tries to take photographs of Kilauea, loses her footing, and nearly falls into the volcano before her friends rescue her. In June, her only sibling, David, dies at age twenty-four. She drops out of USC after completing one year.
1917	On October 13, she volunteers at a Red Cross fundraiser to benefit wounded French and Belgian soldiers. Nan Heron, who would later train Arzner as a film editor, is among the Hollywood women participating in the day-long fête.
1918	On January 26, Arzner participates in a military-themed charity ball in Pasadena. She joins the Los Angeles Emergency Drivers Corps, an organization led by Anna Starkweather and associated with the Drake Section Sanitaire. She hopes to drive an ambulance in France during World War I, but the war ends before she can travel to Europe.
1919	At Starkweather's urging, Arzner meets with William de Mille about employment at the Famous Players-Lasky studio. He offers to hire her once the company's stenographic department has an opening, and in the meantime, she takes a job as a filing clerk and switchboard operator at Joannes Brothers, a wholesale coffee distributor. Several weeks later, a Famous Players offer comes through, and she begins her film career as a typist. She prepares scripts written by others for several months. Late in the year, she tests the Hollywood employment waters by supervising script continuity on the independent Alla Nazimova production *Stronger Than Death*. Among her coworkers is Alice Guy-Blaché, an assistant director on the film. At the end of the year, Arzner returns to Famous Players-Lasky as a script continuity supervisor and assists Nan Heron with the editing of the Donald Crisp film, *Too Much Johnson*.
1920	Arzner edits her first film on her own: Crisp's *The Six Best Cellars*. She edits and "holds script" for numerous films for the studio and its Realart subsidiary over the next few years.

1921	She meets choreographer Marion Morgan while visiting a film set. Their encounter marks the beginning of a deep personal relationship that would last fifty years.
1922	Famous Players-Lasky assigns Arzner to edit the Rudolph Valentino vehicle *Blood and Sand*. She spends a day directing Valentino in a few bullfighting shots that help with her editing. The film premieres in August. Impressed by her *Blood and Sand* work, director James Cruze recruits her to edit his next film, *The Covered Wagon*. It is the first in a lengthy series of Cruze-Arzner collaborations.
1923	Filmed under difficult conditions, *The Covered Wagon* is released in March. That same month, Arzner travels with Cruze and an entourage to Famous Players-Lasky's Astoria studios in New York to shoot interior scenes for Cruze's next film, *Hollywood*. Later that year, she turns down an offer from Cruze to star in his film *To the Ladies*.
1924	Venturing from Famous Players-Lasky yet again, she edits several films for Universal and writes screenplays for Sam E. Rork Productions and Harry Garson Productions. She often collaborates with Paul Gangelin on her scripts.
1925	In January, actor and independent producer George Arthur offers her the chance to direct her first complete film, *Just Plain Buggs*, a low-budget comedy about motherhood. Arthur is unable to secure the necessary funding, and the project collapses. Later that year, she co-writes the script for *The Red Kimona*, produced by Dorothy Davenport. In December, she formally joins the scenario staff of James Cruze Productions, a unit of Famous Players-Lasky. She works under the supervision of Walter Woods, Cruze's principal screenwriter.
1926	She prepares the shooting script for Cruze's *Old Ironsides* and edits the film as well. *Old Ironsides* debuts in December. Later that month, she signs a directorial contract with Famous Players-Lasky. After briefly considering her for the directorship of *Ritzy*, an adaptation of Elinor Glyn's short story, the studio assigns her to direct *Fashions for Women*.
1927	*Fashions for Women* is released in March. Based on its success, Arzner signs a new contract with the studio in April. Her second film as director, *Ten Modern Commandments*, opens in July. Reports surface that Arzner will direct Esther Ralston in *The Glory Girl* and *Good Morning, Dearie*, but Arzner makes neither film. The press reports in August that Arzner has replaced Malcolm St. Clair as the director of *Red Hair*, to star Clara Bow. Arzner, in turn, is replaced by Clarence Badger. Joins the directors' branch of the Academy of Motion Picture

Arts and Sciences during the organization's inaugural year. In summer, Famous Players-Lasky assigns Arzner to direct *Glorifying the American Girl*. The company brings in more than two dozen writers to fix the screenplay, causing major delays. In December, *Film Daily* reports that she will direct Esther Ralston in *Devil May Care* for Universal. The project is dropped. *Get Your Man*, the first of two Arzner films with Clara Bow, is released that same month.

1928 Famous Players-Lasky, now called Paramount Pictures, loans Arzner to MGM in January to direct a film starring Lew Cody. Displeased with the film story given her, she returns to Paramount to direct the long-delayed *Glorifying the American Girl* but is soon removed from the project following creative differences with the studio. She is reassigned to direct *Just Married*, but that arrangement is scuttled.

In October, Paramount announces that Arzner will direct Buddy Rogers and Olga Baclanova in *Two Shall Meet* and Esther Ralston in *The Case of Lena Smith*. She makes neither film. In November, Louella Parsons reports that Arzner will direct Buddy Rogers in *Young Sinners*. The film is not made. *Manhattan Cocktail*, Arzner's fourth film as director, is released later that month. It is believed to be the first synchronous-sound feature film directed by a woman.

1929 In March, the press announces that Arzner is to direct Buddy Rogers and Mary Brian in *The Fighting Coward*, a remake of a film she edited for James Cruze in 1924. The film is reassigned to Richard Wallace. While making *The Wild Party* with Clara Bow, Arzner creates the film world's first boom microphone by attaching a mike to a fishing pole. The film debuts in April, and Arzner's sound-recording technique catches on in the industry. In May, *Film Daily* reports that *Illusion*, another film Arzner was scheduled to direct, has been reassigned to Lothar Mendes. Arzner codirects *Charming Sinners* with Broadway director Robert Milton. The film is released in August. In September, Paramount announces that Arzner and George Cukor will codirect *A Lady in Love* with Evelyn Brent and Clive Brook. This potential collaboration is abandoned.

1930 She completes her second codirected film with Robert Milton, *Behind the Make-Up*. The film premieres in January. Arzner and Marion Morgan move into a house in the hills overlooking Hollywood. In a playful riff on Mary Pickford and Douglas Fairbanks' home "Pickfair," they christen their new home "Armor." *Sarah and Son* opens in March. That same month, Louella Parsons reports that Arzner will direct *Grumpy*, starring Cyril Maude. The film is instead codirected by George Cukor and Cyril Gardner. In April, Paramount releases *Paramount on Parade*, an omnibus film that includes a sequence directed by Arzner, "The Gallows Song," featuring Broadway performer Dennis King. In May, the studio announces that Arzner will direct Ruth Chatterton in *The Right to Love*. In July, Louella Parsons reports that Arzner will instead direct Buddy Rogers in *Molinoff*. Arzner makes neither film. She instead completes *Anybody's Woman*, released in mid-August. In September, she travels to New York City to make films at Paramount's studio facility in Astoria. Paramount announces that Arzner will direct Claudette Colbert in *Strictly Business* and simultaneously codirect her in a French version of the same story. The French version is dropped, but Arzner directs *Strictly Business* under its new title, *Honor Among Lovers*.

1931 She returns to Hollywood and starts working with Ruth Chatterton on *Stepdaughters of War*, an adaptation of a 1930 novel by Helen Zenna Smith. Filming begins, but Paramount shuts down the production after Chatterton departs for Warner Bros. *Honor Among Lovers* is released in March. In July, the trade journal *Film Mercury* honors Arzner and star Claudette Colbert for their work on this film. In July, Paramount announces that Arzner will direct *Break-Up*, to star Sylvia Sidney. Arzner is instead assigned to *Working Girls*, which opens in December.

1932 *Merrily We Go to Hell*, her next film, premieres in June. The press announces that Arzner will direct *The Mirrors of Washington*, starring Tallulah Bankhead and Gary Cooper. This arrangement is abandoned. Refusing to take a salary cut during the next option period of her contract, Arzner departs Paramount in mid-summer. She finds employment at RKO Radio Pictures, where her first directorial gig is to be *The White Moth*, based on an original story by Zoë Akins and to star Ann Harding. By November, the *White Moth* project is dropped in favor of an adaptation of Gilbert Frankau's novel *Christopher Strong* with the same trio of Arzner, Akins, and Harding. In December, RKO producer David O. Selznick moves Harding to a different project and replaces her with relative newcomer Katharine Hepburn.

1933 RKO releases *Christopher Strong* in March. Arzner proposes to direct *Morning Glory*, which would reunite her with Akins and Hepburn, but the film's accelerated production schedule forces her to withdraw from consideration. In September, Samuel Goldwyn recruits Arzner to take over for George Fitzmaurice on the direction of *Nana*, a vehicle for Anna Sten.

1934   *Nana* opens in February. In May and June, the trade press reports that Jesse Lasky has signed Arzner to a Fox contract to direct *Romance for Sale* and *The Captive Bride*. Arzner makes neither film; in fact, she makes no films at all for Fox. In October, she signs a contract with Columbia Pictures as an associate producer and director. Her first project there is to be an adaptation of *Maid of Honor*, which would team her with *Sarah and Son* collaborators Ruth Chatterton and Zoë Akins. However, Columbia's Harry Cohn reassigns the direction to Marion Gering.

1935   In February, the press reports that her first film for Columbia as a producer-director will be an adaptation of I. A. R. Wylie's *A Feather in Her Hat*. The project instead goes to Alfred Santell. In March, she travels to Manhattan with Columbia casting director William Perlberg to search for new talent and conduct screen tests. She discovers Mary McCarthy's comic story "Theodora Goes Wild" and develops it as a property for Columbia.

1936   In March, *Variety* reports that Arzner is negotiating with RKO for a directorial contract. Meanwhile, she completes the Columbia production *Craig's Wife*, released to much acclaim in September. That same month, *Film Daily* reports that Arzner will direct Ginger Rogers in an RKO adaptation of *Mother Carey's Chickens*. MGM production head Irving Thalberg asks her to direct Greta Garbo in an unnamed film, but his death in September 1936 ends the potential Arzner-Garbo collaboration. *Theodora Goes Wild* is released in November.

1937   In mid-January, Arzner signs a contract to direct for MGM, making her unavailable for *Mother Carey's Chickens* at RKO. Following the untimely death of director Richard Boleslawski on January 17, MGM assigns the direction of his in-progress film—*The Last of Mrs. Cheyney*, starring Joan Crawford—to George Fitzmaurice. After Fitzmaurice falls ill, the studio turns the film over to Arzner. She completes it for release the following month. Her next project for MGM is an adaptation of Ferenc Molnar's unproduced play, *The Girl from Trieste*, to star Luise Rainer. By May, MGM has replaced Rainer with Joan Crawford and retitled the film *The Bride Wore Red*. Arzner does her own location scouting in the Sierra Nevada mountains for the film. Released in October, *The Bride Wore Red* is a box-office failure, forcing Arzner into a moviemaking hiatus that lasts several years. Despite her many successes, no studio will hire her.

1938   She becomes the first woman to join the Directors Guild of America and remains a lifelong member.

1939	In March, she directs a half-hour radio comedy-drama, *Tailored by Toni*, starring Carole Lombard, James Stewart, Edward Everett Horton, and Spring Byington. An installment in WABC/CBS's "Screen Guild Show," it is broadcast on Sunday, March 12. In July, she is in the running to direct *The Great Commandment* for Cathedral Films but drops out following a disagreement about the film's overly rapid shooting schedule. Arzner signs an agreement in September to direct *Angela Is Twenty-Two*, an adaptation of the play by Sinclair Lewis and Fay Wray. It is to be the initial film of Knickerbocker Pictures, a production unit within Columbia headed by John Wildberg and Jack Skirball. The arrangement collapses. Arzner joins the Hollywood Theatre Alliance, an organization made up of dozens of film industry denizens interested in producing stage productions that address current social issues.
1940	In the spring, Arzner begins work on an unnamed RKO film with an African American cast. She departs the unfinished project when RKO producer Erich Pommer hires her to replace Roy Del Ruth as director on *Dance, Girl, Dance*. The film is released in August. Officials of San Francisco's Golden Gate International Exposition select Arzner as one of twelve outstanding California women.
1941	She helps promote the work of "The Itinerants," a theatrical troupe made up of young people who recently graduated from Max Reinhardt's Los Angeles-based workshop. In July, columnist Hedda Hopper reports that Arzner has been in talks with Monogram executive Lew Lifton about developing a circus-themed film to be set in Arizona. The project is unrealized.
1942	In December, she begins work on *Commandos*, a Columbia production eventually retitled *First Comes Courage*.
1943	Production on the film comes to a halt in February after Arzner develops a serious case of pleurisy. She is unable to finish the film due to her illness, prompting Columbia to bring in another director, Charles Vidor, to shoot the remaining scenes. In June, the Women's Army Auxiliary Corps recruits Arzner to supervise the production of several training films. The following month, *First Comes Courage* is released.
1944	In May, Arzner asks Preston Sturges if he would consider her for any directorial openings at California Pictures Corp., a new company he founded with Howard Hughes, but the gambit fails. Later that month, Hedda Hopper reports that Arzner will direct a film for United Artists starring dancer/choreographer Katherine Dunham. The film is not made.

1945 On April 29 and for several months thereafter, she hosts a half-hour radio program, *You Were Meant to Be a Star* (sometimes listed as *You Were Born to Be a Star*), broadcast on Sundays over the Mutual Broadcasting System. The show involves West Coast performers enacting dramatizations of domestic difficulties such as "Jealousy" and "Suspicion," followed by solutions.

1948 In October, playwright Alexander Fedoroff asks screenwriter-producer Charles Brackett to read his new drama, *Day of Grace*, noting that Arzner has agreed to direct the movie version. The film is not made.

1949 Arzner is rumored to be Jesse Lasky's choice to direct a lavish Technicolor adaptation of Hugh Studdert Kennedy's *Mrs. Eddy*, a 1947 book based on the life of Christian Science founder Mary Baker Eddy. The project proves too controversial and is shelved. Joins the advisory board for Theatre-for-Children, Inc., in Los Angeles.

1950 Numerous trade journals note in May that Arzner will direct Billie Burke in a stage production of Zoë Akins' *Bright Shadow*, first in an out-of-town tryout and then on Broadway. The project is later abandoned.

1951 She and Marion Morgan move from their home in Hollywood to La Quinta, California. They live out the rest of their lives in this desert community. On June 8, she is the guest on *The Jeanne Gray Show*, a television talk show broadcast on CBS affiliate KTSL (now KCBS) in Los Angeles. That same month, she serves as associate producer for *The Swallows' Nest*, a play staged at the Pasadena Playhouse. The play reunites Arzner with longtime colleagues Robert Milton, Zoë Akins, and Billie Burke. The press reports in the fall that she is developing a television show for Burke.

1952 In August, she is appointed head of the television and motion picture department at the Pasadena Playhouse College of Theatre Arts.

1954 She serves as associate producer for the world premiere of *Mother Was a Bachelor* at the Pasadena Playhouse. Directed by Beatrice Hassel and starring Billie Burke, the play opens on November 11.

1958 In February, she signs on as a consultant with Kenyon & Eckhardt, an advertising agency, to direct television commercials for Pepsi-Cola. Joan Crawford, then married to Pepsi executive Alfred Steele, helps facilitate the arrangement. Working with cinematographer Clifford Stine in facilities provided by Universal-International, Arzner directs dozens of Pepsi commercials.

1959 Late in the year, Arzner is appointed as a film lecturer in UCLA's Theater Arts Department. She teaches directing and screenwriting and on the graduate level supervises film productions.

1964	She retires from full-time teaching at UCLA on July 1 but stays on another year in a post-retirement teaching capacity. Her father Louis dies at age ninety-seven on August 13 in Los Angeles.
1965	On July 1, she finalizes her UCLA retirement. By her estimate, she has supervised more than fifty student films.
1971	Her longtime companion Marion Morgan dies on November 10 at age ninety.
1972	In mid-June, *The Wild Party* is shown at the First International Festival of Women's Films in New York City, prompting a renewed interest in Arzner's work.
1974	She receives more attention after *The Wild Party* is screened at the "Women on Women" film festival, held in June at the American Cultural Center in Paris.
1975	The Directors Guild of America hosts a tribute to her in January.
1976	The Second International Festival of Women's Films, held in NYC in mid-September, features a four-film retrospective of her work: *Anybody's Woman*, *Christopher Strong*, *The Bride Wore Red*, and *Dance, Girl, Dance*.
1977	She is seriously injured in a car accident in La Quinta in February.
1979	She dies of undisclosed causes on October 1 at age eighty-two. Her body is cremated and her ashes scattered.
1986	She posthumously receives a star on the Hollywood Walk of Fame. She is the first woman director to be so honored.
2018	Paramount names a studio building after Arzner. Francis Coppola, one of her former UCLA students, is the main speaker at the dedication ceremony.

Filmography

The following filmography lists every production for which Arzner is known to have served as director, editor, screenwriter, script continuity supervisor, producer, advisor, or some combination thereof. She also worked as a script typist for several months in 1919, but the films based on such labor are unknown.

Anecdotal evidence suggests that Arzner participated in far more films than are listed here. Numerous sources, including several published in this book, claim that Arzner edited dozens of films for Famous Players-Lasky's Realart subsidiary, yet only one Realart film—*Miss Hobbs*—has been verified as of this writing. In addition, Arzner stated in 1944 that she edited all of James Cruze's films over a three-year period following *The Covered Wagon* (1923). If true, she would have cut at least ten Cruze-directed films beyond the ones listed in this filmography. It is quite likely that she edited such films as *Leap Year* (1924), *The Enemy Sex* (1924), and *Marry Me!* (1925), but they are not included in this filmography as her participation in them could not be corroborated by other sources. Nevertheless, there is little question that Arzner edited many films uncredited during the 1920s.

The films Arzner directed are far easier to ascertain, but even here, a number of productions are not included. As noted in this book's chronology, she supervised several training films for the Women's Army Auxiliary Corps in 1943 and dozens of Pepsi-Cola television commercials in the 1950s. None of these productions is listed here due to a lack of available information about them.

During her tenure as a filmmaking instructor at the Pasadena Playhouse College of Theatre Arts and UCLA, Arzner oversaw dozens of student films and occasionally received on-screen credit. A small sampling of the Pasadena Playhouse and UCLA student productions concludes this filmography.

Several filmography housekeeping notes: (1) The listings include alternative/working titles, corrected credits, and supplemental credits whenever such information could be verified. (2) If two companies are listed at the beginning of a listing (e.g., Famous Players-Lasky Corp./Paramount Pictures), the company listed to the left of the backslash was the production company of record, and the one to the right was the film's distributor. (3) Each film's running time is listed in reels, feet, and/or minutes, depending on available information. Generally speaking, a reel could hold up to about 1,000 feet of film and would run approximately twelve minutes.

TOO MUCH JOHNSON (1920)
Famous Players-Lasky Corp./Paramount Pictures
Presenter: Jesse Lasky
Producers: Adolph Zukor, Jesse Lasky. Director: Donald Crisp
Screenplay: Thomas Geraghty, from the play by William Gillette
Cinematography: Charles Edgar Schoenbaum
Editing: Nan Heron, **Dorothy Arzner**
Assistant Director: Frank Richardson
Cast: Bryant Washburn (Augustus Billings), Lois Wilson (Mrs. Billings), Adele Farrington (Mrs. Batterson), Clarence [Charles] Geldart (Joseph Johnson), Monte Blue (Billy Lounsberry), Monty Banks (Leon Dathis), Elsa Lorimer (Mrs. Dathis), Gloria Hope (Leonora Faddish), George Hackathorne (Henry McIntosh), Phil Gastrock (Francis Faddish)
5 reels/4,431 feet
Released January 4, 1920

STRONGER THAN DEATH (1920)
Nazimova Productions/Metro Pictures Corp.
Presenters: Maxwell Karger, Richard Rowland
Producers: Maxwell Karger, Alla Nazimova
Directors: Herbert Blaché, Charles Bryant, Robert Z. Leonard
Screenplay: Charles Bryant, from the novel *The Hermit Doctor of Gaya: A Love Story of Modern India* by Ida Alexa Ross Wylie
Cinematography: Rudolph Bergquist
Script Continuity: **Dorothy Arzner**
Assistant Director: Alice Guy-Blaché
Art Direction: Benjamin Carré
Cast: Alla Nazimova (Sigrid Fersen), Charles Bryant (Major Tristan Boucicault), Charles French (Colonel Boucicault), Margaret McWade (Mrs. Boucicault), Herbert Prior (James Barclay), William Orlamond (Reverend Mr. Meredith), Milla Davenport (Mrs. Smithers), Bhogwan Singh (Ayeshi), Henry Harmon (Vahana), Dagmar Godowsky
7 reels/70 minutes
Working Title: *The Hermit Doctor of Gaya*
Released January 11, 1920

THE SIX BEST CELLARS (1920)
Famous Players-Lasky Corp./Paramount-Artcraft Pictures
Presenter: Jesse Lasky
Producers: Adolph Zukor, Jesse Lasky
Director: Donald Crisp
Screenplay: Elmer Harris, from the novel by Holworthy Hall [pseudonym for Harold Everett Porter] and Hugh Kahler
Cinematographer: Charles Edgar Schoenbaum
Script Continuity and Editing: **Dorothy Arzner**
Assistant Director: Frank Richardson
Cast: Bryant Washburn (Henry Carpenter), Wanda Hawley (Millicent Carpenter), Clarence Burton (Ed Hammond), Elsa Lorimer (Mrs. Hammond), Josephine Crowell (Mrs. Teak), Frederick Vroom (Mr. Teak), Jane Wolfe (Virginia Jasper), Richard Wayne (H. Sturtevant Jordan), Julia Faye (Mrs. Jordan), Howard Gaye (Tommy Blair), Zelma Maja (Mrs. Blair), Parker McConnell (Harris), Ruth Ashby (Mrs. Harris), William Boyd (Holsapple), Olita Otis (Mrs. Holsappel), Allen Connor (Mr. McAllister), Lorie Larson (Mrs. McAllister), Clarence Geldart (Dr. Devine)
5 reels/4,822 feet
Released February 8, 1920

MISS HOBBS (1920)
Realart Pictures Corp.
Director: Donald Crisp
Screenplay: Elmer Harris, from a play by Jerome K. Jerome
Cinematography: Charles Edgar Schoenbaum
Script Continuity and Editing: **Dorothy Arzner**
Cast: Wanda Hawley (Miss Hobbs), Harrison Ford (Wolff Kingsearl), Helen Jerome Eddy (Beulah Hackett), Walter Hiers (George Jessup), Julianne Johnston (Millicent Farey), Emily Chichester (Alice Joy), Frances Raymond (Mrs. Kingsearl), Jack Mulhall (Percy Hackett)
5 reels/4,471 feet/60 minutes
Released May 19, 1920

THE EASY ROAD (1921)
Famous Players-Lasky Corp./Paramount Pictures
Director: Tom Forman
Screenplay: Beulah Marie Dix, from the story "Easy Street" by Hugh McNair Kahler
Cinematography: Harry Perry

Script Continuity and Editing: **Dorothy Arzner**
Assistant Director: Harold Schwartz
Assistant Camera: James Wong Howe
Cast: Thomas Meighan (Leonard Fayne), Gladys George (Isabel Grace), Grace Goodall (Katherine Dare), Arthur Edmund Carewe (Heminway), Lila Lee (Ella Klotz), Laura Anson (Minnie Baldwin), Viora Daniel (Laura)
5 reels/4,982 feet
Working Title: *Easy Street*
Released February 13, 1921

BLOOD AND SAND (1922)
Famous Players-Lasky Corp./Paramount Pictures
Executive producer: Jesse Lasky
Producer: Fred Niblo
Directors: Fred Niblo, **Dorothy Arzner**
Screenplay: June Mathis, from the novel by Vicente Blasco Ibáñez and the play by Tom Cushing
Cinematography: Alvin Wyckoff
Editing: **Dorothy Arzner**
Assistant Director: Frank Fouce
Assistant Camera: Edward Cronenweth
Make-Up: Monte Westmore
Cast: Rudolph Valentino (Juan Gallardo), Lila Lee (Carmen), Nita Naldi (Doña Sol), George Field (El Nacional), Walter Long (Plumitas), Rosa Rosanova (Señora Angustias), Leo White (Antonio), Charles Belcher (Don Joselito), Jack Winn (Potaje), Rosita Marstini (El Carnacione), Gilbert Clayton (Garabato), Harry Lamont (El Puntilero), George Periolat (Marquis de Guevera), Sidney De Gray (Dr. Ruiz), Fred Becker (Don José), Dorcas Matthews (Señora Nacional), William Lawrence (Fuentes), Rafael Negrete (Violinist), Louise Emmons (Old Woman)
9 reels/8,110 feet
Released August 5, 1922

THE COVERED WAGON (1923)
Famous Players-Lasky Corp./Paramount Pictures
Producer: Jesse Lasky
Director: James Cruze
Screenplay: Jack Cunningham, from the novel by Emerson Hough
Cinematography: Karl Brown
Script Supervisor: Walter Woods
Script Continuity and Editing: **Dorothy Arzner**

Assistant Director: Vernon Keays
Music: Manny Baer, Hugo Riesenfeld, J. S. Zamecnik
Costume Designer: Howard Greer
Props: Delmer Daves
Assistant Camera: Irvin Willat
Still Photography: Edwin Willat
Historical Advisors: Ennice Anderson, A. E. Sheldon, James "Yakima Jim" Anson, Ed Jones Native American Liaison: Tim McCoy
Cast: J. Warren Kerrigan (Will Banion), Lois Wilson (Molly Wingate), Alan Hale (Sam Woodhull), Ernest Torrence (William Jackson), Tully Marshall (Jim Bridger), Ethel Wales (Mrs. Wingate), Charles Ogle (Jesse Wingate), Guy Oliver (Kit Carson), John Fox (Jed Wingate), John Bose (Pioneer), Barbara Brower (Pioneer Child), Frank Albertson, Constance Wilson, Chief Thunderbird, Chris Willow Bird, Jack Padjan, Spike Spackman
10 reels/9,407 feet
Released March 16, 1923; rereleased September 8, 1924

HOLLYWOOD (1923)
Presenter: Jesse Lasky
Director: James Cruze
Screenplay: Thomas Geraghty, from a story by Frank Condon
Cinematography: Karl Brown
Script Continuity and Editing: **Dorothy Arzner**
Assistant Director: Vernon Keays
Costume Designer: Clare West
Assistant Camera: Bert Baldridge, Jimmy Murray, "Happy" de Rosselli
Props: Bill Strath, Russell Pierce
Cast: Hope Drown (Angela Whitaker), Luke Cosgrave (Joel Whitaker), George K. Arthur (Lem Lefferts), Ruby Lafayette (Grandmother Whitaker), Harris Gordon (Dr. Luke Morrison), Bess Flowers (Hortense Towers), Eleanor Lawson (Margaret Whitaker), King Zany (Horace Pringle), Frances Agnew (Reporter) [Note: more than eighty Hollywood stars and directors made cameo appearances in this film]
8 reels/8,197 feet
Released August 19, 1923

RUGGLES OF RED GAP (1923)
Famous Players-Lasky Corp./Paramount Pictures
Presenters: Jesse Lasky, Adolph Zukor
Producer and Director: James Cruze

Screenplay: Anthony Coldeway, Walter Woods, from the play by Harry Leon Wilson
Titles: Walter Woods, **Dorothy Arzner**
Cinematography: Karl Brown
Script Continuity and Editing: **Dorothy Arzner**
Cast: Edward Everett Horton (Ruggles), Ernest Torrence (Egbert Floud), Lois Wilson (Kate Kenner), Fritzi Ridgeway (Emily Judson), Charles Ogle (Jeff Tuttle), Louise Dresser (Effie Floud), Anna Lehr (Mrs. Belknap-Jackson), William Austin (Mr. Belknap-Jackson), Lillian Leighton (Ma Pettingill), Thomas Holding (Earl of Brinstead), Frank Elliott (Honorable George), Kalla Pasha (Herr Schwitz), Sidney Bracey (Sam Henshaw), Milton Brown (Senator Pettingill), Guy Oliver (Judge Ballard)
8 reels/7,590 feet
Released September 9, 1923

TO THE LADIES (1923)
Famous Players-Lasky Corp./Paramount Pictures
Presenter: Jesse Lasky
Producer and Director: James Cruze
Screenplay: Walter Woods, from the play by George S. Kaufman and Marc Connelly
Titles: Walter Woods, **Dorothy Arzner**
Cinematography: Karl Brown
Script Continuity and Editing: **Dorothy Arzner**
Cast: Edward Everett Horton (Leonard Beebe), Theodore Roberts (John Kincaid), Helen Jerome Eddy (Elsie Beebe), Louise Dresser (Mrs. Kincaid), Z. Wall Covington (Chester Mullin), Arthur Hoyt (Tom Baker), Jack Gardner (Bob Cutter), Patricia Palmer (Mary Mullin), Mary Astor
6 reels/6,268 feet
Released November 25, 1923

THE FIGHTING COWARD (1924)
Famous Players-Lasky Corp./Paramount Pictures
Presenters: Adolph Zukor, Jesse Lasky
Producer and Director: James Cruze
Screenplay: Walter Woods, from the play *Magnolia* by Booth Tarkington
Cinematography: Karl Brown
Script Continuity and Editing: **Dorothy Arzner**
Cast: Ernest Torrence (General Orlando Jackson), Mary Astor (Lucy), Noah Beery (Captain Blackie), Cullen Landis (Tom Rumford), Phyllis Haver (Elvira),

Raymond Nye (Major Patterson), Richard Neill (Joe Patterson), Carmen Phillips (Mexico), Bruce Covington (General Rumford), Helen Dunbar (Mrs. Rumford), Frank Jonasson (Rumbo), Barbara Brower (Young Girl), Betsy Ann Hisle (Young Girl), Richard Arlen
7 reels/6,501 feet
Released March 14, 1924

THE GAIETY GIRL (1924)
Universal Jewel
Presenter: Carl Laemmle
Director: King Baggot
Screenplay: Frank Beresford, Melville Brown, Bernard McConville, from the novel *The Inheritors* by Ida Alexa Ross Wylie
Cinematography: Charles Stumar
Editing: **Dorothy Arzner**
Music: Sidney Jones
Cast: Mary Philbin (Irene Tudor), Joseph Dowling (William Tudor), William Haines (Owen Tudor St. John), James Barrows (Juckins), DeWitt Jennings (John Kershaw), Freeman Wood (Christopher "Kit" Kershaw), Otto Hoffman (Evan Evans), Grace Darmond (Pansy Gale), Tom Ricketts (His Grace, the Duke), William Turner (Tracy Andrews), Duke Lee (Smythe), George Williams (Sammy Samuels), Roy Laidlaw (Rayburn)
8 reels/7,419 feet
Working Title: *The Inheritors*
Released July 31, 1924

MERTON OF THE MOVIES (1924)
Famous Players-Lasky Corp./Paramount Pictures
Presenters: Adolph Zukor, Jesse Lasky
Producer and Director: James Cruze
Screenplay: Walter Woods, from the novel by Harry Leon Wilson and the play by George S. Kaufman and Marc Connelly
Cinematography: Karl Brown
Editing: **Dorothy Arzner**
Cast: Glenn Hunter (Merton Gill), Viola Dana (Sally "Flips" Montague), DeWitt Jennings (Jeff Baird), Elliott Roth (Harold Parmalee), Charles Sellon (Pete Gashwiler), Sadie Gordon (Mrs. Gashwiler), Charles Ogle (Mr. Montague), Ethel Wales (Mrs. Montague), Luke Cosgrave (Lowell Hardy), Gale Henry (Tessie Kearns), Frank Jonasson (Henshaw), Eleanor Lawson (Mrs. Patterson), Dorothy Wood

8 reels/7,655 feet
Released September 7, 1924

THE ROSE OF PARIS (1924)
Universal Jewel
Presenter: Carl Laemmle
Director: Irving Cummings
Screenplay: Melville Brown, Lenore Coffee, Edward Lowe, Bernard McConville, from the novel *Mitsi* by M. Delly [collective pseudonym for Jeanne Marie Henriette Petitjean de la Rosiére and Frédéric Henri Petitjean de la Rosiére]
Cinematography: Charles Stumar
Editing: **Dorothy Arzner**
Cast: Mary Philbin (Mitsi), Robert Cain (Christian), John St. Polis (André du Vallois), Rose Dione (Madame Bolomoff), Dorothy Revier (Florine du Vallois), Gino Corrado (Paul Maran), Doreen Turner (Yvette), Edwin Brady (Jules), Károly Huszár [Charles Puffy] (Victor), Carrie Daumery (Mother Superior), Cesare Gravina (George), Alice Smith (Governess), Frank Currier (George Der Vroo), D. J. Mitsoras (Major Domo)
7 reels/6,362 feet
Working Title: *Mitsi*
Released November 9, 1924

INEZ FROM HOLLYWOOD (1924)
Sam E. Rork Productions/First National Pictures
Director: Alfred Green
Screenplay: **Dorothy Arzner**, J. G. Hawks, from the story "The Worst Woman in Hollywood" by Adela Rogers St. Johns
Cinematography: Arthur Edeson
Editing: **Dorothy Arzner**
Assistant Director: Jack Boland
Cast: Anna Q. Nilsson (Inez Laranetta), Lewis Stone (Stewart Cuyler), Mary Astor (Fay Bartholdi), Larry Wheat (Pat Summerfield), Rose Dione (Marie D'Albrecht), Snitz Edwards (Old Sport), Harry Depp (Scoop Smith), Ray Hallor (Freddie), E. H. Calvert (Gardner), Janet Chandler, Ruth Sullivan, Marjorie Whiteis
7 reels/6,919 feet
Working Titles: *The Worst Woman in Hollywood*; *Helen from Hollywood*; *The Good Bad Girl*
Released December 14, 1924

THE NO-GUN MAN (1924)
Harry Garson Productions/Film Booking Offices of America
Producer and Director: Harry Garson
Screenplay: **Dorothy Arzner**, Paul Gangelin
Cinematography: Lewis Physioc
Cast: Maurice "Lefty" Flynn (Robert Jerome Vincent), William Quinn (Bill Kilgore), Gloria Grey (Carmen Harroway), Raymond Turner (Obediah Abraham Lincoln Brown), James Gordon Russell (Tom West), Bob Reeves (Oklahoma George), Harry McCabe (Snooper)
5 reels/4,522 feet
Released December 27, 1924

THE BREED OF THE BORDER (1924)
Harry Garson Productions/Film Booking Offices of America
Producer and Director: Harry Garson
Screenplay: **Dorothy Arzner**, Paul Gangelin, from a story by William Dawson Hoffman
Cinematography: William Ivers, Henry Kruse
Assistant Director: Curley Dresden
Cast: Maurice "Lefty" Flynn ("Circus" Lacey), Dorothy Dwan (Ethel Slocum), Louise Carver (Ma Malone), Milton Ross (Dad Slocum), Frank Hagney (Sheriff Wells), Fred Burns (Deputy Sheriff Leverie), Joseph Bennett (Red Lucas), William Donovan (Pablo the Bandit), Raymond Turner
5 reels/4,930 feet
Released December 28, 1924

SPEED WILD (1925)
Harry Garson Productions/Film Booking Offices of America
Producer and Director: Harry Garson
Screenplay: Frank Beresford, **Dorothy Arzner**, Paul Gangelin, from a story by H. H. Van Loan
Cinematography: William Tuers
Cast: Maurice "Lefty" Flynn (Jack Ames), Ethel Shannon (Mary Bryant), Frank Elliott (Wendell Martin), Ralph McCullough (Charles Bryant), Raymond Turner (Ulysses), Fred Burns (Red Dugan), Charles Clary (Herbert Barron), Billy Butts, Doreen Turner
5 reels; 4,700 feet
Released May 10, 1925

WHEN HUSBANDS FLIRT (1925)
Waldorf Pictures Corp./Columbia Pictures Corp.
Producer: Harry Cohn
Director: William Wellman
Screenplay: **Dorothy Arzner**, Paul Gangelin, from the story "The Penalty of Jazz" by **Dorothy Arzner** and Paul Gangelin
Titles: Malcolm Boylan
Cinematography: Sam Landers
Cast: Dorothy Revier (Violet Gilbert), Forrest Stanley (Henry Gilbert), Tom Ricketts (Wilbur Belcher), Ethel Wales (Mrs. Wilbur Belcher), Maude Wayne (Charlotte Germaine), Frank Weed (Percy Snodgrass), Erwin Connelly (Joe McCormick)
6 reels/5,625 feet
Working Titles: *The Penalty of Jazz*; *Don't Tell Your Husband*
Released November 1, 1925

THE RED KIMONA (1925)
Mrs. Wallace Reid Productions/Vital Exchanges
Producer and Presenter: Dorothy Davenport
Directors: Walter Lang, Dorothy Davenport
Screenplay: **Dorothy Arzner**, Dorothy Davenport, from a story by Adela Rogers St. Johns Titles: Malcolm Stuart Boylan
Cinematography: James Diamond
Production Manager: Cliff Broughton
Cast: Priscilla Bonner (Gabrielle Darley), Nellie Bly Baker (Clara Johnson), Carl Miller (Howard Blaine), Mary Carr (Prison Matron), Virginia Pearson (Mrs. Beverly Fontaine), Tyrone Power (Gabrielle's Father), Sheldon Lewis (District Attorney), Theodore von Eltz (Terrance "Freddy" O'Day), Emily Fitzroy (Housekeeper), George Siegmann (Mr. Mack), Dot Farley (The Inquisitive One), Max Ascher (H. E. Reid), Dorothy Davenport (Narrator), Charles French (Jury Foreman), Ellinor Vanderveer, Lottie Williams
7 reels/6,500 feet/80 minutes
Working Titles: *The Red Kimono*; *Gabrielle of the Red Kimono*
Released November 16, 1925

DANCING DAYS (1926)
Preferred Pictures Corp./Famous Attractions
Presenter: J. G. Bachmann
Producer: B. P. Schulberg
Directors: Albert Kelley, William Wellman

Screenplay: **Dorothy Arzner**, Paul Gangelin, from a novel by John Joy Bell and a story by Dorothy Cairns
Cinematography: Lyman Broening
Cast: Helene Chadwick (Alice Hedman), Forrest Stanley (Ralph Hedman), Gloria Gordon (Maid), Lillian Rich (Lillian Loring), Robert Agnew (Gerald Hedman), Thomas Ricketts (Stubbins), Sylvia Ashton (Katinka)
6 reels/5,900 feet
Released September 27, 1926

OLD IRONSIDES (1926)
Famous Players-Lasky Corp./Paramount Pictures
Presenters: Adolph Zukor, Jesse Lasky
Producer and Director: James Cruze
Associate Producer: B. P. Schulberg
Screenplay: Harry Carr, Walter Woods, **Dorothy Arzner**, from a story by Laurence Stallings and a poem by Oliver Wendell Holmes
Titles: Rupert Hughes
Cinematography: Alfred Gilks, Charles Boyle, Harry Perry
Script Continuity and Editing: **Dorothy Arzner**
Assistant Director: Harold Schwartz
Props: Don Greenwood
Special Effects: Farciot Edouart, Roy Pomeroy, Barney Wolff
Art Director: Edward J. Smith
Production Manager: Sam Jaffe
Construction Supervisor: Leroy Shaw
Music: Hugo Riesenfeld, J. S. Zamecnik
Cast: Charles Farrell (The Commodore), Esther Ralston (Esther), Wallace Beery (Bos'n), George Bancroft (The Gunner), Charles Hill Mailes (Commodore Preble), Johnnie Walker (Lieutenant Stephen Decatur), Eddie Fetherston (Lieutenant Richard Somers), Guy Oliver (First Mate), George Godfrey (Cook), William Conklin (Esther's Father), Effie Ellsler (Esther's Mother), Arthur Ludwig (Second Mate), Fred Kohler (Second Mate), Nick De Ruiz (Bashaw), Mitchell Lewis (Pirate Chief), Frank Jonasson (Pirate Captain), Duke Kahanamoku (Pirate Captain), Boris Karloff (Saracen Guard), Tetsu Komai (Saracen), Richard Alexander (Seaman), Richard Arlen (Seaman), Frank Bonner (Seaman), Gary Cooper (Seaman), Frank Darien (Seaman), Jack Herrick (Seaman), Robert Livingston (Seaman), Spec O'Donnell (Cabin Boy), William Bakewell (Young Philadelphian), Dean Harrell (Young Decatur), Norman Robison (Pirate)
12 reels/10,089 feet; 8 reels/7,910 feet
Released December 6, 1926; rereleased March 3, 1928

FASHIONS FOR WOMEN (1927)
Famous Players-Lasky Corp./Paramount Pictures
Presenters: Jesse Lasky, Adolph Zukor
Producer: B. P. Schulberg
Director: **Dorothy Arzner**
Screenplay: Percy Heath, Jules Furthman, Herman Mankiewicz, **Dorothy Arzner**, from the plays *The Girl of the Hour* by Gladys Unger and *La Femme du Jour* by Paul Armont and Léopold Marchand
Titles: George Marion
Cinematography: Kinley Martin
Editing: Marion Morgan, **Dorothy Arzner**
Assistant Director: Dan Keefe
Costume Designer: Travis Banton
Cast: Esther Ralston (Céleste de Givray/Lola Dauvry), Raymond Hatton (Sam Dupont), Einar Hanson (Raoul de Bercy), Edward Martindel (Duke of Arles), William Orlamond (Roué), Agostino Borgato (Monsieur Alard), Edward Faust (Monsieur Pettibon), Yvonne Howell (Mimi), Maude Wayne (The Girl), Charles Darvas (Restaurant Manager), Beth Laemmle, Estelle Etterre, Bess Flowers, Jean Lorraine, Joyce Clark, Ethel Sykes, Lorraine Eddy, Muriel Finley, Constance Finley, Hazel Howell, Edwina Booth, Dixie Davis, Iris Ashton, Doris Hill, Marie Pergain
7 reels/6,296 feet
Working Title: *The Best Dressed Woman in Paris*
Released March 26, 1927

TEN MODERN COMMANDMENTS (1927)
Paramount Famous Lasky Corp./Paramount Pictures
Presenters: Adolph Zukor, Jesse Lasky
Director: **Dorothy Arzner**
Screenplay: Ethel Doherty, Doris Anderson, Paul Gangelin, from a story by Jack Lait
Titles: George Marion
Cinematography: Alfred Gilks
Editing: Louis Lighton
Assistant Director: Otto Brower
Choreographer: Marion Morgan
Cast: Esther Ralston (Kitten O'Day), Neil Hamilton (Tod Gilbert), Maude Truax (Aunt Ruby), Romaine Fielding (Zeno), El Brendel ("Speeding" Shapiro), Rose Burdick (Belle), Jocelyn Lee (Sharon Lee), Arthur Hoyt (George Disbrow), Roscoe Karns (Benny Burnaway), Rita Claire

7 reels/6,497 feet
Working Title: *Modern Commandments*
Released July 2, 1927

GET YOUR MAN (1927)
Paramount Famous Lasky Corp./Paramount Pictures
Producers and Presenters: Jesse Lasky, Adolph Zukor
Associate Producer: B. P. Schulberg
Director: **Dorothy Arzner**
Screenplay: Hope Loring, Agnes Brand Leahy, from the play *Tu m'épouseras!* by Louis Verneuil [pseudonym for Louis Jacques Marie Collin du Bocage]
Titles: George Marion
Cinematography: Alfred Gilks
Editing: Doris Drought
Editing Supervision: Louis Lighton
Script Continuity: Doris Karns
Tableaux: Marion Morgan
Costume Designer: Edith Head
Music Compiler: James Bradford
Business Manager: Henrietta Cohn
Cast: Clara Bow (Nancy Worthington), Charles "Buddy" Rogers (Robert Albin), Josef Swickard (Duke of Albin), Josephine Dunn (Simone de Valens), Harvey Clark (Marquis de Valens), Frances Raymond (Madame Pluche), David Durand (Robert as a Boy), Marion Morgan (Woman in Wax Museum), Tom Ricketts (Man in Wax Museum), Marion Morgan Dancers (Wax Figures)
6 reels/5,718 feet
Working Titles: *You Will Marry Me*; *Will You Marry Me?*
Released December 7, 1927

MANHATTAN COCKTAIL (1928)
Paramount Famous Lasky Corp./Paramount Pictures
Producers: Jesse Lasky, Adolph Zukor
Director: **Dorothy Arzner**
Screenplay: Ethel Doherty, from a story by Ernest Vajda
Titles: George Marion
Cinematography: Harry Fischbeck
Editing: Doris Drought, **Dorothy Arzner**
"Manhattan Skyline" Montage Sequence: Slavko Vorkapich
Music: Victor Schertzinger
Assistant Director: Paul Jones

Choreography: Marion Morgan
Costume Designer: Travis Banton
Costume Jewelry: Eugene Joseff
Music Arranger: Andrea Setaro
Musical Conductor: Irvin Talbot
Recording Supervisor: Max Terr
Cast: Nancy Carroll (Barbara "Babs" Clark), Richard Arlen (Fred Tilden), Danny O'Shea (Bob Marky), Paul Lukas (Boris Renov), Lilyan Tashman (Mrs. Renov), Joe Marba (Stage Manager), Bert Woodruff (Stage Doorman), George Bruggeman (Theseus), Youcca Troubetzkov, Edwina Booth, Larry Steers, Alyn Warren, Richard Cramer, Fred Esmelton, Marion Morgan Dancers
7 reels/6,051 feet/72 minutes
Working Title: *Soubrette*
Released November 24, 1928

THE WILD PARTY (1929)
Paramount Pictures
Presenters: Jesse Lasky, Adolph Zukor
Producer: Lloyd Sheldon
General Production Manager: B. P. Schulberg
Director: **Dorothy Arzner**
Directorial Consultant: Robert Milton
Screenplay: Lloyd Sheldon, John Weaver, from the 1928 novel *Unforbidden Fruit* by Warner Fabian [pseudonym for Samuel Hopkins Adams]
Titles: George Marion
Cinematography: Victor Milner
Editing: Otho Lovering
Assistant Director: Arthur Jacobson
Costume Designer: Travis Banton
Music: John Leipold, Leo Robin, Richard Whiting
Sound Recording Engineer: Earl Hayman
Camera Operators: Cliff Blackstone, Rex Wimpy
Assistant Camera: William Clothier, Daniel Fapp, Albert Myers
Second Camera: Archie Stout
Props: Joseph Youngerman
Still Photography: Eugene Richee, Emmett Schoenbaum
Cast: Clara Bow (Stella Ames), Fredric March (James "Gil" Gilmore), Marceline Day (Faith Morgan), Shirley O'Hara (Helen Owens), Joyce Compton (Eva Tutt), Jack Oakie (Al), Ben Hendricks (Ed), Jack Luden (George), Phillips Holmes (Phil), Adrienne Doré (Babs), Alice Adair (Mazie), Kay Bryant (Thelma), Mar-

guerite Cramer (Gwen), Amo Ingraham (Jean), Jean Lorraine (Ann), Virginia Thomas (Tess), Renee Whitney (Janice Allen), Russ Powell (Pullman Car Passenger), Arthur Rankin (Partygoer), Jack Raymond (Balaam), Lincoln Stedman (Partygoer), William Bow (Partygoer)
7 reels/6,036 feet/77 minutes
Released April 6, 1929

CHARMING SINNERS (1929)
Paramount Famous Lasky Corp./Paramount Pictures
Directors: Robert Milton, **Dorothy Arzner**
Screenplay: Doris Anderson, from the play *The Constant Wife* by W. Somerset Maugham
Cinematography: Victor Milner
Editing: Verna Willis
Costume Designer: Travis Banton
Music: Karl Hajos, Franke Harling
Sound Technician: Earl Hayman
Cast: Ruth Chatterton (Kathryn Miles), Clive Brook (Robert Miles), Mary Nolan (Anne-Marie Whitley), William Powell (Karl Kraley), Laura Hope Crews (Mrs. Carr), Florence Eldridge (Helen Carr), Montagu Love (George Whitley), Juliette Crosby (Margaret), Lorraine MacLean (Alice), Claude Allister (Gregson), Tenen Holtz (Waiter)
65 minutes
Working Titles: *The Constant Wife*; *The Marriage Holiday*
Released August 17, 1929

BEHIND THE MAKE-UP (1930)
Paramount Famous Lasky Corp./Paramount Pictures
Presenters: Jesse Lasky, Adolph Zukor
Producer: Monta Bell
Associate Producer: B. P. Schulberg
Directors: Robert Milton, **Dorothy Arzner**, Henry Hathaway, Rollo Lloyd
Screenplay: Howard Estabrook, George Manker Watters, from the story "The Feeder" by Mildred Cram
Cinematography: Charles Lang
Editing: Doris Drought
Costume Designer: Travis Banton
Casting: Fred Datig
Casting Assistant: Dick Stockton
Music: Franke Harling, John Leipold

Sound Recordist: Harry Mills
Cast: Hal Skelly ("Hap" Brown), William Powell (Gardoni), Fay Wray (Marie Gardoni), Kay Francis (Kitty Parker), Paul Lukas (Count Boris), E. H. Calvert (Dawson), Agostino Borgato (Pierre), Jacques Vanaire (Valet), Jean De Briac (Sculptor), Torben Meyer (Waiter), Bob Perry (Bartender), Walter Huston (Joe)
7 reels/6,364 feet/70 minutes
Working Title: *The Feeder*
Released January 11, 1930

SARAH AND SON (1930)
Paramount Famous Lasky Corp./Paramount Pictures
Presenters: Adolph Zukor, Jesse Lasky
Producer: Albert Kaufman
Associate Producer: B. P. Schulberg
Director: **Dorothy Arzner**
Screenplay: Zoë Akins, Louise Long, from the novel by Timothy Shea [pseudonym for Alden Knipe]
Cinematography: Charles Lang
Editing: Verna Willis
Costume Designer: Travis Banton
Costume Jewelry: Eugene Joseff
Casting: Fred Datig
Casting Assistant: Dick Stockton
Music: Oscar Potoker
Sound Recordist: Earl Hayman
Electrician: Amos Goodall
Business Manager: Henrietta Cohn
Cast: Ruth Chatterton (Sarah "Dutch" Storm), Fredric March (Howard Vanning), Fuller Mellish (Jim Grey), Gilbert Emery (John Ashemore), Doris Lloyd (Martha Vanning Ashemore), William Stack (Cyril Belloc), Philippe De Lacy (Bobby), Edgar Norton (Vanning's Butler), Madame Sul-Te-Wan (Belloc's Maid), Lottie Williams (Kate), Dick Winslow (Kate's Son), Billie and Bobbie Stout (Infant Bobby)
9 reels/7,740 feet/86 minutes
Released March 14, 1930

PARAMOUNT ON PARADE (1930)
Paramount Pictures
Presenters: Adolph Zukor, Jesse Lasky
Producers: Elsie Janis, Albert Kaufman, B. P. Schulberg

Directors: **Dorothy Arzner**, Otto Brower, Edmund Goulding, Victor Heerman, Edwin Knopf, Rowland V. Lee, Ernst Lubitsch, Lothar Mendes, Victor Schertzinger, Edward Sutherland, Frank Tuttle
Screenplay: Joseph Mankiewicz
Cinematography: Harry Fischbeck, Victor Milner
Editing: Merrill White
Art Direction: John Wenger
Music ("Gallows Song" segment only): Helen Jerome, Mana-Zucca
Orchestrations: Abe Lyman, Nat Shilkret
Costume Design: Travis Banton
Production Supervisors: Elsie Janis, Geoffrey Shurlock
Assistant Camera: Cliff Shirpser
Cast ("Gallows Song" segment only): Dennis King (François Villon), Richard "Skeets" Gallagher, Ludwig Berger
13 reels/9,125 feet/101 minutes
Released April 19, 1930
[Note: Arzner was among eleven prominent Paramount directors who helmed brief sequences in this anthology film. Her segment, "The Gallows Song," featured Dennis King reprising his role as *The Vagabond King*'s François Villon.]

ANYBODY'S WOMAN (1930)
Paramount Publix Corporation/Paramount Pictures
Director: **Dorothy Arzner**
Screenplay: Zoë Akins, Doris Anderson, from the novel *The Better Wife* by Gouverneur Morris
Cinematography: Charles Lang
Editing: Jane Loring
Music: Karl Hajos
Sound Recordist: Jack Goodrich
Dance Instructor: Joyzelle Joyner
Cast: Ruth Chatterton (Pansy Gray), Clive Brook (Neil Dunlap), Paul Lukas (Gustave Saxon), Huntley Gordon (Grant Crosby), Virginia Hammond (Katherine Malcolm), Tom Patricola (Eddie Calcio), Juliette Compton (Ellen), Edna Cecil Cunningham (Dot), Charles Gerrard (Walter Harvey), Harvey Clark (Mr. Tanner), Sidney Bracey (Butler), Gertrude Sutton (Maid), William O'Brien (Butler), Buddy Roosevelt (Chauffeur), Mary Gordon, George Reid
9 reels/7,243 feet/80 minutes
Working Title: *The Better Wife*
Released August 15, 1930

HONOR AMONG LOVERS (1931)
Paramount Pictures
Director: **Dorothy Arzner**
Screenplay: Austin Parker, Gertrude Purcell, **Dorothy Arzner**, from a story by Austin Parker and the play *Paid in Full* by Eugene Walter
Cinematography: George Folsey
Editing: Helene Turner
Script Continuity: Pat Donahue
Art Direction: Charles Kirk, Franklin Whitman
Assistant Director: Arthur Jacobson
Costume Designer: Caroline Putnam
Music: Vernon Duke
Music Arranger: Johnny Green
Sound Technician: C. A. Tuthill
Cast: Claudette Colbert (Julia Traynor), Fredric March (Jerry Stafford), Monroe Owsley (Philip Craig), Charles Ruggles (Monty Dunn), Ginger Rogers (Doris Brown), Avonne Taylor (Maybelle Worthington), Pat O'Brien (Conroy), Janet McLeary (Margaret Newton), John Kearney (Inspector), Ralph Morgan (Riggs), Jules Epailly (Louis), Leonard Carey (Forbes), Grace Kern (Party Guest), Winifred Harris (Party Guest), Roberta Beatty (Mrs. Fleming), Charles Halton (Wilkes), Granville Bates (Clark), Si Wills (Waiter), Betty Morrissey (Party Guest), Robert Barrat (Detective), Elisha Cook Jr. (Office Boy), Charles Trowbridge (Cunningham)
6,775 feet/75 minutes
Working Titles: *Strictly Business*; *Another Man's Wife*; *Sex in Business*
Released March 21, 1931

STEPDAUGHTERS OF WAR (1931; unfinished)
Paramount Pictures
Director: **Dorothy Arzner**
Screenplay: Josephine Lovett, Viola Brothers Shore, from the 1930 novel *Not So Quiet: Stepdaughters of War* by Helen Zenna Smith [pseudonym for Evadne Price] and the play by J. Kenyon Nicholson
Montage Sequences: Slavko Vorkapich
Cast: Ruth Chatterton (Kit Smith), Gary Cooper (Geoffrey Hilder), Mary Forbes (Commander), Fay Wray, Jean Arthur, Frances Dee, Juliette Compton
[Note: Arzner shot several scenes for this film, but Paramount canceled it following Ruth Chatterton's departure from the studio. A four-minute excerpt is included in *The House That Shadows Built* (1931), a filmic history of Paramount. The script by Lovett and Shore, dated May 9, 1931, is on file in the Paramount

Pictures Unproduced Scripts collection, Margaret Herrick Library, Academy of Motion Picture Arts and Sciences.]

WORKING GIRLS (1931)
Paramount Pictures
Director: **Dorothy Arzner**
Screenplay: Zoë Akins, from the play *Blind Mice* by Vera Caspary and Winifred Lenihan
Cinematography: Harry Fischbeck
Editing: Jane Loring
Costume Designer: Travis Banton
Assistant Camera: Lloyd Ahern, Robert Rhea
Camera Operators: James Knott, Harry Merland
Music: Ralph Rainger
Music Orchestrator: John Leipold
Still Photographer: Clifton King
Cast: Judith Wood (June Thorpe), Dorothy Hall (Mae Thorpe), Charles "Buddy" Rogers (Boyd Wheeler), Paul Lukas (Waldo Ferguson), Stuart Erwin (Pat Kelly), Frances Dee (Louise Adams), Mary Forbes (Mrs. Johnstone), Frances Moffett (Lou Hollings), Claire Dodd (Jane), Dorothy Stickney (Loretta), Edith Arnold (Verne), Lisa Gora (Elsie), Mischa Auer (Elsie's Boyfriend), Stella Moore (Maude), Marjorie Gateson
8 reels/77 minutes
Working Title: *Stay Up All Night Triple Header*
Released December 12, 1931

MERRILY WE GO TO HELL (1932)
Paramount Pictures
Director: **Dorothy Arzner**
Screenplay: Edwin Justus Mayer, from the novel *I, Jerry, Take Thee, Joan* by Cleo Lucas
Cinematography: David Abel
Editing: Jane Loring
Assistant Director: Charles Barton
Casting: Mel Ballerino, Fred Datig
Casting Assistant: Joe Egli
Assistant Camera: Cliff Shirpser
Music: Rudolph Kopp, John Leipold
Sound Technician: Harry Mills

Cast: Sylvia Sidney (Joan Prentice), Fredric March (Jerry Corbett), Adrianne Allen (Claire Hempstead), Richard "Skeets" Gallagher (Buck), George Irving (Mr. Prentice), Esther Howard (Vi), Florence Britton (Charlcie), Charles Coleman (Richard Damery), Cary Grant (Charlie Baxter), Kent Taylor (Gregory Boleslavsky)
9 reels/88 minutes
Working Title: *Jerry and Joan*
Released June 10, 1932

CHRISTOPHER STRONG (1933)
RKO Radio Pictures
Producer: David O. Selznick
Associate Producer: Pandro Berman
Director: **Dorothy Arzner**
Screenplay: Zoë Akins, from the novel by Gilbert Frankau
Cinematography: Sid Hickox, Bert Glennon
Editing: Arthur Roberts
Montage Sequences: Slavko Vorkapich
Assistant Directors: Thomas Atkins, William Cody, Edward Killy, Robert Margolis
Art Direction: Charles Kirk, Van Nest Polglase
Props: Thomas Little
Costume Designer: Howard Greer, Walter Plunkett
Makeup: Mel Berns
Casting: Fred Schuessler
Casting Assistant: Dick Stockton
Unit Manager: Archie Hill
Production Manager: C. J. White
Special Effects: Vernon Walker
Music: Max Steiner, Roy Webb
Orchestrations: Bernhard Kaun, Eddie Sharpe
Sound Recordist: Hugh McDowell
Sound Technicians: John Aalberg, Murray Spivack
Technical Advisors: Gerald Grove, Del Andrews, Elsie Conde, Captain Francis
Stand-in for Katharine Hepburn: Katherine Doyle
Cast: Katharine Hepburn (Lady Cynthia Darrington), Colin Clive (Sir Christopher Strong), Billie Burke (Lady Elaine Strong), Helen Chandler (Monica Strong), Ralph Forbes (Harry Rawlinson), Irene Browne (Carrie Valentine), Jack La Rue (Carlo), Desmond Roberts (Bryce Mercer)
9 reels/77 minutes
Working Titles: *The Magnificent Affair; The Great Desire*
Released March 31, 1933

NANA (1934)
Samuel Goldwyn Co./United Artists
Producer and Presenter: Sam Goldwyn
Directors: **Dorothy Arzner**, George Fitzmaurice
Screenplay: Edwin Justus Mayer, Louis Weitzenkorn, Harry Wagstaff Gribble, Willard Mack, from the novel by Émile Zola
Dialogue Director: Willard Mack
Cinematography: Gregg Toland
Editing: Frank Lawrence
Assistant Director: Walter Mayo
Art Direction: Richard Day
Props: Irving Sindler
Costume Designers: Adrian, Travis Banton, John Harkrider
Assistant Costume Designer: Fred Zinnemann
Casting: Robert McIntyre
Music: Alfred Newman, Richard Rodgers, Lorenz Hart
Sound Technician: Frank Maher
Cast: Anna Sten (Nana), Lionel Atwill (Colonel André Muffat), Richard Bennett (Gaston Greiner), Mae Clarke (Satin), Phillips Holmes (Lieutenant George Muffat), Muriel Kirkland (Mimi), Reginald Owen (Bordenave), Helen Freeman (Sabine Muffat), Lawrence Grant (Grand Duke Alexis), Jessie Ralph (Zoë), Ferdinand Gottschalk (Finot), Hardie Albright (Lieutenant Gregory), Lucille Ball (Chorus Girl)
10 reels/88 minutes
Working Title: *Lady of the Boulevards*
Released February 1, 1934

CRAIG'S WIFE (1936)
Columbia Pictures Corp.
Producer: Harry Cohn
Associate Producer: Edward Chodorov
Director: **Dorothy Arzner**
Screenplay: Mary McCall, from the play by George Kelly
Cinematography: Lucien Ballard
Editing: Viola Lawrence
Assistant Director: Arthur Black
Production Design: William Haines
Art Direction: Stephen Goosson
Interior Decorations: Babs Johnstone
Costume Designer: Lon Anthony

Music: R. H. Bassett, Emil Gerstenberger, Milan Roder, William Grant Still
Musical Director: Morris Stoloff
Sound Technician: Lodge Cunningham
Cast: Rosalind Russell (Harriet Craig), John Boles (Walter Craig), Billie Burke (Mrs. Frazier), Jane Darwell (Mrs. Harold), Dorothy Wilson (Ethel Landreth), Alma Kruger (Ellen Austen), Thomas Mitchell (Fergus Passmore), Raymond Walburn (Billy Birkmire), Elisabeth Risdon (Mrs. Landreth), Robert Allen (Gene Fredericks), Nydia Westman (Mazie), Kathleen Burke (Adelaide Passmore), John Hamilton (Detective Joseph Catelle)
8 reels/75 minutes
Released September 30, 1936

THEODORA GOES WILD (1936)
Columbia Pictures Corp.
Producer: Harry Cohn
Associate Producers: Everett Riskin, **Dorothy Arzner**
Director: Richard Boleslawski
Screenplay: Sidney Buchman, from a story by Mary McCarthy
Cinematography: Joseph Walker
Editing: Otto Meyer
Assistant Director: William Mull
Art Direction: Stephen Goosson, Jerome Pycha
Interior Decorations: Babs Johnstone
Costume Design: Bernard Newman
Music: Arthur Morton, William Grant Still, R. H. Bassett, Howard Jackson
Musical Director: Morris Stoloff
Sound Engineer: George Cooper
Cast: Irene Dunne (Theodora Lynn, aka Caroline Adams), Melvyn Douglas (Michael Grant), Thomas Mitchell (Jed Waterbury), Thurston Hall (Arthur Stevenson), Elisabeth Risdon (Mary Lynn), Margaret McWade (Elsie Lynn), Spring Byington (Rebecca Perry), Nana Bryant (Ethel Stevenson), Henry Kolker (Jonathan Grant), Leona Maricle (Agnes Grant), Robert Greig (Uncle John), Frederick Burton (Governor Wyatt), Mary Forbes (Mrs. Wyatt)
10 reels/94 minutes
Released November 12, 1936

THE LAST OF MRS. CHEYNEY (1937)
Metro-Goldwyn-Mayer
Producer: Lawrence Weingarten
Directors: Richard Boleslawski, **Dorothy Arzner**, George Fitzmaurice

Screenplay: Leon Gordon, Samson Raphaelson, Monckton Hoffe, George Oppenheimer, from the play by Frederick Lonsdale
Cinematography: George Folsey
Editing: Frank Sullivan
Script Continuity: Wallace Worsley Jr.
Assistant Director: Edward Woehler
Art Direction: Cedric Gibbons
Associate Art Directors: Edwin Willis, Joseph Wright
Costume Design: Adrian
Music: William Axt
Orchestrators: George Bassman, Paul Marquardt
Recording Director: Douglas Shearer
Cast: Joan Crawford (Fay Cheyney), William Powell (Charles), Robert Montgomery (Lord Arthur Dilling), Frank Morgan (Lord Francis Kelton), Jessie Ralph (Duchess), Nigel Bruce (Willie Wynton), Colleen Clare (Joan), Benita Hume (Kitty Wynton), Ralph Forbes (Cousin John), Aileen Pringle (Lady Maria Frinton), Melville Cooper (William), Leonard Carey (Ames), Sara Haden (Anna), Lumsden Hare (Inspector Witherspoon), Wallis Clark (George), Barnett Parker (Purser)
10 reels/98 minutes
Released February 19, 1937

THE BRIDE WORE RED (1937)
Metro-Goldwyn-Mayer
Producer: Joseph Mankiewicz
Director: **Dorothy Arzner**
Screenplay: Tess Slesinger, Bradbury Foote, George Oppenheimer, Waldo Salt, Catherine Turney, Joseph Mankiewicz, from the play *The Girl from Trieste* by Ferenc Molnár
Cinematography: George Folsey
Editing: Adrienne Fazan
Script Continuity: Wallace Worsley Jr.
Assistant Director: Edward Woehler
Art Direction: Cedric Gibbons
Associate Art Directors: Daniel Cathcart, Edwin Willis
Props: Harry Edwards
Costume Design: Adrian
Music: Franz Waxman, Gus Kahn
Orchestrator: Paul Marquardt
Sound Crew Head: Norwood Fenton

Recording Director: Douglas Shearer
Assistant Camera: Harkness Smith
Choreographer: Val Raset
Technical Consultant: Gus Galli
Stand-in for Joan Crawford: Kasha Haroldi
Cast: Joan Crawford (Anni Pavlovitch, aka Anne Vivaldi), Franchot Tone (Giulio), Robert Young (Rudi Pal), Billie Burke (Contessa di Meina), Reginald Owen (Admiral Monti), Lynne Carver (Maddalena Monti), George Zucco (Count Armalia), Mary Philips (Maria), Paul Porcasi (Nobili), Dickie Moore (Pietro), Frank Puglia (Alberto)
11 reels/103 minutes
Working Title: *Once There Was a Lady*
Released October 8, 1937

DANCE, GIRL, DANCE (1940)
RKO Radio Pictures
Executive Producer: Harry Edington
Producer: Erich Pommer
Directors: **Dorothy Arzner**, Roy Del Ruth
Screenplay: Tess Slesinger, Frank Davis, from the story "One of Six Girls" by Vicki Baum
Dialogue Director: Gene Lewis
Cinematography: Russell Metty, Joseph August
Editing: Robert Wise
Assistant Editor: Mark Robson
Assistant Director: James Anderson
Art Direction: Van Nest Polglase
Associate Art Director: Alfred Herman
Set Decoration: Darrell Silvera
Costume Design: Edward Stevenson
Makeup Design: Mel Berns
Music: Edward Ward, Robert Wright, Chester Forrest
Musical Director: Edward Ward
Orchestrators: Wally Heglin, Gene Rose
Sound Recordist: Hugh McDowell
Special Effects: Vernon Walker
Choreographers: Ernst Matray, Marie Solveg
Cast: Maureen O'Hara (Judy O'Brien), Louis Hayward (Jimmy Harris), Lucille Ball (Bubbles White, aka Tiger Lily White), Virginia Field (Elinor Harris),

Ralph Bellamy (Steve Adams), Maria Ouspenskaya (Madame Lydia Basilova), Mary Carlisle (Sally), Katharine Alexander (Miss Olmstead), Edward Brophy (Dwarfie Humblewinger), Walter Abel (Judge), Harold Huber (Kashulian), Ernest Truex (Bailey #1), Chester Clute (Bailey #2), Lorraine Krueger (Dolly), Lola Jensen (Daisy), Emma Dunn (Mrs. Simpson), Sidney Blackmer (Puss in Boots), Vivien Fay ("Morning Star" Ballerina), Ludwig Stössel (Caesar), Ernö Verebes (Fitch)
8,051 feet/90 minutes
Working Titles: *One of Six Girls*; *Have It Your Own Way*
Released August 30, 1940

FIRST COMES COURAGE (1943)
Columbia Pictures Corp.
Producer: Harry Joe Brown
Directors: **Dorothy Arzner**, Charles Vidor
Screenplay: Melvin Levy, Lewis Meltzer, George Sklar, from the novel *The Commandos* by Elliott Arnold
Cinematography: Joseph Walker
Editing: Viola Lawrence
Assistant Director: William Mull
Art Direction: Lionel Banks
Associate Art Director: Rudolph Sternad
Set Decoration: Fay Babcock
Music: Ernst Toch, John Leipold
Musical Director: Morris Stoloff
Sound Technician: Lambert Day
Technical Advisors: Ernst Richter, Wessel Klausen, Frank Schofield
Cast: Merle Oberon (Nicole Larsen), Brian Aherne (Captain Allan Lowell), Carl Esmond (Major Paul Dichter), Isobel Elsom (Rose Lindstrom), Fritz Leiber (Dr. Aanrud), Erville Alderson (Soren), Erik Rolf (Ole), Reinhold Schünzel (Colonel Kurt von Elser)
10 reels/7,742 feet/86 minutes
Working Titles: *Commandos*; *The Commandos Strike at Dawn*; *Attack by Night*
Released July 29, 1943

STUDENT CINEMA PROJECT: O'HENRY III (ca. 1954)
Pasadena Playhouse Productions
Producers and Directors: **Dorothy Arzner**, Dan Bailey
Sets: Gordon Meagher

Part 1: *Jeff Peters, a Personal Magnet*
Screenplay: Dan Bailey, from the short story "Jeff Peters as a Personal Magnet" by O. Henry [pseudonym for William Sydney Porter]
Cast: Frank Dunder (Jeff Peters), James Gilmore (Andy Tucker), Edwin DeBoer (Sheriff), Frank Parker (Bartender), Don MacShane (Hotel Clerk), Charles Veltman (Old Wilson), Clyde Martin (Mayor)
Part 2: *One Thousand Dollars*
Screenplay: Dan Bailey, from the short story by O. Henry
Cast: Edwin DeBoer (Tolman), Clyde Martin (Sharpe), Kenneth Drake (Gillian), Joseph Dunnigan (Bryson), Michelle Adler (Amy), Ellen Ravitz (Lotta Laurier), Robert Dyer (Call Boy), Don MacShane (Stagedoor Jonny), Frank Dunder (Stage Doorman), Nicholas Wallace (Blindman), Mary Armentrout (Miss Hayden)
Part 3: *Psyche and the Pskyscraper*
Screenplay: Patricia Halsey, from the short story by O. Henry
Cast: Robert Dyer (Joe Griggs), Ellen Ravitz (Daisy), James Creson (Mr. Dabster)
50 minutes

THIRD-YEAR CINEMA PROJECT (ca. 1955)
Pasadena Playhouse Productions
Directors: **Dorothy Arzner**, Dan Bailey
Cinematography: Thomas Chapman
Script Continuity: Aileen Koch
Sound Recordist: Felix Masarachia
Technicians: William Weber, Don Meyer, Alphonso Penna
Cast: Herbert Zuckerman (Doc), Clyde Martin (Timmons), Fred Humphries (Cobby), Patrick Miller (Alonzo Emmerich), John Fenneck (Brannon), Alex Finlayson (Louie), Joseph Morrisey (Norman Dix)
38 minutes

THE HOST (1960)
UCLA Department of Theater Arts
Producer, Director, Screenplay, and Editing: Jack Hill
Production Supervisor: **Dorothy Arzner**
Cinematography: Stephen Burum, Jack Hill
Script Continuity: Jean Slanger
Assistant Director: Frank Agrama
Art Direction: Michael Lonzo
Set Decoration: Joram Kahana
Miniature Sets: Donald Shebib
Camera Operator: Peter Good

Gaffer: James Bruner
Music: Ron Feuer
Sound Editing: Dana Gustafson
Sound Recordist: Nils Svensson
Cast: Sid Haig (Fugitive), Sharon Bercutt (Priestess), Joseph Hanwright (Spaniard)
30 minutes

Dorothy Arzner: Interviews

Leave Sex Out, Says Director

Grace Kingsley / 1927

From *Los Angeles Times*, Sept. 18, 1927.

If you are a woman and you aim to become a director, don't think of yourself as a woman director, nor sentimentally of the "woman's touch." Just merely think of yourself as a director. Leave the question of sex out. It will duly assert itself in the right way.

That is the way in which Dorothy Arzner, who has been given her chance by that man of vision, Jesse L. Lasky, and who is making a fine success, thinks of the matter.

"I never think of myself as a woman director, but merely as a director," said Miss Arzner as we chatted in her office—a place as bare looking and businesslike as a man director's office would be.

"And I find in working with men, if you have their viewpoint, play square and don't try to work any of the so-called feminine wiles, you will get along and win all the success you deserve."

And Dorothy might so easily work feminine wiles, one would say!

The director of *Fashions for Women* and *Ten Modern Commandments* is one of these magnetic women, who isn't really pretty, but who looks pretty—which is so much better, really, than being pretty if you don't look pretty. All women will know what I mean, and a few men. She has sparkling, intelligent gray eyes and straight eyebrows, an unremarkable mouth, nose and chin and a good skin, with dark, close-cropped hair. Her beauty lies in her radiant charm, her animated intelligence. She has a keen level outlook on life, loves to analyze situations and people and is a splendid talker. Altogether, you could easily be fooled into thinking that Dorothy Arzner is beautiful.

Dorothy confesses to the fact that she has a strong man to help her over the hard spots in pictures. Probably "confessed" is too strong a word, really, because Dorothy remarked it quite frankly.

"Dan Keefe, my assistant, is my masculine strength. He went in and did all the battling on my first picture," she said.

So that, even if Miss Arzner does "forget that she is a woman director, and remembers only that she is a director," she proves she is keen enough to know it is much better to have a man battle with men for your rights than for you yourself to battle.

"Why aren't there more women directors?" I inquired.

"Well, everything is first an idea," said Miss Arzner. "Somehow the men at the head of firms haven't thought of women as directors. But women are developing power. Take even the children on the beaches, for instance, and, in their bathing suits, it is almost impossible to tell the boys from the girls what with their identical styles of bathing suits, haircuts and more than anything the way they play games and swim."

"But now, just as woman to woman," I inquired. "What are the special qualifications of a woman as a director?"

"Well, I found out one thing, and that was that I never have to ask a woman what her emotional reactions to a situation would be. I always know instinctively. Say what you like, a feminine star carries a huge responsibility in a picture. She furnishes most of the beauty and has the advantage of having the intense interest of women as well as of men, while men are just instinctively a little resentful of a male star who is hugely popular with women.

"Then a woman has an eye for beauty, and beauty is so large a part of the picture. It must naturally be so since the eye is the only avenue by which the audience takes in the picture."

I asked whether men resented being directed by a woman.

"No. On the other hand I think when she goes at her job squarely, they are anxious to help her. That is, if she approaches her job in a manner showing that she is just a worker like themselves and that she has no desire to make the men's roles inferior to those of the women."

I asked Miss Arzner how she chanced to become a director.

And that goes a long way back.

Miss Arzner's father and mother, Mr. and Mrs. Louis Arzner, were owners of the old Hoffman Café on Spring Street near Second, where used to foregather in the old days many of the leading stars, directors, and producers. There, eating the good food and drinking the good wine of the hostelry, could always be found of an evening, all informally clothed in their sports clothes and street dress, such lights as D. W. Griffith, William S. Hart, Sam Rork, Thomas H. Ince, Mack Sennett, Dorothy Gish, Constance and Natalie Talmage, Mabel Normand, Tom Geraghty, and many others.

Not that the small girl, Dorothy, ever saw these people, because she was a quiet little girl who stayed at home of evenings and was put to bed early, or, later, she was off to boarding school. But she did hear her parents speak of the film people.

"When I finished school," said Miss Arzner, "I began to think about my work in the world. The pictures naturally appealed to me. I met William de Mille while driving an ambulance for the army officials here during the flu and confided my ambition to him to do something for the screen. I told him I wanted to begin at the bottom, and he said, 'Well, I'll find you a job at the Lasky studio as a script girl.' He did. And I was awfully bad. If there hadn't been so many workers out on account of the flu and the war, I never could have kept my job. I used to have to retype at night all the stuff I had written during the day, my typing was so bad.

"The first impulse I had toward becoming a director came to me one day when I was watching Cecil B. DeMille direct. It struck me that the director was the brains of the whole concern. But I was still a script girl. I went over to see Mme. Nazimova and obtained a job there as a script girl."

Then Miss Arzner got her chance as a cutter and afterward as a writer for F.B.O. Later, she worked with Laurence Stallings, and was able, through her experience and her store of observation, to help him a great deal, and when he went east, he told Jesse Lasky and B. P. Schulberg that she should have a chance to direct.

She had worked a lot with James Cruze, especially on *Old Ironsides*.

"And I owe him a tremendous lot," said Miss Arzner gratefully. "He always treated me as though I were his son, without any frills but with a sort of comradely friendship."

"Were you frightened the first day you stepped onto a set to direct?" I inquired.

"Just scared stiff," confessed Miss Arzner. "Nobody ever suffered from stage fright as I did, I'm sure. But I kept going doggedly. I grew thin and got a cough. I felt like a rat in a trap. All night I would be figuring out speeches of resignation to make to Mr. Lasky and Mr. Schulberg. But, strangely enough, it seemed to me, the rushes came out all right. I was really putting on the screen just what I meant to. That is the oddest sensation, I believe, a director ever can have, seeing himself, as it were, coming to life on the screen, his own mental attitude and philosophy of life."

"But what handicaps did you find a woman as director has?" I wanted to know.

"Well, here's one thing, I'll confess," said Miss Arzner. "Women are deeply affected by the moods of the players. A man director is less sensitive to these moods. But, on the other hand, this very sensitiveness and a woman's easily impressed sensibilities aid her in getting the meaning of delicate scenes through to the audience."

I asked Miss Arzner if she had any ambition, having worked with Cruze on his big epics, to make any historical pictures.

"No. I just want to put human emotions, philosophy and action on the screen," replied Miss Arzner. "That is the sort of thing that intrigues me, just human drama."

Camera!

Enid Griffis / 1928

From *Independent Woman*, Aug. 1928.

It would be interesting to make a study of chance and the part it plays in the shaping of successful careers. Not that chance alone ever spelt achievement—but ability needs only opportunity! And it was chance that won that opportunity for Dorothy Arzner. If friends from the East had not insisted upon her taking them through a moving picture studio—who knows—she might still be a very efficient secretary in a business firm instead of one of the only two women moving picture directors in the industry today!

Although Miss Arzner has been engaged in directing pictures only for about two years, her contact with the world of films goes back to the days of her childhood. Her father was for many years manager of the old Hoffman Café in Los Angeles, which was the rendezvous of almost every screen pioneer on the West Coast. Long before she realized the importance of the names printed on the backs of the chairs in the alcove off the main dining room—names such as William S. Hart, Erich von Stroheim, D. W. Griffith, James Cruze, Raymond Griffith—she felt the fascination of the world to which these people belonged, and often stood outside the alcove peering through the velvet drapes that screened it from the rest of the room.

James Cruze found her thus one day, and taking her by the hand, he led her to the table and introduced her to the assembled company. From that time on, Dorothy enjoyed the freedom of the private dining room. She absorbed thirstily those bits of conversation and discussion about stories and films and actors that she was able to understand, and resolved that someday, she too would be one of such a group.

In the meantime, there was grammar school to be got through, and after that the Westlake School for Girls, and after that again, the University of Southern California. At the end of her second year in university, Miss Arzner left to take a trip to Hawaii. When she came back from this voyage, America had entered the World War. Anxious to contribute her share of service, she enlisted as a member of the Los Angeles Ambulance Corps and got as far as New York, but the unit to which she was attached was delayed there, and just as Miss Arzner and her fellow workers were about to step on a transport bound for the other side, the Armistice was signed. Inspired probably by her training as an ambulance worker, she returned to Los Angeles and prepared to take a medical course, but abandoned this after a time and secured a position as secretary in a business firm. And it was just about that time that her Eastern friends arrived and clamored to be shown through a moving picture studio.

Through a friend, Miss Arzner obtained a pass, and accompanied them on a tour through the Paramount studios. In the course of the trip, they came upon the set where William de Mille was making scenes for a new picture. Suddenly all the girl's childhood ambitions leapt into life again. She remained on the set, fascinated until the morning's work was completed, and then she approached Mr. de Mille and asked for a job. She offered to begin anywhere. Mr. de Mille took her name and address, and she left the studio.

It was sometime later that she received a call from the studio.

"This is Paramount calling. I understand you are interested in a position with us. We have a vacancy—"

Dorothy thrilled . . .

"—in the stenographic department—typing scripts—"

That was something of a comedown, to one who longed to direct epics of the screen, but she realized that it was an opening and accepted the job without hesitation. After all, a bird in the hand was worth several in the bush, and the work was connected, if humbly, with the profession towards which she aimed. For three months, she worked as a stenographer—and then came her big chance. She was given an opportunity to hold script on a Nazimova company. In this capacity, she remained on the set while each scene was being made, was able to observe the details of production, and saw the story come to life while she held and checked the cold working plans for the director. She was responsible for details in properties, costumes, matching actions, and all the kindred things that are so important to the smoothness of the cutting of pictures.

Faithfulness to her job was its own reward. Within a short time, she became a film cutter and gradually worked her way to a position where she was given an assignment to cut Rudolph Valentino's *Blood and Sand*.

One day while searching through the film laboratory for a room where his latest picture was to be projected in its rough form, James Cruze happened into the darkened room where Miss Arzner was running several reels of the newly cut

Valentino film. He watched it through. Then he demanded to see the cutter, and Dorothy Arzner—whom he had introduced to the company of screen celebrities many years before—presented herself.

Cruze had just finished working on *The Covered Wagon*. He went directly to Jesse L. Lasky and requested that Miss Arzner be given the assignment of cutting his picture. Her work was so successful that she was given a contract, which was the first signed agreement ever awarded a film cutter.

For two years, Miss Arzner continued as film cutter for Paramount, after which she gave up her work and turned to scenario writing. She had just established herself as a fairly successful freelance writer when James Cruze again appeared on the scene. He was about to begin work on *Old Ironsides* and wanted her to edit his picture. Between his persuasive arguing and Miss Arzner's own hankering to be back in the studio, the arrangement was accomplished.

For six months, *Old Ironsides* was in production. Miss Arzner came in contact with Laurence Stallings, author of the story, and with him and Cruze, worked out the action of the picture. Upon its completion, she locked herself up in the studio cutting room and alone executed what is recognized as one of the most nearly perfect examples of film editing in screen history.

While Miss Arzner was buried in the cutting room, forces of which she knew nothing were at work outside. Once, during the shooting of *Old Ironsides*, while the company was out on location, she had confided to Stallings that she would like to direct pictures. Stallings told Cruze, Cruze and Stallings told Jesse L. Lasky, and expressed their confidence in the ability of Miss Arzner to direct if she were given a chance. The upshot was that Lasky offered to give her a trial and made an agreement with her covering a year. Now that her big opportunity had arrived, she felt all her confidence oozing from her. But that did not prevent her from taking the job!

"There were times, even before we started," she confided, "when I felt I couldn't do it. But I didn't let anyone know I was afraid. My first assignment was Esther Ralston's picture *Fashions for Women*. Often at the end of the day's work, I would be convinced that I had failed. My impulse would be to turn over the megaphone to Mr. Lasky and tell him to get someone else. But by morning, some of my courage would have returned, and I would go back to my job. By the time the picture was done, I was a nervous wreck, but the production was a success, and they gave me *Ten Modern Commandments* to do, again with Ralston.

"It was easier this time. Some of the assurance [that] success brings was now mine, and my second picture seemed to show improvement. My third picture was *Get Your Man* for Clara Bow. The successful completion of this brought a renewal of my contract and won me my long-term agreement."

When asked how it felt to be a full-fledged director, Miss Arzner said: "It was hardly a thrill to me when I reached that point. The long, gradual, slow process of seven years of hard work was too continuous in struggles for me to feel that I had been suddenly projected into a realization of my dreams. I knew it was even harder to be a director than to attain that goal, for it is hard work even to make just a *good* picture."

Do Ladies Prefer Brunettes?

Frederick Isaac / 1928

From *Sunday Post* (Glasgow, Scotland), Oct. 28, 1928.

Gentlemen may prefer blondes, but—
Ladies prefer brunettes!
Which may be the reason there are practically no blonde men in Hollywood.
"Women admire virility in their screen heroes more than anything else," says Dorothy Arzner, Hollywood's only woman director. "And women are the greatest supporters of the screen. They want romance. And yet, they want a dash of devilry in their men—the kind, you know, that turns out all right in the eighth reel. There is only one way they can get this, from the virile, vital men, best exemplified in the brunette type."

The epitome of Hollywood opinion, this statement. Stars, directors, producers—practically all are of one mind; that blonde men are not, photographically at least, virile. They lack the warmth and glow and fire of their opposites, the dark-haired, dark-skinned men of fiery temperament.

Clarence Brown—the famous director of *Flesh and the Devil*, you remember—has a word or two to say on the subject.

"Blonde leading men fail by an eyebrow. In other words, the most salient feature in dramatic expression is in the eyes and eyebrows," he says. "Blonde eyebrows do not 'pick up' photographically, and blue eyes photograph almost white, making the face look insipid under the lens. And should an actor darken his eyebrows, the effect would be awful and suggest make-up and artificiality.

"With a woman, make-up is accepted as a matter of course, and a blonde girl with dark eyes and eyebrows is attractive photographically and still accepted as real. But the hero of the play in palpable make-up—it can't be done. That is the reason for the preponderance of dark actors."

But to return to Dorothy Arzner.

"I think people will change their choice pretty soon, as entertainment becomes more aesthetic—I mean away from the body angle—mental romance will replace or overshadow physical passion. Then another type of player will attract the picture-goer into the golden palaces. This new type of hero will be blonder and perhaps slightly effeminate—and as a contrast, a somewhat masculine type of woman will play against him. But remember, I am not talking about the present time."

There is certainly a lack of fair screen heroes to-day; just think of the men you admire, it is difficult to find more than three or four who can claim to be blonde. And all one can say about the coloring of these good chaps is that they are not dark. Bill Boyd and Conrad Nagel, Ralph Forbes and that fellow in *Four Sons*—George Meeker. Those are about the lot.

Yet distinctly dark brunettes are to be found right at the top of the tree and in every studio. There's Adolphe Menjou and John Gilbert, Ronald Colman and Gilbert Roland, Douglas Fairbanks and Richard Dix, Bill Haines and Ramon Navarro—even if one does not step upstairs and peep into the nursery.

I mean, think of the young 'uns—Charlie Rogers, Gary Cooper, Charlie Farrell, and Don Alvorado, Ben Lyon and anybody else you like to think of—they're all dark. Yet when it comes to the flaxen-headed, not many girlish hearts will flutter.

And why not?

Is it that there is a kind of effeminacy about the light-haired boy? Do those who have seen *Four Sons* find George Meeker effeminate? If so, it is a shame; you should see the fellow play tennis.

But had Bill Boyd, the steel-gray blonde, as big a following as dark John Gilbert! No, sir, he has not.

We have a couple of angles to the blonde-lack mystery so far. Dorothy says fans want virility, signified by the dark type of male. Clarence explains how blonde eyebrows look insipid, blue eyes photograph almost white, and men cannot counteract this as the women do, yet look human . . . .

There is some very deep reason for our preference for dark leading men, and it is very possible that Dorothy Arzner has the key to the whole thing. We were sitting in her office again while I was obtaining additional data from her.

"It comes down to symbolism," she said slowly and with thought. "Sunshine, that is—lightness has always suggested the spiritual, the effeminate. The night, that is the dark, suggests the material man.

"Since ever legends have existed, the touch of symbolism seems to have been upheld, and so to-day, when our legends are shown to us, instead of told to us, symbolism is still there. The darkness signifies man—virile, passionate, material—and I do not think that the blonde fellow has a place in the appealing, thrilling, vital pictures people want to see to-day."[1]

Note

1. In a short-syndicated piece published several years later, Arzner shared her perspectives on blonde and brunette women in film. She was quoted as saying that "if the leading woman is a brunette, the 'other woman' is a blonde. This works the other way also. The reason such a plan is used is that each type accentuates the beauty of the other. The contrast is always sought in selecting characters. If a complete cast of blondes were used, for instance, audiences would be conscious of a flatness in the picture although they would not know what had caused it. As a rule it is the blonde who enacts the siren, the fickle one, while the brunette is the one who loves deeply. This is often reversed for the sake of novelty. A few years ago a blonde never had a chance to play any character other than of the sweet young thing. Just why it has finally been decided that the girls with the golden locks are the wicked ones I do not know." For a sample copy of this filler piece, see "Blondes vs. Brunettes," *Singapore Free Press and Mercantile Advertiser*, October 7, 1932.

Only Woman Movie Director

Mayme Ober Peak / 1928

From *Boston Globe*, Dec. 2, 1928.

Women have gained a successful foothold in practically every field of human endeavor. But in the most modern industry—the manufacture of motion pictures—the modern woman has not broken the male monopoly.

Strange to say, there is no woman executive in the motion picture industry and only one woman director, Dorothy Arzner. Lois Weber blazed the trail some years ago, but so far, Miss Arzner is the third, and youngest, woman who has traveled it and survived.

Recently, Mrs. Wallace Reid directed one of her independent productions. "Wally's" widow, however, has no official studio connection, while Dorothy Arzner is under contract to Paramount Studios, which recently renewed it under long-term agreement after a year's trial.

Director Arzner, like Lois Weber, learned the mechanics of moviemaking from the bottom up and did not arrive overnight as did many of her lordly colleagues. On the theory that the first requisite is to get inside a studio, she crashed the gates with a typewriter, pounding her way to the top from the script department. "The kindergarten of motion picture education," she called it. Here she took her first step toward handling a megaphone by typing script, considered the blueprint and very foundation of movies.

Having a college-trained, analytical mind, a goal that stood out like a beckoning mountaintop, Miss Arzner wasted no time detouring. Studying the creative work of the different writers and the various minds with which she came in contact, she absorbed knowledge as a sponge does moisture and, in due time, graduated from typist to script clerk, scenario writer, cutter, film editor and thence straight to director. No assistant directorship for her!

Five minutes' talk with this young woman director will tell you why she is successful. In fact, you don't have to talk to her at all. To look at her is sufficient. If you could have seen her the day I interviewed her at Paramount Studios, swinging down the concrete walk of the big lot, planting her tan oxfords firmly with each step, shoulders and head up, cool gray eyes alert, you would have recognized the surefire qualities that make for success.

She stepped into the publicity office where I had been delayed, shot a keen glance at me, and came forward with a strong grip of the hand. At once I thought, Here's a woman who could run the studio if she had a mind to!

Not that there is anything aggressive about Dorothy Arzner's manner. She isn't masculine. Neither is she especially feminine. Just one of those modern college girl types with a certain air of boyishness and an awful lot of confidence.

Her black hair was cut in a boyish bob and brushed straight back from a strong forehead. She wore a slip-on sweater and skirt of tan; a soft silk blouse with Buster Brown collar. If I remember rightly, a gay striped scarf was twisted about her neck.

She was between pictures, so we had time for an uninterrupted talk. To have it, we went to Miss Arzner's office in Directors' Row. The room was almost prim in its neatness. The usual wall spatter of stills and autographed pictures was missing. Above the director's desk hung the original artist's sketch of her first "set"—a café scene in Paris.

Dorothy Arzner turned out to be a delightful person to talk to. She has a mind that isn't single-tracked on pictures, and we switched about considerably, so much so that it was difficult to get her to tell me her own story. In telling it, along with her philosophical observations, she told me why there aren't women directors.

"Women haven't come around to thinking they can undertake the task of directing," she said. "So far, women haven't wanted to be directors. They had rather write or act. I wanted to be a director the first day I entered a studio—the man at the top, he seemed to me, and that was where I meant to be. I got there not by merely believing I would be, but by almost being, a director. When I was on the set as script girl, I always was visualizing how I would be doing the scene regardless of how the director was doing it!

"There will be more woman directors," she went on, "in motion pictures when more women build their careers in that direction. After all, the only limitation is in the mind. If your mind is set on a thing and you know you can do it, you are not going to feel any physical lack on account of your sex. I heard C. B. DeMille say once that a woman couldn't stand under twenty hours of directing. From a man's point of view, that meant a woman lacked physical and moral stamina for long location trips and such demands!"

Dorothy Arzner gave a little chuckle. "If the present generation continues its gymnastic stunts, physical culture, swimming and tennis, a woman's body will be as sound and healthy as a man's. A woman will be able to throw handsprings around many men; all she will need will be strength of mind to undertake any task.

"The mistakes so many women are making now is trying to do two jobs. The sooner women get somebody else to run the home while they go out and work, the more successful they are going to be, because they will bring to it more strength of mind and body."

"What can a woman bring to the job of directing pictures that a man cannot?" I queried.

"Men as a mass have been free and selfish. Women for centuries have been shackled and serving, giving, bearing children. They have learned discipline, gained a knowledge of living that goes deep. I feel that women can bring more knowledge than men.

"But there is something of the woman in all the best men directors. Woman is primarily creative and the men who succeed best are those with the characteristics of creativeness so often associated with women. The ideal combination would be a man and woman working together. A woman who understands direction is valuable on a set during the filming of any production.

"Try as man may, he will never be able to get a woman's viewpoint into telling certain stories, which is important when you come to think that 75 percent of picture audiences are women!"

Miss Arzner declared she had experienced no sex prejudice in working with men or difficulty in giving orders to the small army of technicians required on every set. But she admitted a bad case of stage fright the first day she wielded the megaphone when there were 200 extras to direct in a café scene in Paris, when she had never been to Paris in her life.

"Since talking to men, I find that they had it, too," she said, "for their first picture, and most men, you know, have been assistant directors first.

"Never before had I been in a position to tell others to do something. I was petrified. Every night I would go home thinking I couldn't come back tomorrow, lying awake making up speeches of resignation. But fear never overcame me. The assistant director knew I was panicky. He watched for some indication of it but told me afterward he never saw any. My voice was low. I moved slowly and deliberately. Mr. Schulberg would look out of his office window and see me passing through the lot, and he'd say, 'She acts like a veteran!'"

As luck would have it, Miss Arzner's first picture was *Fashions for Women* starring Esther Ralston. But the problem wasn't altogether clothes, although an elaborate fashion show was one of its sequences. A score of mannequins had to be selected to wear the stunning creations—tall and symmetrical.

Because the camera favors the small woman, Miss Arzner found that among the thousands of girls in Hollywood, the tall, symmetrical ones who walk gracefully and know how to wear clothes seemed to be scarce. The executive offices select the star for a picture, but the remainder of the cast, ranging from featured players down to bits, are largely selected by the man behind the megaphone, who decides whether they fit his pattern.

Then there is the ever-present bugaboo of budget—the consumption of limited time and money, too. This was another worry for director Arzner to map out a schedule that would use the fewest number of camera days and the smallest number of high-salaried people who were not under contract to her studio. Story conferences had to be had with the star, the scenarists, the wardrobe and property departments. Small wonder that Dorothy Arzner was near collapse before she even started shooting!

It is now a matter of record that she "clicked" with this first directorial effort, which she assembled in the cutting room at the end of just thirty days. *Ten Modern Commandments* was her next picture, then *Get Your Man* starring Clara Bow. After that, there was nothing to it. Dorothy Arzner knew her stuff, and the studio knew it, so they gave her a long-term contract. Under the latter, her first picture was *Manhattan Cocktail*.

There have been several interesting press yarns about Dorothy Arzner that I got her to sift down to the truth. Honesty, I found, was one of her characteristics—that, and directness—two of the most disarming qualities one may possess, especially a woman.

"Honesty was the policy by which I became a director," she explained, "and I haven't seen any reason to change it. When I made a mistake, I never tried to alibi it! I went straight to the seat of the trouble and corrected it."

Born in Oakland, Dorothy came to Los Angeles as a small child when her father became manager of the old Hoffman Café—the rendezvous of every screen pioneer. At the far end of the café was a velvet-screened alcove, where members of the film colony gathered at a round table. On the back of the chairs were painted such names as William S. Hart, D. W. Griffith, Charles Chaplin, Mack Sennett, Lew Cody, and James Cruze.

One of the prettiest stories about how Dorothy first became interested in the movies stated that one day James Cruze discovered her peeping through a slit in the velvet curtain; that the now-famous director brought out his future *confrère* and introduced her to the industry in which she was soon to shine; and that thereafter little Dorothy sat on Cruze's lap [and] listened enraptured to discussions of stories and acting.

But here's the truth straight from headquarters. "I was never allowed to go to the café," she said. "I may have heard my father talking about the picture people, but it made no impression on my childish brain.

"I grew up out of step with other children. I was restive and had something of the spartan in me. I thought I wanted to study medicine, to help people out of pain. After I finished at the Westlake School for Girls, I went to the University of Southern California to take a medical course.

"Shortly after, the war broke out. I enlisted in the Los Angeles Ambulance Corps. Our unit got as far as New York en route to France when the Armistice was signed, and I found myself back home still not knowing what I wanted to do.

"One day the commander of the Ambulance Corps whom I had driven for months asked me: 'Now what are you going to do? Why not go into the movies, that's a modern industry for a modern girl like you.' She told me she would make an appointment for me with Mr. William de Mille, whom she had known in our intelligence department, and a few days later fairly dumped me outside his door.

"'Here I am,' I announced, 'I suppose I want to work.' Mr. de Mille gave me a searching look and told me to turn my head this way and that. 'Oh, I don't want to be an actress,' I said.

"'Well, maybe you could be a set dresser,' he suggested. 'What's the period of this furniture?'

"I was struck dumb. I didn't know any kind of furniture but Italian, which I liked because of the simplicity and purity of its design.

"'It is Franciscan,' Mr. de Mille advised me. I will never forget it, I assure you!

"When he saw I would be no good as a set dresser, he told me to look around for a week, go anywhere I wanted. I thought that would be grand and give me a chance to see how pictures are made. I looked around, and I went back to Mr. de Mille. 'If possible,' I told him, 'I would like to start to work at the bottom.'

"'Where do you think the bottom is?'

"'Typing script.'

"'Go to the head of the class,' he said and sent me away with the promise of the first opening.

"I went home, never thinking there would be one. But I mastered the mechanics of the typewriter and determined now to go into business. I obtained a job through a girlfriend at Joannes Brothers coffee house as a filing clerk at twelve dollars a week. I had a grand time. I learned to run the switchboard and all phases of the coffee business. If I had kept on, I probably would be president of that coffee house."

Business palled on Miss Arzner, however, and when a call came from the studio for [a] typist position, she jumped at it, although she honestly admits that maybe the fifteen-dollar weekly salary as against the twelve dollars she was getting may have had something to do with it.

The first day at the studio she says was a nightmare.

"The woman in charge had left a pile of typing. I thought it had to be done at one time, and I worked all day and night to finish it, thinking, goodness me, I'll never be able to hold this job! If it hadn't been for the typist sitting next to me who took compassion on me and helped, I might not have gotten by.

"I held that stenographer's job just three months when I realized it was time for the next step. It was like seeing a mountaintop. The only way you can go to it is to move along. But I had learned a great deal. I had not only come in contact with directors and so-called important persons around the studio but in typing scenarios, I had observed the minds of all the different writers and studied their creative work. I would read the original story or novel from which the scenario was being made, see the finished picture and compare it with my own ideas, and watch audience reactions at the previews or studio projection room.

"I learned that placing stories on the screen is quite different from the ability to write them. Description might cover up a multitude of weaknesses in a written story, but this is not possible on the screen, which requires action [that] will photograph."

Dorothy Arzner's next step was to hold script on a Nazimova picture. Here on the set, while holding and checking the mechanical working plan for the director, she watched the story come to life; [and] was responsible for details in properties, costumes, matching actions, and other things important to the smoothness of cutting the picture.

Then she advanced cutting and assembling the finished film, which required dramatic feeling and sense of "situations." Pictures are made up of more than one thousand scenes or camera set-ups. Cutting is like gathering material for an essay; all scenes are perfect in telling their part of the story but cannot be used because of time limit[s]. The dramatic discrimination of the cutter can make or mar the picture.

Dorothy Arzner worked under the head cutter to a position never before held by a woman. She was signed to an agreement—something unheard of among cutters who had always been men. The result was she showed what a woman could do in this department, and now most of the cutters are women in the various studios.

One day, Miss Arzner was cutting Valentino's *Blood and Sand*, in which she introduced a new method of film editing now pretty generally adopted. James Cruze stumbled into the darkened projection room. He stood in amazement, looking at the flickering picture, its dramatic course holding him to the end. He immediately asked to see the cutter and the young lady, whom that nice yarn had it used to sit on his lap when a child, walked out.

Cruze had just finished work on *The Covered Wagon*. He went to Jesse Lasky with the request that Miss Arzner be given the task of cutting his picture. She made such a good job of it that when, later, Cruze began work on *Old Ironsides*, he went to Dorothy Arzner's office where a little sign had been hung out announcing her a full-fledged scenario writer, with the request that she edit his production.

Miss Arzner, who hadn't been any too successful as a freelance writer, closed her office and went on location with [the] *Ironsides* company—the only woman among a small army of two thousand men. Together with Laurence Stallings, who wrote the story, and with Cruze, she worked out the action. When the picture was completed, she locked herself in the studio cutting room and single-handedly executed what is declared to be one of the most nearly perfect examples of film cutting in the history of pictures.

During their work together, Miss Arzner had confided to Stallings her ambition to be a director. He and Cruze went to the powers that be and declared they knew a woman who would make a good director if given the opportunity. And you know the rest!

Of course, Dorothy Arzner has ideals about picture-making, but she says, "[I]f you know what is perfect and carry that perfect picture in your mind, you have the terrific job of trying to get that perfection from many people working with you. That is what drives the sculptor crazy. He takes the dead, silent medium [that] is stone and tries to carve into it the life and spirit he sees."

She believes the screen will become "the most spiritual medium" we have and that eventually, it will be something fine if man doesn't try to limit it. "I discovered a great truth in slapstick," she said, "that the screen is very spiritual. There is no time, no space. It can be illustrative of the fourth dimension. In slapstick, we show a man leaping from the top of a building. He falls completely dead and then immediately comes to life. He can be ground under the wheels of a train and come to life. The theory of all philosophers is that there is no death.

"The screen is not limited, but man is going to limit it just as he has limited himself because he wants to make the people on the screen like himself instead of giving it the spirit of its own. As yet, the most spiritual medium is music. You can hear it and feel [it], but you can neither touch nor see it."

From here, she branched off to the philosophical awakening, as evidenced in the interest in the writings of Wells, Durant, and others, and how it would affect the screen, and talked on until dusk. I came away, after an instructive two hours, more convinced than ever that Dorothy Arzner has enough brains to run a whole movie plant. And I'm not so sure that all a woman has to do is to "think" she can direct movies and then go do it!

"Dot" Arzner Proves Talker Ability

Howard Hall / 1929

From *Sound Waves*, April 1, 1929.

Men, the discoverers of new worlds through untold centuries, have had their ranks invaded by a small slip of a woman with calm, serious eyes.

The feminine Columbus has just made one of the most important discoveries of the year—a revelation [that] will prove more interesting to millions of people the world over than would the finding of a new comet with a tail ninety million miles long.

For this woman, Dorothy Arzner, has discovered a new star in Hollywood!

She has disclosed that Clara Bow, fiery red-haired star of the silversheet, is an even greater stellar light in talking pictures then she was on the silent screen.

Entrusted with the important task of directing Clara Bow's first talking picture—the production by which [the] public and critics will judge the voice of the screen's greatest feminine star—Miss Arzner went ahead with plans for filming *The Wild Party* with the same cool judgment and executive foresight [that] have characterized her work in other pictures. The fact that it was also Miss Arzner's first talking picture did not create any mental hazards but increased her determination to make it her greatest directorial achievement.

And now Dorothy Arzner has the distinction of being the only woman director of talking pictures in the film industry!

"When Jesse L. Lasky gave me the chance to direct Clara Bow in a talking production," Miss Arzner declares, "I believe I was even more thrilled than the day when, several years ago, he gave me a contract to direct *Fashions for Women*, starring Esther Ralston. Prior to that first directorship, I had been working in various capacities around the Paramount and other studios. Typing scripts for the Alla Nazimova Company was my first job, and it taught me a great deal about the mechanics of picture making." Miss Arzner quit the script job to enter a studio cutting room.[1]

"I was thrilled beyond words when the office decided I should cut *Blood and Sand*," Miss Arzner continued. "Rudolph Valentino was starred in it, and I was terribly frightened and amazed to think I had been assigned such an important task. And then, I remembered that it was only through the accomplishment of important things that I could reach the goal I had set for myself—that of a director."

Her work stood out so well that James Cruze, then a Paramount director, praised it to Lasky and other studio executives. Cruze picked her out to cut his first big production, *The Covered Wagon*.

That gave her her great chance. After this, she applied for a place in the scenario department, writing several stories. After a period of freelancing, she rejoined Paramount. This was the turning point in her career.

Jesse L. Lasky had a long talk with her. He learned her ideas on various subjects and was impressed by her firm belief in her own abilities. The result of the meeting was a contract. Paramount liked her first picture, and so did audiences. She followed it with *Ten Modern Commandments*, *Get Your Man*, *Manhattan Cocktail* and then was assigned to her first talking picture, *The Wild Party*.

Her life story has the aspects of a Cinderella tale.

"I'll admit I'm a Cinderella," she declares. "And I have a fairy godmother, too. Yes, and that godmother's name is—Hard Work!"

Note

1. Arzner typed scripts for Paramount before serving as a script continuity supervisor on a single Alla Nazimova film, *Stronger Than Death*, in 1920.

Hollywood's One Woman Director

Washington (DC) Evening Star / 1929

From *Washington (DC) Evening Star*, July 7, 1929.

"Now kiss!"

Then fifteen seconds later by the stopwatch: "Break!"

And another Hollywood ga-ga girl has been brought one kiss closer to stardom, thanks to Hollywood's girl-with-brains and only woman director, Dorothy Arzner.

For movie kissing isn't the impetuous pastime it appears to be. In fact, it's an exact science. In the words of the song that is considerably older than cinema kissing technique: "Every little movement has a meaning all its own"—and also a time limit.

A perfect kiss never lasts longer than fifteen seconds—at least not in the movies, according to director Dorothy Arzner. And only the most heavily scented moments can stand a kiss of that length. Not because movie wooers who can't get into that length of time all the emotion any scene requires are not efficient enough at the business to have their efforts immortalized in celluloid, but because even the loveliest heroines and nicest heroes look ridiculous if this matter of osculation is overdone.

But do not get the idea that timing kisses is a movie director's principal occupation.

"A director's job really isn't nearly as easy as many persons seem to think it is," Miss Arzner says. "In many ways, the success or failure of a picture lies in the director's hands. When a theater audience sees a picture, it thinks only of what the characters are doing and not of the guiding hand behind that action.

"For example, in a love scene, few people stop to consider the technical action behind it," Miss Arzner explains. "When a man kisses the girl, that act is all that registers. Yet, if the kiss were a little too long or too short, it might ruin the entire scene.

"Kisses must be of various durations, depending upon circumstances. I would say that the average screen kiss should last from five to seven seconds, although there are many times when a two-second kiss is more effective. That is a thing the director must decide for his players. He must visualize the effect that kiss will have upon an audience and time it exactly right. A seven-second kiss in a spot that calls for one of fifteen seconds would be just as bad as overdoing it.

"Another very important factor which must be decided by the director is the amount of highly emotional acting, commonly known as 'sob stuff,' a film requires. That is one of the most difficult questions to decide because people vary so greatly in their like or dislike for this type of acting.

"Women, as a rule, like considerable emotion in a picture," she continues. "If they shed a few tears while they are in the theater, the film is a success. Men, on the other hand, prefer comedy. Consequently, we must have enough sob scenes to satisfy the women, but not enough to overcome the humorous side of the film [that] appeals to the men."

Dorothy Arzner's view of movie matters [is] interesting because she is the only woman in Hollywood who is in a position to express them, as it were, through a director's megaphone. And for nearly eight years, she has been associated with the business of producing pictures. So, although she has never acted, she knows the cinema art—and business—from every angle.

Two years ago, she achieved her greatest ambition by becoming a director. Only one other woman, Lois Weber, who has since retired, ever wielded a movie megaphone.

Miss Arzner is considered one of Hollywood's most interesting notables. She is credited with having more brains than many of the so-called big men of the industry. And she easily holds her own in competition with the horde of male directors. Yet her entry into the movie business was purely accidental.

"If anyone had told me I was going into the picture business a year before I did, I would have promptly told him he was crazy," Miss Arzner says, although much of her early life was spent around theatrical people.

Her father was a prominent San Francisco café owner before the 1906 earthquake. After his business was wiped out by that disaster, he came to Los Angeles to start over again and opened a café in connection with one of the leading theaters in the city, which became popular.

About that time, Dorothy was enrolled in the Westlake School for Girls, located on what was then the outskirts of the city. She completed her grammar and high school courses there.

She was in the midst of her second year at the University of Southern California when the United States entered the World War. Along with several other girls, she left school and joined the Red Cross Ambulance Corps. However, she saw no overseas service. Her detail was assigned to transporting sick soldiers and sailors between San Pedro and San Diego.

Very shortly after she was mustered out of the ambulance service, Miss Arzner had her first taste of life within a film studio, although she still had no desire to pursue a cinema career. In college, she had studied sociology and medicine with the idea of following the medical branch of sociology work.

"A girlfriend of mine literally shoved me into picture work," declares the director. "She thought I was well suited for it, so she made an appointment for me with Cecil B. DeMille. Then she drove me over to the Paramount studio and dumped me out in front of the main office. There was nothing left to do but go in, although I still had no idea what I wanted to do."[1]

When the more or less abashed young girl entered his office, DeMille inquired, "What can I do for you?"

"I want a job," Dorothy replied.

"Let me see your profile," said DeMille.

"Oh, I don't want to be an actress," she hastened to assure him.

"What do you want to do?" he asked.

"I don't know."

That closed the short interview. For the next week, Miss Arzner spent her entire time prowling around the studio, learning what she could about the art of making pictures. It was during that week that she became ambitious to be a director. She saw DeMille walking around the lot and decided that he was the "big shot" with a comfortable seat right on top of the world. So she went back to his office and told him she wanted to go to work.

"Do you know yet what you want to do?" he inquired.

"Yes. I want to start at the bottom," she replied.

"What do you consider the bottom?" was his next question.

"Typing scripts," she replied.

DeMille promised her the first opening in the studio's typing department, and about a week later, she was called to start work. Then followed jobs as a script girl and finally as a cutter.

"My first picture as a cutter was Rudolph Valentino's *Blood and Sand*," she says. "I was given a pretty free hand on the picture, and the studio officials liked my work well enough that they gave me a permanent job as a cutter. But I wasn't satisfied. I wanted to become a film editor, so I quit and went to work as an editor for Universal."[2]

"I was always quitting my job at Paramount to go somewhere else and always came back again," Miss Arzner says. "I soon learned that there is a lot of truth in the old proverb, 'a prophet in his own country is without honor.' Nobody would recognize my ability to do bigger things in my own studio. I had to take the bigger job at another studio and then come back to Paramount.

"Finally, I decided I wanted to be a scenario writer. So I quit my job again, rented an office, and set myself up as one—but there were no scenarios to write. I was just about ready to give up when I got a job adapting six Western stories for an independent producer.

"Just as I was getting nicely established as a scenario writer, Jim Cruze asked me if I would come back to Paramount and cut *Old Ironsides* for him. After I finished cutting his biggest success, *The Covered Wagon*, I told him that if he ever wanted me to edit another picture for him, I would. When I finished on *Old Ironsides*, I decided it was time for me to achieve my great ambition and become a director, so I tried to quit my job again."

But this time, Paramount would not let her, and when she clung to her determination to be a director, the Paramount executives decided to give her a chance.

Her first picture was *Fashions for Women*, in which Esther Ralston was starred.

"I shall never forget it," Miss Arzner declares. "I never had called 'camera' before in my life. Most assistant directors have the opportunity to direct small scenes, but I never had had that training. Outwardly I guess I was perfectly calm. But inside, I was in a turmoil. On the very first day, we shot a cabaret scene with about five hundred extras in it. Nobody said anything, but I know everyone on the set sensed a certain tenseness for about two weeks.

"I have not found, however, that men object to taking orders from a woman. In fact, I don't believe they consider it in that light [at] all. I have never thought I was working for anyone but myself, and I believe most people are in that same frame of mind.

"Then, too, I don't believe there is such a thing as sex in thought, and thought is the prime factor in making a picture. I had thoughts to transfer to the screen, and the people working with me accepted those thoughts at their face value without any consideration of sex whatever.

"One often hears remarks about good direction, but in reality, it is the actors who are good," Miss Arzner contends. "You can only bring out of people what they have in them. If they don't possess a certain quality, nobody can bring it out. That is why some directors are better than others. They know better just how to bring out the qualities in their players. It is impossible to make a character appear noble on the screen unless he has a noble streak in him somewhere, even though it may not be developed.

"Nothing is surefire in pictures," director Arzner has found. "We can guess at what type of material will make successful pictures, but we never know until we find out how many people are paying their money to see the film.

"I have never yet attempted to make the type of picture [that] we term great. My idea is that the public goes to a theater to be entertained, and if we don't entertain them, we aren't giving them their money's worth, no matter how great the production might be. If a film is wholly entertaining, people will overlook its minor defects."

Notes

1. In other accounts, Arzner credited Drake Section Sanitaire Director Anna Starkweather for making the appointment. In addition, Arzner or her interviewer misidentified William de Mille as his brother Cecil.
2. Arzner edited dozens of films for Paramount's Realart subsidiary before editing *Blood and Sand*. She did, however, edit at least two films for Universal in 1924.

Directed by Dorothy Arzner!

Julie Lang / 1929

From *Screenland*, Aug. 1929.

The only woman director to wrest consistent success from a megaphone job. The only woman director under long-term contract to any studio in Hollywood. The only woman to rise in the span of a few years from a typist's job to that of making Clara Bow's first dialogue picture.

Would you like to meet her?

Would you like to know what sort of a person this Dorothy Arzner is?

Of course you would! So, through the pages of *Screenland*, let me introduce you to a quiet-voiced, dreamy-eyed girl, just under medium height, heavy dark brown hair worn smartly off forehead and ears, small mouth and nose, enormous gray eyes.

Very attractive, you say?

You discover that she is gracious without any studied effects with which to impress new acquaintances. But where is that dominance, that aggressiveness, you ask? Is she cleverly hiding her generalship and putting on this artful feminine fantasy?

No, the Arzner dominance is entirely mental; and as for aggressiveness, she shrinks from its contact. Field marshal tactics have never been employed by Dorothy Arzner, on the set or off; but cleverness, a great capacity for absorbing knowledge, and a genius for accomplishing grinding, nerve-crushing mountains of work have brought very satisfying results.

Now you will want to talk to her but be prepared to do most of the chattering yourself. Naturally, the first question will be on her break into the movies. Yes, ask her that one—everybody does!

"Very colorless, I assure you," she will answer. "A visit to the Paramount studios with the Commander of the Los Angeles Emergency Ambulance Corps."

Yes, yes, but what had that to do with her career?

"Well, I had never felt any desire to visit a studio, although I had lived in Los Angeles all my life," she will reply very slowly and softly, "and when I first stood on a klieg-flooded set, I suddenly knew that my future was inside those studio gates."[1]

Now there is an interesting story about Dorothy's many and conflicting ambitions before that eventful visit to the Paramount studio, but you will never get her to elucidate on the subject, so I'll tell you.

During the war, Dorothy enlisted in the Ambulance Corps and was about to embark for the front when the armistice was signed. When she returned to Los Angeles, she enrolled in the University of Southern California.

After graduation came the dilemma. "Where do I belong? I must do something." Although Dorothy's family was anxious that she stay at home and elect the playful routine of a debutante, she cast about for an occupation. The business world loomed up as a colorful globe to conquer, so she hied herself to secretarial school (lucky thing she did, as we shall see later) and got herself a job secretarying. But business proved to be a mundane affair of mussy carbon copies, dull letters, uninteresting indexes, and innumerable filing systems. So Dorothy pleased her family for a few months by attending social gatherings. But that old germ ambition gnawed at her peace of mind.

The next Arzner enthusiasm was medicine. To become a renowned physician, to help alleviate the suffering and misery of human beings became her goal, and she enrolled in a medical college.

It was during this adventure into the land of bacteria that the eventful tour changed the destiny of Dorothy Arzner. She had anticipated the studio visit with boredom but left the gates with her future a tangible object.

"I pried open the studio gates with a typewriter," she says laughingly, "for my knowledge of typing brought about an opportunity to get on the studio payroll as a typist in the scenario department. After four months of exhausting work, a spark of encouragement brightened the horizon in the form of promotion to the reading department. Step number one, said I!

"I knew that every day's work brought me a little nearer that canvas chair lettered 'director'; each task finished was that much knowledge stored away for the big job that would come someday. A year later, I found myself back of the cameras as a script clerk. Step number two! Out on the sets at last, at the side of a director, thousands of new details to learn. I asked questions constantly, of the electricians, the prop boys, the cameramen, and the director when he was not too busy. I suppose many of those boys put me down as a dreadful pest!"

Script work led to cutting, and although that was a step away from the sets, it meant more valuable knowledge to Dorothy for her ultimate job. Every successful director knows how to cut his productions. As a cutter, she won unusual fame. James Cruze heard of her prowess and asked her to cut *The Covered Wagon*. From that time, the sailing was a bit smoother.

While working on this production, Dorothy confided her secret to Cruze, the first person to know of this very young person's astounding ambition.

"Well, if any woman can direct, you're the one to do it, Dorothy," was his encouraging reply.

The next year was spent cutting and writing while she patiently waited for that opportunity. James Cruze again summoned her help on *Old Ironsides*. During this production,

Cruze told Dorothy it was high time she tried her hand at directing and then slyly let the subject drop. But when the last inch of film had been cut and spliced, Dorothy was called to the offices of B. P. Schulberg, general manager of West Coast production for Paramount.

"We have watched your work for several years," Schulberg told her, "and we have all the confidence in the world in your ability to direct. Your first assignment will be Esther Ralston's next production, *Fashions for Women*."

That is the story of one girl's break. Now perhaps you would like to go out on the set and watch her work.

A petite woman in charge of a company of several hundred persons with the responsibility of a tremendous production on her shoulders and the popularity of a famous star in the palm of her hand, Dorothy Arzner is as quiet on the set as in the drawing room. Her natural poise is always evident. She dresses in quietly clever tailored suits that blend perfectly with her personality. A vagabond felt hat is usually pulled down to shade her eyes from the glare of the lights. She sits back in that canvas chair lettered "director" or walks about slowly, talking with the players or the crew. She keeps herself and her personality in the background, for she believes that the players should dominate the set, never the director.

When a scene is about to be "shot," Dorothy talks over the work at hand with the players. She never goes through the gestures or repeats the lines for them to illustrate the tempo or the effects desired. Through subtle suggestion, she gets the players to feel the mood of the scene so that their work will have the spark of spontaneity and not the woodiness of imitation.

How simple it all appears to the onlooker—all those men and women to assist her with the work! Yet the most simple things have complicated foundations. Let us delve into the simplicity of Dorothy Arzner's job. Five weeks before a single foot of film is shot on any production, she is working in her office at the studio from nine every morning until ten and eleven at night.

Doing what, you ask?

Story conferences, outlining work for sets, making out shooting schedules, okaying wardrobes, selecting casts, and a thousand other unfilmed details that go into the making of our movies.

During actual shooting, Dorothy averages a sixteen-hour working day and uses the intervening Sundays and holidays to help with the cutting and editing. After production is over comes the labor of trimming and finishing the film. Hours in the projection room running the reels over and over again, catching every incorrect detail, revising, rearranging, until the last snip of the scissors is heard and the films packed in their respective cans and shipped to the exchanges for the date of distribution.

Then a few days of rest and she's off again on another production.

You won't be able to resist asking her about marriage and her future plans.

"Marriage is natural for both men and women and does not interfere with one's career or ambitions," will be her answer. "Matrimony travels a much less rocky course when both parties are occupied in some sort of work during the day. But then the subject of marriage or careers for women is such a hackneyed one that I try to avoid it. I will probably marry someday, and I hope I will make a success of it when I do."

But there is little need for conjecture as to whether Dorothy Arzner will make a success of marriage or any other job she tackles. Her spirit will ever be restless; she will always be searching for mental stimulation, but she is gifted with the patience and the intelligence to work, struggle, even suffer to attain her ideals. And it follows that she does attain them, and what is more important, retain them.

Note

1. Arzner was born in San Francisco but moved to Los Angeles as a child.

Custom Restricts Women

Elena Boland / 1930

From *Los Angeles Times*, March 23, 1930.

Why are there so few women directors in pictures? In fact, now, there is only one—Dorothy Arzner. To her, it is not a question of women being unsuited to directorial responsibilities but a question of tradition. Each profession, through the law of custom, has certain positions [that] it is taken for granted that men will fill; certain other capacities are sought by women. The reason there are not more women picture directors, Miss Arzner thinks, is that women do not aspire to be directors. They accept this convention that directorship is a man's job, and they find their work elsewhere.

The reference is to motion pictures; there is, for contrast, the theater. During recent years, an increasing number of women have taken over both the directing and producing end of play presentation. Why, then, in the theater and not the films? Again Miss Arzner draws on tradition as the solution. The theater is older; it has held women important far longer than have the pictures. Women have had time to move up the scale to the most influential position of all—director.

Dorothy Arzner is a philosopher, self-professed. She is not a feminist, nor does she harbor any theory about masculine and feminine viewpoints.

"Thought is sexless, and creation comes through thought. I don't class society as men and women. There are only individuals and mind. A woman's mind is often more masculine than a man's; men, though most might resent this, are thinking more femininely. There is, however, a difference between feminine and effeminate.

"Women have intuition; men, reason. That, I think, is their great distinction. Intuition leaps directly to the point. Reason figures out the steps along the way. Reason is more often right, hence men [are] more useful. Intuition arrives at a conclusion, say, for instance, this—the man went home. Reason attacks that—brings it down to practicality. Thus the man went out that door and around that corner, so could not have gone home. Men's logic, then, is sometimes more valuable practically than intuition. But complete and perfect thought must have in it both elements. That will come together; that will come after men and women work together longer."

The impersonal attitude is what Miss Arzner strives for in directing; that, and absolute naturalness. To a degree, she believes she has accomplished both in *Sarah and Son*, now at the Paramount Theater.

"A picture or a play is the director's product. Only insofar as he is capable is the production good. The fine actor is but a willing instrument. A director can put nothing of himself into an actor, though he can draw out, almost limitlessly, that actor's possibilities. But the director, his personality must not be seen at all.

"I like to direct women. I know their emotions and reactions. *Sarah and Son* is a woman's story; it was adapted for the screen by Zoë Akins. I liked it, and I liked directing Ruth Chatterton. She is intelligent and, I think, the finest actress on the screen.

"It is a quiet story, done entirely in restraint. It has no emotional display. It is natural, I can say that. It has been so stripped of all artificiality that it has the effect of realism. The last sequence is the best. It is held down to a monotone, ended unfinished, and leaves the audience a little breathless."

So often it is complained that pictures are too commercial to be artistic, that an artistic success must be a box-office failure. Dorothy Arzner does not agree. She holds the classic belief that greatness has a universal quality appreciated, if not understood, by all. Artistry, therefore, does not necessarily imply greatness but comes within the jurisdiction of criticism.

Very few of her pictures Miss Arzner considers good. The human mind is still too occupied with effects, she contends, when it is the cause that matters. For that reason, she hopes someday to bring Wagner to the screen, for in his operas, especially in *The Ring*, he has harmonized all the causes of creation. It is Miss Arzner's belief that the music Wagner wrote was already in the spheres. He happened to be in tune and heard it, as we tune in a radio. He was the impersonal medium in translating a universal thought. And that, in her opinion, is the future mission of the motion picture.

Hard for Girl to Become Film Director, Dorothy Arzner Says

Jessie Henderson / 1930

From *Springfield* (MA) *Republican*, April 13, 1930.

"It's a new field," explained Dorothy Arzner. "That's why women directors are rare in the motion picture business. Women gained equality—if they have yet gained it—so recently that a woman still has to be twice as good as a man in any field before she wins recognition or even a chance. Twice as good, or make people think so. She must make them think she's twice as good a script girl, twice as good a cutter, before she has any opportunity to be just as good a director."

Miss Arzner, a young San Franciscan with very steady gray-blue eyes and remarkably long eyelashes, is the only woman director on the Paramount staff. She is only the third woman director so far in the movie industry. Eight years ago, she decided that picture direction should be her career, and as the first step, she took a job as stenographer in the Paramount offices. It was eight years of hard labor at learning the inside of motion pictures, but her reward came when they asked her to direct *Ten Modern Commandments, Manhattan Cocktail, Get Your Man, The Wild Party*, pictures starring Esther Ralston, Nancy Carroll, or Clara Bow.

And now here she is, an alert but unassuming person in a tan sports suit who rises at six each morning, drinks a cup of coffee with you in the little restaurant opposite the movie lot, says with a simplicity strangely impressive that she believes "all roads lead to God," and packs more ideas into five minutes' chat than the average author puts into a book. She has just done a beautiful piece of work on *Sarah and Son*, in which Ruth Chatterton starred.

"A woman's viewpoint is important for certain pictures and scenes, especially since 75 percent of picture audiences are women," Miss Arzner continued over the coffee, "but when it comes to actual directing, I can't see that it's a question of male or female, but of ability. There's no reason why women should not have such ability as well as men. The reason there aren't more women directors is not because men in the picture business resent taking orders from a woman; it is merely that the job is new, and few women have so far learned—or earned it. In pictures, as in all big enterprises, the trained brain counts, regardless of sex.

"The single thing which holds women back at this stage from full opportunity with men is a matter of physical strength. Women have not yet developed the sheer strength which enables a man to go on when he is tired out, like a captain who, after days on the bridge during the storm, is physically able to stay on that bridge until he brings the ship into port. Women have not developed this last ounce of endurance, just as, generally, they have not developed the habit of analytical thinking. Until lately, they hadn't much need for either.

"But women did develop intuition, the faculty by which a woman often arrives at the right conclusion before a man reaches the same conclusion through logic. I think that, for some reason, a woman's brain gets from the air the vibrations that bear on her problem. This sounds complicated. But it's no more complicated than the radio. Just the fact that millions of people are thinking about a particular thing has, I believe, a tremendous effect."

Then in that commonplace restaurant over a commonplace cup of coffee, Dorothy Arzner said an extraordinary thing. "It is my belief that each human being has in his makeup the potentialities of every talent. We all have the latent ability to be artists or inventors. If the world in general desired sculpture more than anything else today, I honestly believe its concentrated thought could make a potential sculptor of any child, and practically instantaneously. To me, a human being is neither more nor less than the means through which the life force behind the world, and the thought force behind the world, find expression."[1]

Note

[1]. Arzner's comments in this nationally syndicated interview drew the admiring attention of Gottfried de Purucker, renowned head of the California-based Theosophical Society. "Dorothy Arzner has said a great deal of truth here," he stated in a public lecture on May 18, 1930. See Gottfried de Purucker, *Questions We All Ask: Lectures Delivered by G. de Purucker in the Temple of Peace, Point Loma, California* (Pasadena, CA: Theosophical University Press, 2000). https://archive.org/details/questions_we_all_ask/page/n929/mode/2up.

Woman Movie Picture Director

Eileen Creelman / 1930

From *New York Sun*, Sept. 23, 1930.

"A motion picture director can bring out of screen players only what they have in them. If they don't possess a certain quality, no director in the world can make them portray it realistically. The public hears much discussion about good movie direction, but in the final analysis, it is the actors who are good. Some directors are merely better able than others to understand and bring out the undeveloped potentialities of their players."

So says Dorothy Arzner, whose views on the motion picture industry are interesting because she is the only woman in Hollywood who is in [a] position to express them, as it were, through a director's megaphone. Only one other woman, Lois Weber, who is now retired, ever successfully told the darlings of the screen, both male and female, how to act.

Miss Arzner's climb into the front rank of picturedom would supply the plot for a feminine Horatio Alger story that might well be [titled] "From Typist to Movie Director, or How One Girl Took a Job and Grew Up with It," yet her entrance into the picture business was quite accidental.

Since shortly after the war, when she was mustered out of a Red Cross Ambulance Corps, which she carefully explains never got overseas, Dorothy Arzner has been associated with the business of making motion pictures. She knows the business literally from the story manuscript to the gala premiere and is credited by those who know with having more brains than many of the best-yessed men in Hollywood.

"In the beginning, I hadn't the faintest idea of doing motion picture work." Miss Arzner explained across the breakfast table at her hotel soon after her recent arrival here to work at the Paramount New York studio. "I had gone to Westlake School for Girls in Los Angeles and later, to the University of Southern California. Then along came the war, and I joined an ambulance corps shortly before the armistice was signed. When I was mustered out, I was at loose ends, like many other girls, with no definite idea of what I wanted to do. A friend suggested that I go to see Cecil B. DeMille, and it sounded interesting, so I went down to his studio."

Miss Arzner's dark eyes twinkled and her heart-shaped little face lighted up with smiles as she told about her first talk with DeMille. She has a rare faculty of drawing definite word pictures, and as she talked, it was easy to visualize the diffident, abashed young girl who stood before the great producer and announced that she wanted a job but that she hadn't the faintest idea what she wanted to do.

"Of course, that interview was brief," she said. "But for several days, I prowled around the studio and watched the making of pictures, and I soon made up my mind that what I wanted to do most of all was to direct.

"So I went back to Mr. DeMille and told him I'd like to start at the bottom and learn the business. He gave me a job typing scripts, which certainly was beginning at the bottom, and that's the way I went to work."[1]

All that was nearly nine years ago, and since then, Miss Arzner has worked in the production end of the movies until she knows it from every angle. From typing, she graduated into a script girl and then became a cutter. The first picture she cut was Valentino's *Blood and Sand*, and from then on, she was established as a cutter.

After a time spent at cutting, she worked as a film editor and then as a scenario writer. At the request of James Cruze, she returned to cutting long enough to cut his biggest success, *The Covered Wagon*.

"I quit my job at Paramount several times to go to other studios when chances for advancement came, but I always returned to Paramount again. It was like the old proverb, 'a prophet is not without honor, save in his own country,' for nobody would recognize my ability to do bigger things in my own studio.

"After the Cruze picture, I decided I was ready to begin directing, so I tried to quit my job again, but Laurence Stallings advised I be allowed a chance to direct, and they gave me *Fashions for Women*, with Esther Ralston starred. And I've been directing ever since."

As simply as that, Miss Arzner outlines the beginning of her career as a director, and you have to learn from others that she did such a good job on her first picture that Esther Ralston was made, and so was she. Since then, she has handled many of the leading figures of the screen—Clara Bow, Nancy Carroll, Clive Brook, Ruth Chatterton, and other big box office attractions. Probably her most notable picture was *Sarah and Son*, which was hailed by the critics as one of the outstanding pictures last year. She recently finished directing *Anybody's Woman* and now cherishes a secret desire to put *Green Pastures* onto the screen.

This is Miss Arzner's first job at the Eastern studios, all her work having been done heretofore on the West Coast. She will direct Claudette Colbert in her next picture, the title of which has not yet been announced.

The fact that she occupies a job [that] puts her entirely in competition with men concerns Miss Arzner very little. She doesn't believe there is such a thing as sex in ideas and thought, and those, she says, are the prime factors in making a picture. Electricians, cameramen, actors, and actresses accept orders from her at their face value, she contends, without any consideration of sex whatever.

"I've never directed the type of picture called great," she said. "I believe that the public goes to the theater to be entertained, and I strive to make my pictures entertaining. Of course, no one knows in advance what type of picture will be financially successful. We just have to do our best and then sit back and hope the public will like our efforts."

Miss Arzner is convinced that there is a field for women in motion picture directing, just as there is in other directions. She says that the woman with capabilities can make a place for herself anywhere, providing she is willing to begin at the bottom and work. And mere onlookers cheerfully concede that, for Dorothy Arzner herself is an A1 example of how the rule works.

Note

1. As in several other accounts, Arzner or her interviewer mixed up William de Mille with his brother Cecil.

Meeting Miss Dorothy Arzner, Screen's Only Woman Director

Marguerite Tazelaar / 1930

From *New York Herald Tribune*, Nov. 16, 1930.

[All ellipses are in the original text.]

The only woman director in the "movies" pondered gravely before answering. She sat quietly—a slight, almost frail figure. Black, short hair, with here and there a thread of gray, was brushed smoothly back from her wide, thoughtful forehead, and blue eyes under heavy brows looked at one steadily and directly. The face mobile and sensitive harbored a strength and power for some reason rather surprising.

"I don't know why there aren't more women directing pictures unless it is that this is a transition period for women. They are just beginning to get a foothold in business and in the professions. There are only six women in the new company. I can't explain why there aren't more.

"I have found no obstacles in my own progress made by men. I have had their entire cooperation, their willing assistance. I have been treated on equal terms with other directors and have never encountered resentment in the actors I have had to direct . . . men have helped me, never hindered me in my job . . . the things that hinder you in anything are within yourself, not in the world about you."

Dorothy Arzner—the name does not seem to fit her exactly—reminds one of certain studies of early pioneer women in whose faces the artist has suggested a musing abstraction, determination, and dreaming reach toward the future. Though she prizes activity, she is herself introspective and idealistic, and replied when asked what she liked to do when she wasn't directing pictures, "I like to think," adding a little shyly, "Yes, I enjoyed reading, and right now am reading Plato; only don't mention this, for I will be put down as a highbrow. I read also such things as *Queer People*, though, as a rule, I don't care much for fiction. I go to the theater, too. *Green Pastures* and *Lysistrata* have been my favorites so far."

"If you had all the money and leisure you wanted and could do as you pleased, what would you do?"

"I would give it all away so that I wouldn't have any leisure," she smiled. "I would rather be active, be working, than anything else. I think that the best thing which could happen to people who want to be rich and have nothing to do would be to let them have their wish . . . they would soon see how empty it is.

"The future of women in the arts and sciences? They will go as far as they like as long as they desire to realize their ambitions. But as soon as women have undisputed freedom in any field, have the indifferent permission of men to be in the running, they will no longer desire to compete. Because when men, either voluntarily or by force, become the weaker sex in the economic struggle or any other, women, who desire above all things strength and virility in their men, will no longer find the race worth the prizes . . . though I believe they have proved they can combine careers with homemaking. One example is Norma Shearer, the arrival of whose daughter scarcely interfered with her acting routine, and who also makes an excellent home for her husband.

"The sexes complement one another. The thing to be desired, it seems to me, is for the perfect understanding and cooperation between them. Art in itself has no sex, no more than have ideas or thought. A woman or man creating beauty belongs to mankind rather than to either sex. The created thing should be the same in its standard of perfection, whether a man or woman conceives it. Masculinity stands for power, strength, virility; femininity for intuition, ideas. It is for the future to work out a successful way of combining these qualities."

Miss Arzner, who is the first and only woman ever to become a director of pictures,[1] was born in San Francisco and educated in Los Angeles at the Westlake School for Girls and at the University of Southern California. The year after she left college, the war broke out, and she enlisted as an ambulance driver in a women's volunteer corps, seeing active service in Los Angeles and in New York. Following the armistice, she returned west and took a position as script typist with William de Mille, then a Paramount director.

Later, she was graduated to film cutter and not long afterward, started writing scenarios and continuities for the screen. She was making progress as a freelance writer when James Cruze, at that time making *Old Ironsides*, asked her to edit the picture for him, which she did. Feeling now that she was ready to direct, the goal she had been steadily striving for, she went to the Paramount executives and asked them to let her try her hand at a picture.

They offered her *Fashions for Women*, starring Esther Ralston, and she accepted the assignment and made good, as the saying goes. She has since directed

Ten Modern Commandments, Get Your Man, with Clara Bow; *Manhattan Cocktail, The Wild Party*, and *Sarah and Son*, recently released, with Ruth Chatterton. Her first picture to be made here in the East will be *Strictly Business*, with Claudette Colbert and Fredric March, which she will begin late this month.

She does not view her success as unusual. She says that producers will offer anyone who has proved himself or herself work waiting to be done, and that only when he or she has failed will they cut off assignments. She has no preference in types of plays. If a light comedy interests her when she reads it, she wants to make it. If it is a drama that catches her imagination, she is just as eager to direct it. She says the combination of story, direction, photography, and performance results in the quality of picture, though the story, since it is the groundwork for the rest, is of first importance.

She believes pictures are a permanent art form, that they will never return to silence, but that they will continually be undergoing change and experiment. Color will be popular when it is improved, and she said there probably would be inventions having to do with the penetration of the ether, which will give screen shadows substance for the spectator so that the old form of the theater, with characters moving out into space, may then supersede the flat screen. She has little interest in making pictures for the few; she makes them for the masses and believes they have, during the last ten years, improved the taste, the dress, and the manners of these masses. She also firmly believes they have, as have aviation and other modern inventions wiping out time and space, drawn people all over the world closer together and into a closer understanding of one another.

Note

1. Numerous women preceded Arzner as film directors.

She Thanks Her Lucky Stars

Dora Albert / 1931

From *Silver Screen*, Feb. 1931.

Ruth Chatterton is like a skilled musician who, when inspired, knows what strings to play; she can consciously play on certain emotions of her audience. Clara Bow is at her best when she acts spontaneously, at her worst when she has to repeat a scene over and over.

These are the views of Dorothy Arzner, Paramount's only woman director, and for that matter, the only woman director of the talkies. She says she tries to live her life utterly without reactions. Positive action is all she is interested in.

It was Dorothy Arzner who directed *The Wild Party*, *Sarah and Son*, and *Anybody's Woman*. She has directed Ruth Chatterton, Clara Bow, and, in the days before the talkies, Esther Ralston and Nancy Carroll. She has also worked with such general favorites as Fredric March.

"Fredric March," she said, "is a very sincere worker, very natural and very much of a man. I believe he feels the emotion he portrays, which is most unusual for a man!

"Unlike some actors, he does not stand aloof from his part. He really gives himself to his work. He has great freedom of movement and no inhibitions. If he has to shout, he shouts. If he has to run up and down stairs, he runs. But he doesn't fall in love with the women to whom he makes love in the films. He is in love with his own wife, Florence Eldridge."

Of the women stars, Dorothy Arzner confesses that she particularly enjoys directing Ruth Chatterton.

"She knows her business. She is a skilled technician. She knows what instruments to play on in order to awaken emotional response.

"Sometimes, of course, it is impossible for the actress to know just what reaction she will get. When Ruth Chatterton in *Anybody's Woman* played the scenes where she had to get Clive Brook to come out of his drunken spell, we believed these scenes were farce and that the pathos of the situation would not come through. Ruth Chatterton's audiences saw something more in these scenes than just comedy. There were tears very close to the laughter.

"It is sometimes said that women are more emotional than men. I think that men players are more restrained, but it is a natural restraint.

"I should like to direct some of the men stars, particularly Maurice Chevalier. He would be fun. I suppose the reason I am always given women stars to handle is because that's a man's idea of what a woman's work in pictures should be.

"Most of the pictures I have done have been pictures of feminine appeal. I thought that *Sarah and Son* would appeal chiefly to women because of its theme, but more men than women personally told me that they liked the picture. I asked them what they liked about it, and almost invariably, they said it was the little boy. Men like boys—in pictures, anyway.

"Men are more sentimental than women, but women like sentimental pictures better than men do. Women like great human stories that treat of the life they know. As a rule, they do not care for pictures of the underworld because it is a stratum of life with which most women have had no contacts. But most men have brushed against the underworld in one way or another, and their imagination is more open to pictures of this kind. Pictures like *Underworld*, *Journey's End*, and *Gentlemen of the Press* are essentially man pictures.

"But pictures that are most successful must strike major notes. *Sarah and Son* dealt with the universal theme of mother love. I liked it personally because it was the human document of Sarah. I was interested in Sarah as a human being rather than just as a mother.

"The most universal theme of all is love. That is why it is used in almost all pictures.

"Because pictures strike these universal notes, movie fans have sometimes been described as having little intelligence. Personally, I think that's libelous. The people who attend movies know what they want better than the people who make them.

"If you find something really good, the mass will like it. None will be led astray who consults its tastes. We are all sufficiently alike, so that if a director considers what appeals to him as a human being when he isn't being snobbishly arty, he'll get what appeals to other human beings. Few good pictures have ever failed.

"Talking pictures are more interesting to direct than silent pictures because they bring you closer to the mind of the player. But silent pictures were more difficult to direct because it is hard to tell a story entirely in pantomime.

"I never try to impose on the stars. I direct my vision of how a part should be played. First, I let them interpret a scene as they themselves think it should be portrayed. They act the scene out without interruption. This is called walking through a scene. Then changes are made if necessary.

"And yet—directing is compromise. The director has her own vision of just exactly how everything should be done. Ideally, the director is like the conductor of an orchestra, and all the players work in perfect harmony.

"I've been told that there is a good deal of jealousy on the movie lots, but I have never seen it. I have never looked for it."

We talked next about the pictures which Dorothy Arzner herself has directed. She criticized them as impersonally as though they were completely the work of another person.

"*The Wild Party* was a poor picture. The sound apparatus at the time was very unsatisfactory. We had to take the same scenes over and over and over again. Now, Clara Bow works best when she works spontaneously. When four o'clock in the afternoon came and she was limp from doing the same thing over a dozen times, you can imagine what happened.

"*Sarah and Son* was a good picture," she said, "but there wasn't anything wonderful about it. The end was badly motivated.

"If I were doing the thing over the way it should be done, I'd try to find some better explanation of why the boy knew his own mother as soon as he awoke to consciousness.

"I knew it would go over all right because people were terribly anxious to see those two get together and didn't care how it was done. But the end comes almost too quickly. If I were doing it over and doing it right, I'd develop better water scenes and make the ending more plausible."

Dorothy Arzner has even less affection for *Anybody's Woman*, though she admits liking the character of the burlesque queen played by Ruth Chatterton. "But the story was not developed well. I never cared for it from the beginning.

"Players sometimes complain of the poor parts that are given to them. That's nonsense. Players draw toward themselves exactly the parts that represent the kind of thing that they have become in pictures. Poor parts gravitate toward poor players. If a part is poor, it is because a player has made it poor. A player can make anything out of his part that is in himself. A director cannot draw anything out of a player that is not in him. Some directors are merely better than others at drawing out certain potential abilities that are in the stars they direct."

Though she did not, of course, say so, Dorothy Arzner is the kind of director who can get the most out of a player. Since Clara Bow has been directed by others, her star seems to be setting. Miss Arzner, even in *The Wild Party*, brought out the pathos that is in Clara.

Miss Arzner, nevertheless, will not attempt to explain why she has been so successful as a director when every other woman who has tried to direct, with the possible exception of Lois Weber, who is now out of pictures, has been a flop. But it is the writer's opinion that Miss Arzner has clicked where the others have failed because she possesses a combination of shrewdness and imagination to a degree not yet attained by any other woman who has ever penetrated behind the scenes in the picture world.

The Secret of Personality

Dorothy Arzner / 1931

From *La Opinión*, May 13, 1931. Translated by the editor.

[The following item appeared under Arzner's byline in *La Opinión*, a Spanish-language newspaper published in Los Angeles. Newspapers often carried ghostwritten articles attributed to celebrities, and "El Secreto de la Personalidad" may have been one of these instances. It is included here, however, since it contains material quite consistent with Arzner's views and does appear to be written by her. Readers might compare the thoughts expressed in it with ones in the Martin and Wilcox interviews and Arzner's "Starlight" essay, among this book's other pieces.]

For a very lucky few, personality is not a secret but a part of their nature, not unlike the supreme good they brought into the world at birth.

For the vast majority of individuals, however, it's a result of a constant repression of the intelligent will's dominance over instinctive impulses.

It generally happens with women who think of themselves as perfect and incapable of improvement. These women spend most of their lives looking for reasons why other people are so ignorant or so awful. That is, they seek in others those things that are within themselves. Under such conditions, personality can only be a constant and debilitating hindrance.

If you, dear reader, can honestly answer the following questions negatively, your personality doesn't need any reform or guidance:

1. Do you dislike more than six people, either in your private life or at work?
2. Are you unwilling to do favors for people who don't know how to return them?
3. Do you only like those people who are interesting to you, or do you treat others who seem insignificant to you in the same way?
4. Do you enjoy imposing your will rightly or wrongly?

5. Do you impose yourself on your family and friends?
6. Are you easily irritated by the pushiness of salespeople?

Answer these questions honestly, and don't be discouraged by the results. Personality, like beauty, can be developed through constant effort.

However discouraging the conclusions that you reach may be, you have time to correct yourself, to change yourself completely. The path isn't difficult, especially considering that every effort you make will bring its own reward. Here's the remedy: promise yourself that for the next forty-eight hours you won't be sarcastic with anyone, will greet each person you meet with a pleasant smile, and will have a word of encouragement for everyone. Does this sound like an easy task? Don't believe it. If you can achieve it the first time, or the second, or the third, you can be satisfied.

A calm tone of voice will win a woman more friends than all the gifts she can give. Gentle gestures can make her more attractive than her lovely cheeks. In general, I can assure you that the secret of personality is nothing more than the kindness we show to the people around us and our interest in making life pleasant for them. With these qualities, any woman is beautiful and endears herself to the most demanding people around her.

Do You Want a Studio Job?

Mabel Duke / 1931

From *Picture Play*, July 1931.

A girl looking for short hours and little work, or a chance to break into acting through a business job, won't find what she wants at a studio. But there are many positions open to women requiring hard work, skill, and endurance. Some of these are described in this article, together with the bright girls holding them.

Studios are fun.

Outside a newspaper editorial room, I can't think of another workaday office atmosphere that is more exciting and interesting than a studio. And there are plenty of other girls who feel the same way about it, judging from the thousands continually storming the studio gates for a chance to work inside.

Most of these girls, of course, are ambitious to act. But all screen-struck girls aren't actresses. Nor even ambitious to act. The goal of a vast number of them lies on the other side of the camera—in the business offices, writing scenarios, cutting pictures, costuming players, directing pictures, or in another of the scores of glamorous positions connected with picture making.

Then there's a third group of youngsters just dying to get a job by which they can work in the same studios, eat in the same commissaries, and mingle on the sets with their screen favorites. They are the stenographers, typists, telephone girls, and beauty operators who apply for work at the studios with no particular ambition beyond just a job in the magic fairyland of movies.

There are many positions open to women in this fascinating industry. Some of these are twice as exciting as making faces before a camera and, while the financial returns are not as large as an actress enjoys, the jobs last years longer than an actress's professional life.

A girl looking for an easy berth with short hours and little work, or a chance to break into acting through a business job, won't find what she's looking for at a studio. Working until the wee small hours—without overtime pay—is far from unusual. While as for breaking into the acting business, girls with such ideas are taboo in the business end of the movies. Alice White did it, but she's a rare exception.

For a girl ambitious to succeed in any number of lines, from directing to costume designing, the movies offer varied opportunities. While competition in the beginners' jobs is keen, the competent worker finds opportunity for advancement, and the higher she goes, the less competition there is in numbers, but the keener it is in the matter of ability.

Although it is smaller, the Paramount studio in Astoria, Long Island, is really more fun than the West Coast studios. There exists a camaraderie, a democratic spirit throughout—on the set, in the lunchroom, and in the business offices. A trip through the studio reveals scores of these ambitious girls and successful women.

Alone on a pinnacle unapproached by any other woman in movieland is Dorothy Arzner, the only woman director. In addition to this distinction—or rather because of it—she is also the inspiration for every aspiring stenographer, script girl, and cutter in the studio.

"Look at Miss Arzner!" they insist. "She used to be a script girl and cutter. Why can't I do what she's done?"

And Dorothy encourages them. She firmly believes that a woman can be anything she desires and refuses even to consider the possibility of prejudice against feminine workers.

"Prejudice is ignorance," declared Miss Arzner. "There is no prejudice against women as women. There does exist a prejudice against them because they are often poor workers. Women generally want to think instead of work.

"When you mention hard work as the only route to success, they think of brain work. But when it comes to actual physical exertion—staying on the set until three in the morning and returning next morning at nine, or cutting film until your muscles are numb and your eyes red and smarting—those are the jobs that come under 'hard work.' And that's the sort of thing most women don't like. They want regular hours of mental effort and no physical exertion."

Dorothy Arzner has a right to her opinion, for she has reached the position she holds through long years of hard work. She was just out of the University of Southern California when she went to work in Paramount's West Coast studio typing scenarios for twelve dollars a week. This, in Miss Arzner's opinion, is the ideal beginning for one aspiring to any branch of the production of motion pictures. Here, she says, one gets the "feel" for stories and characters.

Although her job consists only of typing the original manuscript and nothing more, the girl who is ambitious will watch for this picture on the screen, sit through it two or three times to study carefully how it was treated, what changes were made in the plot, and how the situations were handled. That's the way

Miss Arzner worked, and, with such application and study, it wasn't long before she was promoted to script girl, then to cutter, continuity writer, and finally to director.

Her first picture was *Fashions for Women*, starring Esther Ralston. She made Clara Bow's first talkie, *The Wild Party*, and two of Ruth Chatterton's most successful ones, *Sarah and Son* and *Anybody's Woman*.

"Miss Chatterton is a skilled technician," she declared. "She can play a scene for all it is worth, can squeeze every ounce of dramatic potentiality from it, and yet never overact for an instant. She is a perfect trouper, considerate of others, willing to work, quick to grasp the director's ideas. She plays upon her emotions as a musician plays upon a harp.

"Clara Bow is a madcap and a delight to work with. That girl has an amazing amount of energy, and when she is at her best, she keys everyone else to the same high pitch. But Clara hates rehearsing. Her first spontaneous reaction has fire. Repetition deadens her.

"Claudette Colbert, like Ruth Chatterton, is an artist in getting the most from a scene, no matter how often she has to repeat it. It is probably the stage training that Ruth and Claudette have had that gives them this ability. When a stage actress plays the same role over again night after night for months, she has to learn to reawaken her enthusiasm for the role each evening, no matter how weary of it she may become."

Although Miss Arzner is at present the only woman director, there are many who would like to follow her example. One of them is Ruth Chatterton. Ruth declares that when her star begins to fade, she will leave acting and learn to direct, just as Dorothy does.

In a little square room on the top floor of the Paramount studio on Long Island, twelve little girls sit at twelve little desks and peck away at typewriters all day long, typing manuscripts, copying dialogue, listing production schedules, and a hundred other items of studio detail.

It is of this room, or ones just like it on the West Coast, that Dorothy Arzner speaks when she advises ambitious beginners to start at the bottom. It is from this room—and similar ones—that most of the script girls and several cutters and writers in the studios have emerged in the last few years. In this room at present, the twelve little typists work like bees with their eyes glued on the road of promotion which their predecessors have traveled. Here these girls get their first idea of what the movie business is all about and then advance to position as secretary to an executive, script girl, publicity writer, or what have you.

Clara Bow to Recover Fame, Director Says

Duane Hennessy / 1931

From *San Bernardino Sun*, Aug. 30, 1931.

The woman who directed many of Clara Bow's most successful pictures had a few words to say here on the future of the fiery little redhead.

"The talkies took away a lot of Clara's impetuosity, and she didn't reach out to the audience like she did in the silent days," said Dorothy Arzner. "Clara worried about her dialogue so much that it robbed her of something that is hard to explain.

"Perhaps it was partly the fault of the dialogue that was given her. It was so perfect that it was not natural for Clara. She had to watch herself every minute. She was so afraid that she would say something wrong."

Miss Arzner added that she believed there was no reason why Clara Bow cannot resume her work this fall after her present rest to regain her health.

"Clara can conquer the talkies if they will give her the kind of dialogue, even though colloquial, that is natural to her. She can say any kind of lines in rehearsal, but once a scene is being shot, she goes to pieces. She must have something that will come natural to her. That will give her back her old fire, and once more, she will reach out and capture the audience."

Miss Arzner is the only woman director to survive the arrival of the talkies. She has a woman's viewpoint on the making of pictures. Her observations are of unusual interest.

"There are no true movie fans among the men," she said. "Women are the real fans. They are more critical.

"I don't say that men don't like to go to picture shows. What I do say is that women are more appreciative of everything that the picture tells and of everything that goes to make it up—players, sets, costumes. To sum it up briefly, men like to go to shows because it is someplace to take a woman. And the woman decides what show they will go to."

She said that when she makes a picture, she tries to make one that men will like. "You know," she said, "there is one thing that arouses a man's sentiment. Give him a picture in which there is a young boy. The man will look back upon his boyhood days, and he'll go away thinking not of the star but of that boy."

How to Become a Woman Director

Dorothy Arzner / 1932

From the *Hollywood Reporter*, May 16, 1932.

[During her career, Arzner received countless letters from young women seeking advice on breaking into Hollywood. She wrote the following open letter in the hope that it would stem the tide of inquiries and cut down on the personal replies she felt she needed to make.]

There is only one way to become a woman director. You have to be a woman. Then you must get your chance.

Directing, like writing for the screen, is something most easily obtained by someone on the outside who has achieved prominence as a stage director or an author. It took me eight years to get my first chance, and I have about concluded that the hardest part about directing is getting the studio job that may lead you to this goal.

If you can get a job inside a studio, you are already half a director. It doesn't matter what your first job is—watering lawns, sweeping offices, dressing hair, operating telephones, or punching a typewriter. Once you are inside a studio, you can work toward your ambition. I pried the studio gates open with a typewriter. But I had had a bit of professional experience before that.

A woman's intuition isn't worth two hoots in Hollywood. A director has to think analytically in order to make his story hold water.

All fish swim in water; men swim in water; therefore, men are fish. That's a little problem in logical thinking that most women know is wrong through intuition, but men find the answer by determining that everything that swims isn't a fish. The conclusion is wrong, and I had to learn to reach my conclusions like a man so that my story conclusions would be correct.

When I finished school, I wanted to get into some business or profession in which I could make a success. It occurred to me that a secretarial position might lead to something interesting, so I devoted several months to absorbing the mechanics of stenography. But I couldn't get a job and had to rely on family connections. A friend of my father's put me to work in his office.

When I could no longer stand the routine and the same dull monotony day after day, I resigned. My employer still doesn't understand why I left.

I decided next to be a doctor and became an assistant in a physician's office. The work at first fascinated me, and I enrolled in pre-medical courses. The constant stream of complaining humanity, talking about pills, operations, disease, and suffering was giving me a gloomy outlook on life. I quit before I became a confirmed pessimist.

The war came along, and I started on a great adventure. I joined the ambulance corps. We got to New York, ready for embarkation when the war ended.

When I returned to Los Angeles, I relaxed into a coma of boredom. Then some relatives came from the East and wanted to see a studio. I had never been inside one. My father obtained a pass to Paramount Studios, and I went along.

I was like a screen-struck youngster, only I had no desire to act. When I saw William de Mille directing, I knew that was what I wanted to do. Apparently, he caught the expression on my face, for he asked me if I was interested.

Well, within three weeks, I wasn't a star or a studio official, but I walked through the gates every morning to a typewriter in the stenographic department.

For three months, I typed scripts. I studied them and tried to figure out why they were successful or not. I analyzed everything I typed, trying to learn all there was.

I discovered the only way of telling whether or not a script will make a great motion picture. That is by making it into a motion picture.

I was a script clerk next, first on a picture starring Nazimova. I worked at this for months and decided that writing stories for the screen should be my next step. After long days at the studio, I worked on stories at home at night, and surprisingly, I sold several, which brought me a job in the scenario department.

When an opening came as a film editor, I felt a yearning to get a pair of scissors in my hands and hack film into pieces. The importance of a good cutter was brought home to me. Many a picture had been saved by good editing, and many a good one ruined by poor editing.

My first [big] film was *Blood and Sand*, starring Rudolph Valentino. I cut thirty-seven productions in one year but still wanted to be a director. I also edited *The Covered Wagon* and *Old Ironsides*. During the latter, James Cruze asked me what my ambition was. I told him.

B. P. Schulberg, managing director of production, sent for me several months later and floored me by asking, "How would you like to direct?"

I had real stage fright during the first weeks of *Fashions for Women*, which starred Esther Ralston. I wanted to quit. I rehearsed speeches of resignation. I couldn't eat or sleep. I didn't feel comfortable until I found myself back in the cutting rooms.

The men I work with never forget I'm a woman. It's their innate chivalry, I suppose. I was deeply moved when I found a tremendous basket of flowers in my office just before starting my second picture. Everyone on the staff had a share in that basket.

I've had a lot of publicity because I'm the only active woman director. Women flagpole sitters and feminine soldiers get publicity, too. I don't mind.

"Get Me Dorothy Arzner!"—Samuel Goldwyn

Adela Rogers St. Johns / 1933

From *Silver Screen*, Dec. 1933.

Dorothy Arzner is the only woman picture director in Hollywood. More than that, she is the only woman who ever directed a talking motion picture.

The aura of success surrounds Dorothy Arzner.

She belongs among Hollywood's six greatest women because she is a pioneer, because as a woman she broke down an age-old tradition against women because she is definitely one of the most successful executives of one of the biggest industries in the United States, and because she fought her way to the top with courage, hard work, and sheer ability.

Almost two years ago, Samuel Goldwyn, one of Hollywood's greatest producers, brought to America a girl named Anna Sten. Nobody in this country knew much about her; she had never made an American picture.

Yet upon this unknown girl, Mr. Goldwyn, who is a very shrewd businessman in spite of the fact that he has an artistic temperament, was ready to gamble something better than a million dollars. And her arrival in the cinema capital was trumpeted loudly.

Miss Sten was the first movie actress to come out of Russia completely and entirely trained in the Soviet State stage and screen institutions, a product of the great new artistic experiments of the socialist era.

Her new career did not start upon the silver screen. With infinite care and at great cost, Mr. Goldwyn started out to make a new star second to no one. He believed in the girl's ability and her personality, and he determined she should have every chance. The entire resources of his organization were thrown behind her. Fifty-one tests were made of Anna Sten, where as a rule, a dozen suffice. The best directors, cameramen, and dressmakers were called in—and Miss Sten made tests for lighting, for hair and make-up, for clothes, to determine exactly the best way to make the most of her unusual beauty. Tests for dramatic ability, comedy, diction, singing, and dancing were filmed and carefully studied in the projection room by the experts. And tests, though you may not know it, cost a very great deal of money. To make those fifty-one tests, as much money was spent as often goes to make a whole production.

In fact, a fortune went into her sixteen months of training on the United Artists lot.

Then Mr. Goldwyn, after his staff had searched for months, selected a story—the French classic tragedy drama, *Nana*. He engaged the best writers to make a screen adaptation—and good writers do not come cheap.

At last, they were ready to make this important picture, a picture which they hoped would be a sensation and which would introduce a new dramatic star to the movie audiences of the world. Expensive sets were built, a fine cast selected, a well-known director placed in charge.

But somehow, things didn't work out right. After three weeks of shooting—and many pictures are entirely finished in that time—Mr. Goldwyn called a halt.

I haven't the exact figures, but as near as I can find out, over $280,000 had gone into the motion picture *Nana*, and they still didn't have a lot of film to send out to the theaters. And the enormous cost of the actual picture itself was still to come. More than that, the future of this young Russian girl, upon whose great future Mr. Goldwyn had gambled so heavily, was still in the balance.

Had all that time and money been wasted?

What could be done to salvage it, to absolutely ensure that the magnificent talent of Anna Sten would reach the screen at its height?

Mr. Goldwyn, worried almost out of his wits, picked up his desk telephone and said, "Get me Dorothy Arzner."

And into the hands of this young woman, still in her early thirties, Mr. Goldwyn put the whole responsibility for *Nana*, the future of Anna Sten, and the chance of getting financial returns on the fortune already spent and the vast amount still to be spent.[1]

Something of the same kind happened at Radio Pictures Corporation when the fate of Katharine Hepburn was at its most crucial stage.

Hepburn had made a totally unexpected and unlooked-for hit in *A Bill of Divorcement*. Brought out from New York, where she had scored a success on the stage, she played the role of John Barrymore's daughter. Studio executives knew she was a competent actress, but they were not prepared for the sensational success [that] she achieved. A wave of real enthusiasm swept the fans of the country.

As the fan letters, the exhibitors' reports, the columns of newspaper praise poured in, David Selznick, then head of Radio Pictures, realized that here was a girl who might be one of that small group of really great stars—and it is a small group.

Whether she achieved that great place, whether she turned the skyrocket hit she had made into something solid and lasting, or whether she joined the ranks of those who have made one great hit and then drifted into mediocrity, depended largely upon her second picture, in which, of course, she would be starred. The public, openly anxious to see Hepburn again, would go to see that second picture, whatever it was. But whether they would go to see the third and fourth would depend upon its success. Her hold wasn't strong enough then to stand a bad picture. It was vital to bring out the great Hepburn personality, to impress it completely upon the favorable mind of the public.

What should they do to ensure her future?

They sent for Dorothy Arzner to direct the first Hepburn-starring vehicle, *Christopher Strong*. Today, Hepburn is one of the greatest stars in the game.

It was also Dorothy Arzner who directed that picture upon which Ruth Chatterton's great popularity was largely built, *Sarah and Son*.

Yet Dorothy Arzner is the only woman ever trusted with the direction of a talking motion picture, and she is one of the only three women in all film history who ever directed any kind of a picture at all. The other two were Lois Weber, who made pictures many years ago, and Frances Marion, who, for a brief period, codirected her own stories in the silent days.[2]

"It can't be done."

That was the way the studio powers always dismissed the very idea of a woman as a motion picture director. Usually, they didn't even take it that seriously. They just laughed as though the idea were utterly absurd. Women just weren't considered possible for that particular job. Let them act—write—even supervise. But directing was something else, something too difficult and important.

Yet, as Mr. Goldwyn told me when I asked him why he selected Dorothy Arzner, there are certain things a woman has to bring to direction that perhaps a man has not, a certain understanding of feminine psychology, of the tricks, humors, emotions of a woman in love that a woman can bring out better than a man.

Dorothy Arzner alone succeeded in breaking through that set prejudice against women directors—and to understand that prejudice, it is necessary to understand something of what a director means, what he is and does. (You see, it becomes natural to refer to directors as "he" because, with the shining exception of Miss Arzner, all of them are "he.")

In the final analysis, the director is the single person who bears the entire responsibility for a motion picture. The production itself is upon his shoulders. Other people have to know one thing at a time—the director must know everything. The writer has to create the story, the star has to act, the cameraman has to photograph, the art director has to design the sets, the production manager has to arrange locations and mechanical details, the business office has to make budgets. But the director has to know more about each job than the expert himself, he has to pronounce judgment on each one and see that it is properly done and carried through. He has to weld all those things together successfully—he has to transfer the story to the screen in its totality.

Any picture can be only as good or as bad as its director.

Dorothy Arzner is one of Hollywood's great directors, and we have seen it recognized by the industry itself. Praise and kind words are all very well, but the real test is whether or not a major company will entrust the terrific amount of money and the reputation of a great star in a director's hands.

What kind of person is this woman who completely controls such a vast undertaking, with its magnitude of details and knowledge, its enormous financial investment, its effect upon important careers?

We had lunch together the other day, and though I have known her well for almost twenty years, I found myself studying her more carefully in the light of this astounding success that has come to her.

She is a slight little thing with a boyish figure and a rather boyish manner, a result of dealing on her own with a man's world. Her eyes are steady and clear and meet yours with much more directness than the average. Her hair is dark and short, and she wears tailored clothes and immaculate white shirts, which she adopted as suitable for her work. There is an air of quiet and control about her that suggests complete command of herself and of everything about her, but it is never a passive quiet. And, in spite of it, you feel a strong emotional force and one of the keenest intellects you had ever encountered.

The first time I ever saw Dorothy Arzner, she was a slim little kid with black pigtails. In those days, I was [a] cub reporter [for] the *Los Angeles Evening Herald* in Los Angeles. Just around the corner from the office was the old Hoffman Café, famous for its German cooking and—that being before Prohibition—for its beers and wines.

The Hoffman was a favorite meeting place for what, in those days, we referred to as a "Bohemian" gathering. Newspaper men, actors, writers liked to sit about its cool, quiet room and talk over huge steins of golden beer. And the men who were important in those very early days of pictures often spent long evenings there. Charlie Chaplin, Bill Hart, Erich von Stroheim, Mack Sennett, Wallace Beery, Ford Sterling, Chester Conklin, Lew Cody, Victor Fleming, Frank Lloyd, and Jimmy Cruze were among the many I used to see there when I dropped in after my day's work.

The Hoffman Café was owned by Dorothy Arzner's father, and the youngster used to slip out of the office and stand peering around, watching the many interesting people. Soon many of them came to know and like her, and Charlie Chaplin or Jimmy Cruze would call her out to join the circle, and she would sit and listen hour after hour to talk about motion pictures, about the future of pictures, about the early struggles and discoveries in the then-new film art.

That was where she developed her great interest in the motion picture art and decided that someday in some way, she would be a part of it.

She went to finishing school, to the University of Southern California, and during the war, drove an ambulance.

And when that was over, quietly, with complete determination, with a definite objective, she started her motion picture career.

"Sometimes," she told me the other day, "I think that pride is the greatest obstacle to success. A silly false pride that keeps people from being willing to learn, from starting at the bottom no matter how far down it may be, and learning every step of the way up.

"When I went to work in a studio, I took my pride and made a nice little ball of it and threw it right out the window."

Dorothy Arzner started at a very small salary and in a very minor position as a stenographer typing scripts in the Lasky studio. William de Mille got her the job.

It isn't because I admire Dorothy Arzner greatly and, as a woman, am very proud of what she has done that I say I believe she knows more about motion pictures and how they are made than ninety percent of the men directors. It happens to be true.

For, from typing scripts, which she had the ambition and good sense to study carefully as she typed them, she became a script girl. A script girl sits on the set while every single foot of film is shot. She keeps a stenographic record of every scene, just what is done, worn, said, and where and when. Dorothy held script on a good many pictures for a good many fine directors, and she never missed anything. She wasn't by any means content just to do her own work and collect her paycheck. She studied the methods of directors, of actors; she studied the cameramen—absorbing every detail with that quick, active brain of hers.

And finally, she went to Mr. Lasky and asked him to let her try cutting for a while.

Now, cutting is one of the most important parts of picture-making. When the film is shot, it has to be assembled. The reels and reels of films have to be put together with infinite care, and it isn't a mechanical job alone by any means. It takes a keen dramatic sense and a lot of vision to cut successfully. The cutter must know just how and where action fits together, what scenes can be left out, where the action begins and ends.

"I learned more about pictures in the cutting room than anywhere else," Dorothy Arzner told me.

Such pictures as Rudolph Valentino's *Blood and Sand* and *The Covered Wagon* were entrusted to her to cut—the latter by her old friend Jimmy Cruze.

When he felt that she had learned all from that work that she possibly could, Dorothy gave up a fine salary and a good contract and decided to become a scenario writer. That, she felt, was [an] experience she must have, because by this time, she had fixed her goal, she knew exactly what she wanted to do. She wanted to be a director, and the fact that there wasn't any such animal and that everybody told her "it can't be done" when she mentioned it didn't alter her course one degree.

The writing game proved a hard struggle—to get a job as a writer, you are supposed to have written something. But though her savings vanished and the months dragged by, she kept at it—asking for a chance everywhere she could. Of course, she got it.

And when she had written a certain number of successful scripts, she made an appointment one day with Jesse Lasky.

Quietly but completely, she explained to Mr. Lasky what she wanted to do and why she thought she could do it.

"I want a chance to direct a picture," she said. "Will you give it to me? I believe a woman director could be very valuable, that she has something different to offer."

And then she told him about all the things she had done, all the experience she had had, and just what her plans and ideals were. Mr. Lasky, who had the vision and the ability [that] successful executives must have to take a chance and grasp a new idea, decided to take a chance on this slim, quiet young girl.

He gave her a picture to direct—not a very important nor expensive one, of course. It was called *Fashions for Women* and starred Esther Ralston. As pictures go, it wasn't to cost much—but then, the most inexpensive picture runs up around a hundred thousand dollars, and that isn't chicken feed. It was a big chance Mr. Lasky took—but he won.

"I never had any obstacles put in my way by the men in the business," Dorothy told me. "They all tried to help me. Men actors never showed any prejudice against working with me. All the men who help—cameramen, who are so terribly important—assistants, property men, actors, everybody helped me."

I asked her how she felt about "careers for women."

She was thoughtful a moment; she is apt to think before she speaks.

"It all depends on the woman, it depends on each individual woman," she said. "The place for a woman isn't necessarily in the home if she is more valuable and happier elsewhere.

"But I do believe that if a woman has a particularly good chance for a career, and a talent and an ambition to succeed in a career, she shouldn't marry. Women have as much ability as men—how they wish to use it is their own personal choice. Mine, as it happens, was for a career—I wanted to be a motion picture director—and so I have not married."

She still lives quietly at home with her father and mother, in the same house where she lived when she was a little girl.[3] Parties don't appeal to her, but she likes people, in small groups, and good conversation.

We had a standard for the six great women of Hollywood, didn't we?

They must be outstanding in their own job. They must, of themselves, be great women who would have succeeded in anything they chose to do and whose characters are fine in themselves. And they must have impressed themselves upon the art and industry of the motion picture in a valuable way, have done something important to further this great art.

There can be no question but that Dorothy Arzner qualifies.

There should be women motion picture directors. They have, quite definitely, something to give to this world of entertainment. They have certain qualities which might have a great meaning in the interpretation of life—the presentation of women and their problems—which no man can have.

Dorothy Arzner has blazed the trail.

Notes

1. Decades later, Arzner described her professional relationship with the tempestuous producer. She said she "liked working for Sam Goldwyn. Oh, he would blow his top and the writers would be carted off to the hospital with ulcers, but I'd just wait for him to settle down and then I'd explain why things couldn't be the way he wanted them. You have to learn how to handle producers. Goldwyn gave me everything I wanted in the way of sets, lighting, cameramen and costumes, but he also gave me the job of making Anna Sten look like a great actress. He had spent a year grooming her, telling everyone that she would be greater than Dietrich, greater than Garbo, and then when she opened her mouth, out came these monosyllables. The only thing I could do was not let her talk so much." Arzner quoted in Guy Flatley, "At the Movies," *New York Times*, August 20, 1976.
2. Numerous other women had directed films during the 1910s and '20s besides the three mentioned here.
3. In 1930, Arzner and her partner Marion Morgan moved into a hilltop home overlooking Hollywood.

Clothes Do Not Make the Stars

Alice Tildesley / 1933

From *Oakland Tribune*, Dec. 17, 1933.

One of Hollywood's favorite indoor sports is naming the ten best-dressed women of the screen. Pages are devoted to outlining the reasons for the claims of this or that actress to knowing how to wear clothes; more pages are filled with fashion photographs proving these claims. Girls and women everywhere are induced to buy copies of garments worn by these exalted clothes models in the hope that they will look as lovely.

"But what have clothes to do with acting?" demanded Sam Goldwyn, who has selected many successful stars.

"I think it's a foolish business, picking the screen's ten best-dressed women," he continued. "The screen shouldn't demand exotic style creation. It shouldn't make style freaks or clothes horses of its women.

"Show me Hollywood's ten best-dressed women, impartially selected for no other reason than that they are smart and chic and know how to wear clothes, and I'll show you at least seven completely unimportant actresses. Being smart and chic is a business, an absorbing occupation in life. It isn't something that is incidental to being an actress.

"I believe that great elegance in clothes would disqualify anyone from being a great actress.

"It's the same way in other lines. The most fashionable and the most socially acceptable player is usually a second-rater as far as artistic or popular standing goes. You know that the fellow who is funniest in the dressing room or at lunch is often a pretty dull entertainer on the screen.

"My latest importation, Anna Sten, has no interest in things to wear. She tells me that where she comes from, a woman washes her face and puts on her hat, and then she's ready to go out. No fussing around for hours in a beauty parlor. No worrying about which dress to put on.

"She can act, because she has had to depend on acting and not on what she has on in order to be a success!"

So, instead of picking out the ten best-dressed women of the screen, Dorothy Arzner, Hollywood's most famous woman director, has chosen the ten women in Hollywood to whom clothes are relatively unimportant.

"I do not mean that these women are not well dressed or that they do not know about clothes," explained Miss Arzner carefully, "but none of them needs to rely upon what she wears in order to be effective on the screen. They are Marie Dressler, Greta Garbo, Anna Sten, Miriam Hopkins, Ruth Chatterton, Katharine Hepburn, Beulah Bondi, Helen Hayes, Judith Anderson, and Louise Fazenda."

There is no argument about Marie Dressler. "Marie Dressler hasn't the face or figure of a clothes horse," says Miss Arzner, "but even when she was young, what she wore was never so important as what she did.

"Greta Garbo is foolproof so far as clothes go," points out Miss Arzner. "She can wear anything, no matter how weird it is and still make herself seen and felt. Witness the fantastically exotic raiment of Mata Hari or the shabbiness of Anna Christie. You never feel clothes-conscious when Garbo is on the screen."

Greta seldom bothers about style off the screen, for that matter. She likes to wander about in a covert coat and old beret, which effective disguise permits her to stand in line at the box-office before a theater showing one of her own pictures with[out] being recognized.

"Being beautiful," said Greta in an interview granted in the days before such things were prohibited, "is too very much trouble!"

As to Anna Sten, she is the first actress to come to America from Russia, trained entirely in Soviet State stage and screen institutions. Her picture *Karamazov* gave her world prestige.

Mr. Goldwyn, after signing her, worried lest she, a distinctly Slavic peasant type, earthy and feline, should be lost in Hollywood among the pink-and-white dolls, the young goddesses and the sophisticated artists. He gave her sixteen months training, made fifty-one tests for lighting, for hair, for dramatics, for diction, for singing, and for dancing, before she even began her first picture.

Then, when she had worked for three weeks on actual picture-making, he wasn't satisfied. He threw out everything that had been made, crossed off the investment, and engaged Dorothy Arzner as director to begin all over again.

"Most Hollywood directors know sex as a series of pretty pictures," complains Mr. Goldwyn. "They know how to give women that glazed, lovely look they have on the covers of magazines or candy boxes.

"That isn't what I want from Anna Sten. So I employed Dorothy Arzner, who is not content with pretty pictures, as you might set a thief to catch a thief. She should be able to get the complex psychology of this woman."

Anna refuses to believe that clothes have any importance. When she was in Berlin, she posed for some pictures for Chanel, who rewarded her with a suit specially designed for her, a beautiful thing of beige with a rainbow vest and small cloche hat. Anna arrived in New York wearing this suit and a pair of tennis shoes! "The shoes are comfortable; why not?" she replied to amazed protests.

When she was invited to her first Hollywood party, where she would presumably meet the important stars of the film city, she wore a sweater and skirt and no make-up. She fails to see why an actress should be expected to display gowns. That, says she, is for the girls who sell them.

Anna is tall, slender, and svelte, with heavy, silky yellow hair and wide blue-gray eyes and a face that seems to mirror her thoughts. She is the Russian intellectual, cold or fiery at command of the mind.

"And what," she queries, "have clothes to do with acting?"

"You can't bury personality under styles," commented Miss Arzner. "Miriam Hopkins wears clothes well and is often seen in parts that require dressing, but she is at her best as a gamin-urchin type, as in *Dr. Jekyll and Mr. Hyde*."

Offscreen, Miriam is as casual about clothes as Greta Garbo or Anna Sten, except upon occasion, when she can be as exquisitely gowned as the best of our Hollywood pets.

"Ruth Chatterton and Helen Hayes have played roles in which they go from youth to old age. They have demonstrated, in different pictures, their freedom from the power of clothes by playing characters who never put on anything but a nurse's uniform or plain gingham frocks.

"Neither of these girls is particularly interested in fashions, and yet both are hailed as chief among our screen actresses," the young director observed. "Katharine Hepburn can dominate any dress she chooses to wear. Fortunately, she attempts no ostentation in clothes. In her latest and biggest success, she had only one important gown. The rest were meant to be a blank."

Silk Underwear Feelings and Nail Polish Effects

Philadelphia Inquirer / 1934

From *Philadelphia Inquirer*, March 11, 1934.

[A Goldwyn publicity writer worked with Arzner on this brief piece.]

Dorothy Arzner, who directed *Nana*, now at the Aldine, is the most successful woman director of the industry, and one of the foremost, regardless of sex. She was selected by Samuel Goldwyn for the job of handling Anna Sten's debut in an American-made picture because he felt that the story needed the sympathetic understanding of a woman.

Miss Arzner has her own ideas about making pictures and is not at all averse to airing them.

"Hollywood has been a fool about pretty pictures and has been so crazy about beauty that it has idealized life instead of painting it realistically," says Miss Arzner.

"Softly diffused lights, mist-hung images of surpassing loveliness, girls too beautiful to be alive, men consciously handsome, virile, charming, romantic, with an imaginary (or maybe real) multitude of adoring females in their wake—these are in Hollywood's chemistry.

"Sets recreate homes that are dazzling examples of the interior decorator's art. Girls wear clothes that naïvely suggest Schiaparelli or Chanel. They never get away from the silk underwear feeling or the nail polish effect. The screen has not yet discovered that people actually drive automobiles that are four and five years old.

"*Nana*, which I had the honor to direct, has a richly atmospheric period for its setting. It is the gaslit Paris of 1870, excited, decadent, and overfed. Paris had just become the city of light. Her newly laid boulevards were the talk of the world. The streets were gay with the songs of its music halls, bright with the charm of the day.

"In this setting, in the life of the Paris boulevards, Nana lived and had her being. The screenplay is an unromanticized account of her rise and fall. In her costumes and in the living screen that serves as her background, her career is to be seen, first as the little street brat, then as the grabbing little careerist, and onto her budding success as the demimondaine of the music halls, to her opulence as the greatest courtesan of her time.

"This, to us working on the United Artists lot, was an opportunity for the 'naturalism' that Zola spoke about. The finished production is, we believe, a natural and human picture, and we sincerely hope that the theater-going public will agree with us.

"Motion pictures have been taking on the universal language of the dialogue writer. It is good, but it is too calculated, too precise in its dramatic effect.

"Beauty can't be shrill and hysterical and dramatic all the time. There must be arid periods for catching breath, for a change of pace. Grays are needed to set off the bright glint of Hollywood's dramatic Christmas tree ornaments. For anyone can get tired of too much rainbow."

Women Directors Are the Outlook, Says the Only One

Marguerite Tazelaar / 1936

From *New York Herald Tribune*, Oct. 4, 1936.

There will be more women directors in Hollywood soon, says Dorothy Arzner, the only woman film director, whose *Craig's Wife*, the picture version of George Kelly's Pulitzer Prize-winning play, starring Rosalind Russell and John Boles.

"Intelligence has no sex," says Miss Arzner. "Year by year, the number of women who do creative work in the studios has increased. Women scenario writers, art directors, costume designers, film editors, and publicity workers have been successful in the studios, and there is no reason why they should not succeed as directors."

Miss Arzner started her film career after the war as [a] stenographer in a scenario department and became, in succession, manuscript reader, script girl, cutter and editor, and scenario writer. Then she had an opportunity to direct, her first picture being *Fashions for Women*.

"One of the important lessons that must be learned by anyone who wants to be a director," Miss Arzner says, "is that motion picture directing is not just telling people how to act. The director must know the business of making motion pictures from the ground up. He must be thoroughly familiar with the mechanical phases of the studio because motion pictures are based on mechanics. Shooting schedules, and the reason for them, production costs, film cutting, the qualities that go to make up a good scenario—they must all be as familiar to the director as to the producer himself."

Miss Arzner is known as one of the quietest directors in Hollywood. Her voice is low, and she has never been known to indulge in fits of temperament. This same temperament, she declares, is the greatest obstacle in the way of women who want to become directors.

"If women can overcome the tendency to become flustered under pressure," she says, "they'll find that they are removing one of their greatest handicaps. Self-confidence and knowledge of the mechanics of picture-making are a necessity if one wants to become fortified with the poise that goes a long way toward rendering unimportant this so-called feminine trait. I don't believe in histrionics on the part of the director. I want my company to be a smooth-running machine."

Miss Arzner feels that some pictures, such as *Craig's Wife*, definitely need women directors. "This picture," she says, "is typically a woman's picture. Its entire premise is feminine psychology. It takes a woman to interpret that properly. When you consider that motion picture audiences are predominantly feminine, why shouldn't women in every phase of production be capable of producing entertainment for them?"

Woman among the Mighty

New York World-Telegram / 1936

From *New York World-Telegram*, Nov. 21, 1936.

Dorothy Arzner is a phenomenon in Hollywood, a woman who doesn't believe that something glorious and glamorous is going to happen to her late this afternoon. Or tomorrow at the latest. She is quite content with what she is—the only woman director in the movie capital.

"There ought to be a lot more of us women directors," she said pensively. "I don't understand why at least a few dozen women don't enter the field every year."

An ex-ambulance driver and stenographer, she is cool, tolerant, and extremely patient. Sightseers never see her in the Troc, Lamaze's, the Beverly Derby, or the other fashionable rendezvous of Hollywood's elite. She is dubious about publicity for a very good reason.

"I want my work to be judged on its merit," she says. "Why should I be pointed out as a strange creature because I happen to be the only woman director? Intelligence has no sex."

Men predominate in the seats of power in Hollywood, men of fifty and sixty who believe that woman's place is in the home—if it isn't *facing* the camera. They look on women as poor executives, which made Miss Arzner's rise fairly arduous. And that is why she detests anything that emphasizes the fact that she is Dorothy Arzner—not Arzner, the director.

"It puzzles me why more women don't deliberately set out to become directors," she says. "Of course, there are going to be many of them sooner or later. There are plenty of women writers, art directors, costume designers, film cutters, and publicity workers in pictures now."

She is in her middle thirties with glints of premature gray on her dark hair, which she wears brushed back from her ears. She is slender, medium-tall, low-voiced, and amiable. She generally wears dark tweed or serge tailored suits. On the set, hard-boiled camera crews treat her deferentially. When a scene is to start, she says "Go" quietly instead of shouting the traditional "Roll 'em!"

She okays final camera adjustments herself. When an actor spoils a scene, she waits until it has been played through, then strolls over and holds a whispered conference with the offender, so subdued and neat that you'd think she was asking for a cigarette.

She has a quick, slightly awry grin. In story conferences, she is silent for long stretches, then speaks in a rush of words.

She gets along well with actors. Her last job was directing *Craig's Wife*. The star, Rosalind Russell, who is supposed to be temperamental and did not want to play the part to begin with, willingly worked through lunch and dinner, [and] limped around ten days on a sprained ankle.

She has been an enigma to Hollywood because there is no gossip to relay about her. She pursues her trade like a conservative bank executive.

Usually, she asks to have the writer of a picture on the set with her, to suggest dialogue changes and discuss changes she herself may think of. Nine out of ten other directors make arbitrary decisions and will endure no one on the set except their personal errand boys. This makes Dorothy Arzner popular with the screen writers.

She straightens her cuffs, lights a cigarette, and tells you, "I'm where I want to be, and I have no further special ambition. In getting where I am, I suffered a good deal. It was not much fun then."

She entered the motion picture business after leaving the University of Southern California, where she had studied to be a doctor. Her first job was driving an ambulance.

"At that time," she says, "I was inspired with the idea of serving humanity as a physician. I wasn't calm about it. I was excited."

One day, she went through a studio on a sightseeing tour. She knew nothing of the stage or film construction, but she decided she was going to be a director. A week later, she landed a job as a twenty-dollars-a-week stenographer at Paramount. She kept asking for more work. She was allowed to synopsize published stories. A year of this and she became a script girl, sitting on the set and checking script for directors as they shot it. For several years, she was a cutter, putting film together in its sequence after various scenes had been made. Then an executive made her an assistant director. It sounds fairly exalted but means no more than serving as a flunky for the director, seeing that stars reached the set on time, scampering for their lunches and such.

Then Paramount gave her a chance to direct curvy Clara Bow from Brooklyn in *Get Your Man*.[1] She has had assignments ever since. She has directed Katharine

Hepburn, Fredric March, Claudette Colbert, and Ruth Chatterton, and her next job may be with James Cagney.

She rides and walks strenuously, priding herself on being in hard trim always. She weighs 115 pounds and is five feet, four inches tall and becomingly tanned. She is not married.

"The hard way is the right way to do anything," she says. "I'm glad I took the road I did. I know all I need to know to direct. There is no question that can come up that I will ever have to bluff on. I hate bluffing and all bluffers. I expect I am going to have a good many more hard knocks, but I don't do any worrying about tomorrow."

Although she has been directing several years, she never has had the bullheadedness of old-timers whose practice always was—and is—to be an absolute despot. She does not even have a chair on the set with her name stenciled on its back, and there are no inch-deep carpets in her office. A converted dressing room underneath the stairs will suit her.

In Manhattan, you never find her with the stage-movie-writing set at the 21 [Club], the Stork Club, or the Rainbow Room, or any of the places people go to be seen. When she takes a vacation around New York, she prefers (a) hiking the West Shore of the Hudson if it isn't too hot, (b) the front row of the balcony of every play in town, (c) riding the subways watching and listening to people, and (d) the main library at Fifth Avenue and Forty-Second Street.

"If a moving picture is bad, the director should be blamed and no one else," she says. "If he accepts a bad script, it's up to him to work with the writer to make it a good one.

"As for the chances young women have of becoming directors—the trouble is, many who might have the talent haven't the patience or the downright guts for the long and painful years, the years when it looks as if they'll be stuck where they are for good."

Note

1. *Get Your Man* was actually Arzner's third film as director, not her first as implied here.

The Screen's Only Woman Director

Marky Dowling / 1936

From *Movie Classic*, Dec. 1936.

Meet Dorothy Arzner, and you understand why she is one of Hollywood's ace directors!

Chat with her—and you understand why so little is known, even in the cinema colony, about one of our most fascinating personalities! Ask her a personal question, and often, without any attempt to evade, she will answer straightforwardly, "I really wouldn't know!"

Her concentration is directed outward, away from herself, and it is the minds of others that she finds interesting—not her own!

But don't think her own mind is inactive!

Maybe that's why producers choose her for their most difficult assignments. She just finished *Craig's Wife*, in which Rosalind Russell plays one of literature's meanest women.

Now she is doing *Mother Carey's Chickens*, with Ginger Rogers essaying her first straight dramatic part.

"Oddly enough," she told me, "I like directing stars in pictures that prove to be turning points in their careers." And she has done it often. But she added modestly, "The roles, really, effected the change—rather than my direction."

Her first picture, *Fashions for Women*, was Esther Ralston's first starring picture. Reviews read: "A triumph for both star and director."

Wild Party, Clara Bow's first talking picture, brought Fredric March a contract with Paramount.

Sarah and Son, one of Miss Arzner's most brilliant pictures, made Ruth Chatterton world-famed and gave her the title "First Lady of the Screen."

Merrily We Go to Hell was outstanding for both Fredric March and Sylvia Sidney.

Refer to these pictures of the past, and Miss Arzner says, "As far as I am concerned, they are ancient history and serve only as an instrument to be used for better work now. It's what I am doing now that counts."

Amazingly enough, Hollywood does not limit her to "woman's angle" stories, and if you call her the screen's "only woman director," she will refuse the title and tell you a list of other women who have made their marks in the production field. She has foresight, vision, and imagination, and she has the authority of any man director.

How does a girl start out to become a director? She receives hundreds of letters asking that question. Her own route, from cutting room to director's chair, proved successful also for Lewis Milestone and Josef von Sternberg. Miss Arzner herself hesitates to discuss her rise from studio stenographer to top director. "The incidents of themselves are of value only insofar as they are alive and active now," she says. But her progress from typist, script girl, cutting room assistant, head cutter, writer of original stories, and then director is easily explained by the fact that she fills each job so thoroughly, giving it the whole of her amazing energy, that she just naturally rises to a better one!

In the studios, they call her type of direction "the Dorothy Arzner system." She works with the writer upon the script. She directs. Then she supervises the cutting. And the whole becomes a Dorothy Arzner product throughout.

Unusual assignments, making new demands on her talents, interest her most. (She was offered a producer's job with one studio but prefers to concentrate completely upon a single picture.)

Always self-effacing and modest, Miss Arzner was called upon in her first scene to handle a group of sixty extras, as well as the principal players.

"For ten days, I was so nervous that I couldn't eat," she admits.

Then a friend took her into a projection room one morning and showed her the previous day's rushes of all directors, with her own rushes at the end.

"That's how I lost my fear," she says. "He proved to me that my own work was as good as the rest."

The other side of the story illuminates her extraordinary modesty, for at that moment, producers, executives, and other directors were marveling at the ease—the *veteran's* ease!—with which this astonishing girl was handling her difficult assignment.

Right now, *Craig's Wife* is speaking rather loudly. It may be the turning point in Rosalind Russell's career. When you see it, look behind the action and the characters upon the screen, and add to your pleasure by thinking of the level-eyed and composed woman who sat in the director's chair!

Would You Be Master of Your Fate?

Alice Tildesley / 1937

From *Springfield* (MA) *Republican*, Jan. 3, 1937.

Are you satisfied with your life, pleased with the way it is going, and hopeful about its future? Or are you disappointed, disillusioned, forced to adopt a "what's the use" attitude toward it?

It's not an unattainable ambition, thinks Dorothy Arzner, the only woman director in motion pictures, who has proved that she could achieve her ambition in the face of a widespread belief that it couldn't be done.

She is the sort of young woman for whom the adjectives "quiet" and "strong" might have been invented. She has short, thick, wavy black hair, serene gray eyes, and a transforming smile.

"I believe the present is the only time that counts," she stated definitely. "We should live always in the present—today—not forever yearn backward toward the past or strain forward toward the future. Otherwise, we missed the actual living.

"The latest picture of mine—*Craig's Wife*—happens to be a hit, but why should I talk about it and think about it now? It's finished. I'm through with it. There is nothing more I can do about it, so why should I dwell on it? The important thing for me is WHAT am I doing today?

"People can get into the habit of sitting back, looking at their triumphs or achievements, thinking that after all, they are pretty good, see what they've done! Nobody thought they could do this, but they did it! Everyone said they couldn't do that, but they did it! So they all sit back and let the part carry them.

"That's wrong. Forget the thing that's past. Live NOW!

"This is true—perhaps even more true in a sense—of that habit of living over past injustice, unkindness, unhappiness. We all suffer what we consider injustice or unkindness at times, but when it's over, the thing to do is to close that chapter, forget it. Go on from there.

"Don't permit yourself to dwell on either the unpleasantness of yesterday or the delights of the past, for what matters is today. The future will take care of itself if we live as we should live now."

In her smartly tailored gray suit, immaculate white shirt, and tie, she looked like the 1937 model in *Independent Woman*, especially so against the background of "ancient castle" that happens to be Hollywood's present fad in cafés.

"I don't believe in piling up goods or bank accounts or large estates for yourself and for the future," she declared. "It's my theory that if you do your best today, tomorrow will be provided for lavishly. You needn't even think of the future in relation to your own need. For I believe, implicitly, that giving is the act that results in getting. If anyone asks for help, give it . . . Of course, I am speaking for myself in this. I am not wise enough to tell other people what to do, so I hope you'll understand that all my remarks apply to myself. I know that if anyone came to me and asked, the only thing for me to do would be to give.

"Youth today seems to be afraid of life. This is a new thing in my experience, for a few years ago, the most noticeable thing about youth was that they didn't know what Fear was. You couldn't discourage them. You said, 'No!' today, but they were back again tomorrow, undismayed. It was this inability to take 'No' as an answer that created their success.

"I think the new attitude of youth is our fault. We have allowed the impression to go forth throughout the land that there are no jobs, that there are so many unemployed that nobody could hope to get work, that no one can possibly get anywhere. As I drove over here today, I saw billboards with enormous figures on them, overstating the number of unemployed.

"It's not true! It never was true! There is a place for everyone.

"The youth of today must learn that the secret of getting is to ask for what they want. Maybe they won't get the exact thing they think they want the first time they ask, but they must ask anyway; ask, keep on asking, don't be discouraged.

"Keep on asking, and presently, they will be given something—maybe at first not the ideal thing they asked for, but a way will open to the goal if they do not lose faith in themselves and their ability.

"I think all youth should take to heart the message 'ask and ye shall receive.' How can you get what you want if no one knows you want it? Don't give up! Ask is the only active part of that message."

There is, Dorothy is certain, no such thing as a dead end for anyone.

"You are the director of your own career," she pointed out. "If you are true to yourself, you can't fail. You must not allow yourself to be stopped by any sense of failure. Go ahead, with courage. As director, you can say to yourself *do this*, and you will do it.

"The way I think that 'dead-end feeling' can be dealt with is this: treat it as we would treat an experience on a journey when we went off the right road. When we are traveling in a car and find ourselves on the wrong road, what do we do? We say: 'Where did I get off the road?' We retrace our path, perhaps we find a shortcut to take us to the right road, but at any rate, we don't just sit there on the wrong road and bemoan our fate.

"Why should we sit helplessly down and believe we can't get back on the right road in life?

"If we find ourselves in a rut, depressed, following a hopeless trail or up against a seeming dead end, the thing to do, I believe, is to get off by ourselves, sit down quietly and think things out.

"I usually take a pencil and paper, and presently, I have written myself into a new start. But that happens to be my method because I feel easy with a pencil in my hand. Another woman might merely sit down quietly and think: 'Here I am in this room, facing the fact that there seems no way to turn, nothing to do. What shall I do? What can I do?'

"The thing to do is to go on from here, to get out of my rut. Now, how shall I do that?

"Then listen, listen with all your might to the voice in you. In each of us, there is a voice that will direct us if we will listen to it. Listen carefully—don't set up a defense of 'I hate doing that!' or 'I can't possibly do this!' Or 'I know I wouldn't like that!' The voice will guide you.

"No, it won't be an actual voice, of course. It will be a thought that will come to you, a thought that will insist on breaking through, whether we like it or not. We can follow it to an answer, if we will.

"I know I have often fought against the voice, thinking that it will mean I must do something I dislike very much, but if I have conquered this feeling and gone ahead as the voice suggested, I've found myself at my goal."

Her voice is low, and she seldom raises it, but there is a note of authority in it that carries.

"Women in small towns, who are tied to their homes by the care of small children or because they must wait on invalids or have no means, often complain that there is no way out of their ruts," she observed. "I feel that I have been unusually fortunate in my life because I haven't been up against the hardships and difficulties of some other women.

"But I do know this: it's not the hardship or the difficulty that matters; it's our attitude toward it.

"To the woman in the small, dull town who longs for the way out, I think the thing to do, while waiting for the way out to be made clear, is to prepare for the life you hope for. Get ready for it, as if it were a sure thing."

A listener at our table put in, challengingly, that there was nothing ahead for the woman whose child had turned out badly.

"I know a family," said she earnestly, "who devoted themselves to their only son, who sacrificed everything for him, pinned all their hopes to him. He began to drink; his dissipation killed his mother, and now it looks as if it would kill his father. What would you do if your child turned out like that?"

The young director smiled.

"I have no children, so I don't know how they might turn out," she argued, "but I believe that if a child turns out well, most families will take credit for it. Don't you think that the spoiled child might blame his parents a bit?

"I should think it would be the case of the car on the wrong road again. Just where did we turn off the road with our son? Maybe we can retrace our steps. If not, isn't there a shortcut to the right way?

"It is easier to spoil a child than not, if you love him, because it is your pleasure to please him. But no one can decide the problem of someone else. We are all individuals. We must walk by the light we happen to have. We all know what is right, according to the light we have, and we all know we are wrong if we don't follow it."

Hollywood's only woman director was born in California and educated in Los Angeles, where she studied medicine, hoping to serve humanity as a doctor. The war came while she was at school, and she joined the Los Angeles Emergency Drivers Corps, hoping to go to France. Older girls were given the calls, so she did not leave the country.

Driving an ambulance led to her career in motion pictures, for her corps commander introduced her to William de Mille, at the time an officer of the Intelligence Service, and as a result of this meeting, she went into his studio as a typist.

After looking over the new field, the girl decided that the most important person connected with a picture is the director. He is the one individual who is responsible for the success or failure of any film. Therefore, quite simply, Dorothy determined to become a director.

From typist, she rose to script girl, to scenarist, to script reviser, to cutter, to assistant director, and at length, her ambition was achieved.

"Women can't direct pictures," they said in Hollywood.

"But I can!" decided Dorothy. And she does!

Hilltop Tenant: Dorothy Arzner Thus Looks at Films with a Clear Eye

Grace Wilcox / 1937

From *Screen & Radio Weekly*, Jan. 17, 1937.

"If you, as the director, are sufficiently inspired, you can make good actors out of bad ones. You can make an exciting and successful picture from a mediocre script. You can invent a situation [that] may change the tempo of an entire sequence. You can lighten a dreary scene or put drama into one that is too trivial. There is one catch in all this—most directors are not consistent in their inspirations. There is too much work to do and too little time in which to do it."

Dorothy Arzner, Hollywood's only woman director, speaking. She is one of two women to make good behind a directorial megaphone—to actually direct a picture from beginning to end. The other one is Lois Weber of the silent days.

Miss Arzner knows what it takes to qualify in the moving picture field of men. She speaks with conviction:

"Physical endurance, mental alertness, a willingness to shoulder responsibility, the ability to stand the gaff and to play the game."

Miss Arzner and I were having dinner at Levy's Tavern the other night. Al Levy prides himself on having catered to three generations of Los Angeles folk, most of whom are still alive.

In Miss Arzner's childhood, her father, proprietor of the Hoffman Café, was Al Levy's competitor, so it is not surprising to learn that three old Angelenos must go in for a spell of reminiscing before ordering the soup.

Besides, it gave me an opportunity to get a good look at our only woman director without a coterie of cameramen, electricians, script girls, and players surrounding her. Hers is a very satisfying face, brilliantly alive; her skin is clear and healthy, without aid of cosmetics; her eyes are a deep, violet-blue, shadowed with long lashes, and I should hate to be the one to double-cross or try to fool those eyes.

They see straight through with the uncanny insight of the Scotch, and she confesses to a distinct partiality for everything pertaining to the land of Burns and Stevenson. She wears a severely tailored tweed suit, with mannish shirt and tie, when working. She orders her shirts by the dozen from a New York firm and says she feels this is the only sort of costume suited to her job.

After Al Levy, Dorothy Arzner, and myself had taken several of the local inhabitants apart and put them together again in their proper places, she and I fell into a discussion of what constitutes the difference between a good picture and a bad one.

"Neither producer, director, players, technicians, or cameramen can produce interesting screen entertainment from a story which may be all right on the printed page but all wrong for filming purposes." Miss Arzner forgot to go on with her dinner, as she got well launched in one of her favorite subjects.

"Because a story reads well, it doesn't always follow that it will film well," she said, "but if the right adapters get hold of it, such a story may turn out brilliantly. The author, however, usually fusses a good deal at the results. No director, inspired or otherwise, can cope with dreary dialog and sixteen pages of introspection or descriptions of states of mind. If there isn't action to carry along the characters and make them clear, then the whole thing is hopeless."

She looks very fragile to have tackled some of the important talking pictures she has brought to the screen. These include *Sarah and Son*, with Ruth Chatterton; *Honor Among Lovers*, with Claudette Colbert and Fredric March; *Merrily We Go to Hell*, with Sylvia Sidney and March; *Christopher Strong*, with Katharine Hepburn; *Nana*, with Anna Sten, and recently *Craig's Wife*, with Rosalind Russell and John Boles.

Miss Arzner is of the opinion that a director can do a great deal to bring out the acting ability of a player. "After all, if a director doesn't know the effects he is aiming for, how can he hope to get them from his actors? If he knows exactly what he wants, he can explain the scenes so clearly that the players immediately get them and give him what he is trying to achieve. Actors are sensitive; otherwise, they wouldn't be actors. They are interesting and willing to learn, at least most of them. Sometimes just a hint turns the trick."

Miss Arzner has some interesting ideas on the subject: Personality or acting—which is the more important?

"It has been pretty well proven," she reflected, stirring her coffee slowly, "that some of the most talented and brilliant actors fail to make good in Hollywood. They flash on the film horizon for a few months or a year and then disappear. Others make good and keep getting better at the box office. Unless a player has personality, a certain something that comes through, he may be the best actor in the world and yet not make good on the screen.

"This is equally true of men and women. In the case of women, it is not necessarily beauty, but it is something that is at once individual and arresting. In men, it is the power to project themselves through the camera lens in such a way that they are unforgettable."

We spoke at length of such outstanding personalities as Robert Taylor, Gary Cooper, Clark Gable, Greta Garbo, Joan Crawford, Marlene Dietrich, Carole Lombard, Claudette Colbert, and others. She admires those who, having personality, have worked hard to perfect themselves in the art of acting.

Perhaps if you or I had the Arzner experience, we too might be able to direct a picture. She did not arrive by easy stages at her present high place in the Hollywood sun.

She is a fine example of the young woman of wealth and financial security who set out on her own to do something in the world. Her early ambition was to become a doctor, but she was still taking a general college course when the World War broke out. She joined the Los Angeles Emergency Ambulance Drivers Corps, hoping to get to France, but the older girls were sent, and she remained at home.

During this time, her corps commander introduced her to William de Mille, who at the time was an officer in the Intelligence Service. She told him of her desire to get into some department of motion picture work, and at the close of the war, he put her to work in his studio as a typist in the scenario department.

While working in the studios, Miss Arzner decided the director was the most important single unit in the business, so she decided to become a director.

From typist to scenarist, story writer, script reviser, assistant cutter, cutter, script girl, and finally, to director indicates the thorny path along which Miss Arzner learned by experience how to shoot a scene and how to handle temperamental actors.

Her first picture was *Fashions for Women*, starring Esther Ralston. In this, she incorporated her system of working with the writer, directing the picture, and supervising the cutting.

She does not like to be considered a "woman's angle" director but prefers not to be limited to any particular class of story. At the moment, she is anxious to try a costume picture and has one in mind. She works very hard while the picture is in production, but afterward, she likes to go in for rather strenuous exercise for a while in order to let down from the mental activity. She rides horseback, swims, plays golf and tennis.

There is something strong and self-reliant about Dorothy Arzner. I can't imagine her losing her calm, poised attitude. She is well read, well informed, crisp, and her voice is well modulated but firm. She lives on a hilltop near Hollywood and looks at the sea of city lights before going to sleep.

I am told that those who work in a picture with her like her, admire her, and that the men do not in the least object to being directed by her. Around this town of ten million wonders, she is said to "know her onions," which is high praise indeed.

"You are your own world," she said sometime during dinner, which tells you better than I can the sort of person she is.

Woman Film Director Needs Tact

Alma Whitaker / 1937

From *Los Angeles Times*, Feb. 21, 1937.

Women motion picture directors must never be bumptious. They must not yell, "What the hell?" or a sprinkling of *damn*s. They must be gently explanatory, fulsomely "reasonable."

So confided Dorothy Arzner, lone woman film director, now entering her tenth year on the job. She still treads her way as though walking a narrow plank over a deep chasm.

Hence, although she was picked to complete *The Last of Mrs. Cheyney*, starring Bill Powell, Joan Crawford, and Bob Montgomery, after the death of Richard Boleslawski, and it rates Grauman's Chinese and Loew's State showing, she is all retiring modesty.

"I contributed so little to the picture. The scenes, the characters were all set. All I did was to try to carry out Boleslawski's ideas," she said.

At the same time, she has won a long-term contract with MGM, due in large part to *Craig's Wife*, her previous picture for Columbia, which caused her also to be selected to finish *The Last of Mrs. Cheyney*. She is slated to direct Luise Rainer in *Once There Was a Lady*, which calls for the sensitive, gentle direction of a tragic theme.

Albeit Dorothy is the boyish type, wears her hair in a mannish cut, and favors men-tailored suits and low-heeled shoes; she remains judiciously feminine. The destinies of various actresses have hung upon her ability. The first picture she was ever allowed to direct was *Fashions for Women* in 1927, Esther Ralston's first starring feature. Later, it was *Christopher Strong*, Katharine Hepburn's initial "starrer" after *Bill of Divorcement*, over which she assumed sway.

"I always feel that the writer is the real creator, far more important than actors or directors, and I regard myself as just a translator," she said. "I wish I could cultivate a more authoritative manner and wasn't afraid of hurting people's feelings. I'd love to be able to snap 'Out!' without being tactful when something displeases me."

Dorothy went to a fashionable girls' school. "But I preferred playing baseball with the boys. I'm a swell pitcher," she bragged. In college, she had medical ideas, but the urge to get out and earn her living in a hurry spoiled that. Someone sent her to William de Mille, who thought her movie-struck. She told him she only wanted to decorate sets.

She blushes to recall how he asked her what period the furniture in his office was, and she didn't know. He let her sit on a set while he directed: "And I promptly decided directors were the whole cheese." Her first job was in a wholesale coffee firm at twelve dollars a week. From this, she was lured with a fifteen-dollars-a-week offer as a typist at Paramount.

When a script clerk was needed on Nazimova's set, Dorothy asked for and got the job at thirty dollars a week. Presently, she was cutter for James Cruze and wrote and sold a series of Westerns on the side. It was when she had a better offer from a rival studio that Dorothy teased Paramount into letting her direct.

Miss Arzner has a pretty good sense of humor now but confesses she had to cultivate it persistently. "When I could begin laughing at myself, it gave me a new sense of independence," she says.

A Woman's Touch

Pauline Gale / 1937

From *Motion Picture Studio Insider*, July 1937.

Sidelights on the character of one of the screen's best directors, who believes that women should try this new field in motion pictures. Dorothy Arzner's success lends her words weight.

"The story of life is a woman's story. The men, of course, are participants in the action of this great stage but reduced to their ultimate fundamentals, the motivating forces of nearly every human act are feminine-inspired. Every art should recognize that fact, and the finished creation to be valid should be presented from the subtler, more intuitive point of view of the female of the species."

Gravely, succinctly, firmly, Miss Dorothy Arzner expounded her philosophy, a creed that has taken her from typist through the various positions of scenarist, script reviewer, assistant cutter, script girl, and assistant director to her present position as one of the screen's ablest directors.

As a girl, Miss Arzner aspired to be a doctor. At the university, she studied medicine until the war came with its patriotic fervor and romantic appeal. Then she joined the Los Angeles Emergency Ambulance Drivers Corps as a driver, hoping to go to France. As the older girls received the first calls, she never left Los Angeles.

Being an ambulance driver, however, became Miss Arzner's stepping stone into the picture business. The corps commander introduced the college girl to William de Mille, who at the time was an officer of the Intelligence Service. As a result of the acquaintance, Miss Arzner went into de Mille's studio as a typist in the scenario department. As Miss Arzner became familiar with studios, she decided the director was the most important single unit in the business and promptly decided to become one.

The climb was long and arduous, but for the last ten years, Miss Arzner has been responsible for some of the cinema's best. Competition, though keen, has not embittered her but rather made her the more tolerant and the more understanding of human foibles and failings.

Deep thought brooding in her steel-gray eyes, she continued: "Because women as a whole play such a decisive part in life's drama, I believe that women directors should be as successful as men. They, being of the same sex as the women stars, can more readily survey the depths and understand the workings of a woman's soul, thus bring to the screen a subtler and defter touch.

"Please do not consider, while I am saying this, that I am speaking of myself as an example, because when anyone works for me in a picture, they consider me not as a woman but as a director, and the fact that I do happen to be a woman is merely incidental. Good directors, of course, can be either men or women, but I am discussing the ideal situation.

"I believe picture history will bear me out when I say that men directors who have had some of the better feminine characteristics have been the greatest artists and have made the greatest contributions to the advancement of technique. On the other hand, men have qualities, those of firmness and of positiveness, which are vital in order that success may be obtained. Perhaps I can attribute my own position to the fact that I possess to a definite degree those masculine characteristics."

Miss Arzner leaned forward in her chair, a smile lighting her finely chiseled features as she continued to explain her point of view.

"My reason for saying the foregoing is that I am firmly convinced there is as great an opportunity for women behind the camera as there is in front. After all, the director is completely in charge of the picture. When I am on a production, I sit in on every conference from the time the story is first conceived until the picture is previewed. Throughout, the responsibility is mine, the same as it is any director's. Story, casting, treatment—all come within my province. When more women are similarly placed, it is my belief that the motion picture will eventually reach the status of a true art."

There being as many definitions of "true art" as, perhaps, there are people, we asked Miss Arzner to outline her conception. Her low, slightly husky voice made ready answer.

"True art is not reality because neither people nor things are entirely as they appear on the surface. We must probe beneath the veneer that casts a protective cloak about souls as well as events and there find an approximation [that] is neither stark reality nor sheer imagination but is woven of the warp and woof of both. This approximation appears more real than reality itself, and that, to me, is true art. This can be translated on film when we learn to cast a picture in a certain style and sustain that mood throughout, not only in *dramatis personae* but also in their clothes and dialogue and the sets in which and against which they move."

With swift strokes, she illuminated her remarks by pointing out the stark classicism of *Craig's Wife*, her last picture, and how it had been obtained. How even in a modern world and in an ultra-modern art it was possible to attain and maintain classic simplicity. That picture is a monument to her penetrating insight and the clearness of her views.

"Even though this picture was laid in Beverly Hills, we used gowns whose lines harked back to ancient Greece. The dialogue of the participants was couched in [a] simple tone, and even the furniture of the various rooms was styled for the same effect. We tried to have each component part of the production so designed and constituted that a certain definite rhythm was established, so that each contributed toward making it a harmonic whole."

She went on to say, "Every picture, of course, is the product of the combined efforts of a group of artists, but I believe it should be even more so. I believe that in the industry, everyone from a prop boy to producer should be privileged to offer any ideas at any appropriate time. Less fear and less jealousy should rule. Individuals should not be so afraid of their jobs, so subservient to the will of those above them, but should contribute any suggestions they might have to enhance the quality of the finished production."

That Miss Arzner follows this practice is gratefully attested to by all who have worked with her. Her quiet, winning charm welcomes assistance, and her aides find her easy to approach.

At present, Miss Arzner is busy getting ready to go into production on Luise Rainer's newest picture, *Once There Was a Lady*. We feel safe in saying that with Miss Arzner directing such an actress, both will attain new pinnacles of success.

Woman Director!

Jackie Martin / 1937

From *Washington* (DC) *Times*, Nov. 26, 1937.

Do you know the melody that runs through Cesare Franck's *Symphony in D Minor*? Hum it to yourself. Do you feel the strength and the spirit of it? Close your eyes and hum it again. Is the blue smoke of its sad melodic gentleness in your eyes and seeping through your heart and mind? Then hold it, hold it, for we're going back to get Dorothy Arzner. I want you to meet Hollywood's only woman director.

And when you two meet, I want that melody wrapped about you—for her sake and your sake.

The publicity man is guiding me through the maze of sets, storehouses, offices, and laboratories that make up the MGM lot. His name is Otto Winkler. And there is a closeness between us, for he has just left the *Examiner* and is now working for Howard Strickling, MGM's publicity boss.

"What's she like, Otto?" It's getting colder here.

"Quiet. Does swell work." Oil spots on the pavement.

"Young?" Whatta place!

"Yes. About thirty-five or thirty-six." A little city all of its own.

"Popular?" Gravel in my sandals.

"Everyone that's worked with her thinks she's swell."

We come to a halt in front of a little white bungalow.

"Here we are. Hope you get a swell interview and pictures. Come back to the publicity office when you finish, will you?"

Otto's broad back disappearing down the path. Well, here you are. You've admired this woman's work for a long time. You've wanted to meet her. All right, get the lead out of your feet and go on into that office. But the pictures I've seen of her. She looks nearly hard, cold. Suppose she is pompous? Overflowing with egotism. Suppose she's like a lot of these others I've seen—shallow, unkind? Suppose she's—oh, nuts to this! Get on up there and find out! What do you think you are here for, anyway?

I knock on the door. The secretary (Eunice from Kansas. Lives here with her family. Has for a long time. But still doesn't think that California is the ONLY state in the union. Pardon, Eunice, a little gold star for you) lets me in. Opens another door. Announces me. Then closes the door behind me.

Dorothy Arzner is sitting on a low leather couch. Gets up and greets me with a simple "Hello." About five-four, I should say. Wide shoulders. Athletically built. Her hands a combination of the workman's and the artist's. A dark, well-fitting suit. White blouse with Dutch collar on the outside. A flowing artist's tie.

"Have a smoke?" Nice voice.

"No, thanks. Don't smoke." That sounds smug, Miss M.

"I shouldn't either." Dark blue-gray, level eyes.

"Why not?" This is a funny interview.

"It's a habit." What's that terrific quietness about her?

"I don't think it's so bad." Sort of remote, isn't she?

"All habits are bad. I shouldn't do anything because it's a habit. I want to be always aware of the things I do." Careful, Miss M. Don't get into deep water. You'll enjoy it, but you won't have an interview—and what's more, you'll take a licking.

"Tell me, Miss Arzner. How long have you been a director?" Those photographs lied. Nothing hard about her.

"Eleven years." In fact, there is a definite gentleness about her.

"There's a picture, the direction of which made a great impression on me. I'd like to tell you how I felt about it, and then I'd like to know if you directed it. It was *Christopher Strong*, the picture, to my way of thinking, which set Katharine Hepburn for stardom. She was directed to a terrific quietness and intensity [that] I think she never since has reached. There wasn't any emotional flutter about her. Was that your picture?" Certainly an intelligent face.

"Yes. I'm delighted you liked it." Her smile is shy. Strange to find a Hollywood director modest. What rare, good taste. She lights another cigarette and continues: "Katharine Hepburn is a fine girl. Just as Clara Bow was the personification of the spirit of her day, so Hepburn has been the personification of hers." What a shame Hepburn hasn't stayed under the direction of this woman. She would be greater.

Miss Arzner leans back in her chair and looks at me in that contemplative way—

"How long have you been in Hollywood?"

"About a week." Who's getting interviewed?

"Like it?" She isn't passing the time of day. She's driving at something.

"No." Doesn't beat around the bush much.

"Why not?" She knows, so you might just as well go ahead and tell her.

"Something in the air. I sensed it the minute I got off the train. It beats me down. For the first time in my life, I have an inferiority complex. Too many beautiful women. Too many handsome men. Too many block-long cars. Too many silver foxes. Too many umph-umph personalities." She's watching all this time in a sort of gentle, understanding way. It's the smile of a mental attitude that belongs to someone much, much older. A very sensitive person has it. One who has known bitter suffering has it. Suffering that takes away the crackling fire and leaves in its place a gentle flame.

"You mustn't feel that way. You see, it isn't real—this thing that is worrying you. If Hollywood itself didn't have an inferiority complex, it wouldn't put on such a show. Just reach inside and hold onto the worth of you and look at things and people around you for exactly what they are. Just because you're in Hollywood, don't let your sense of values become distorted . . . ."

She went on talking to me out of her own calm philosophy, which is based on no particular religion or creed. A philosophy, the essence of which is kindness, gentleness, and a forgiving down to its very depths.

It is true. I had been feeling very lonely. Very depressed. Very inferior to these super—super everythings out here. But I wouldn't have let on to you had it not been for Hollywood's woman director.

Out of her sympathy came peace—and as I listened to her setting me straight (but not at the expense of others but at the death of a false idea), that melody of Franck's [that] to me has always symbolized universal compassion flowed through my mind.

I got up and took a turn around the little office.

"Thanks. That was good of you. But you better tell me something about yourself that I can write. This would make you look too good. They wouldn't believe that you're like this. Better give me something I can sink my typewriter into. Don't you love to cook and really, really, really make supper when you go home?"

"No." That slow smile.

"Don't you have a collection of elephants or match boxes?"

"No." Amusement.

"Don't you crave to get away from it all?"

"No." A snicker from Hollywood's only woman director.

"Haven't you adopted some children? That's always a good one."

"No." The face was a little sad.

"What am I going to do with you? You're not giving me anything to write about! You know I can't very well say, 'Amazing, folks, but this dame has a soul!'"

The woman who has bossed Joan Crawford in *The Bride Wore Red*, Rosalind Russell in *Craig's Wife*, Esther Ralston in *Fashions for Women* and *Ten Modern Commandments*, Clara Bow in *Get Your Man* and *The Wild Party*, Nancy Carroll in *Manhattan Cocktail*, Ruth Chatterton in *Anybody's Woman* and *Sarah and Son*, Katharine Hepburn in *Christopher Strong*, Anna Sten in *Nana*, Claudette Colbert in *Honor Among Lovers*, Sylvia Sidney in *Merrily We Go to Hell*, and many others—threw back her head and laughed. And then looked a little embarrassed.

"Well, just say: 'There is nothing to say about Dorothy Arzner.'"

But there is—lots.

She drives a swell-looking car—and drives expertly, smoothly. Loves her car and treats it as if it were human. Consequently, she says, it never has been unfriendly enough to have a flat at just the wrong moment. And with that remark, Miss Arzner didn't even knock on wood!

At the Brown Derby, I asked her about the story that she had a collection of hundreds of cufflinks.

Between speaking to this actress and that actor, this producer and that executive, she said: "No, that wasn't true. The fact is, I have one pair of little gold cufflinks, which I have worn for many, many years. They were given me by the head of the department I was in at that time. It was Christmas. All the other girls were getting all sorts of presents. But I had been there only a month and didn't expect any presents. But anyway, I felt pretty out of it. So you can imagine how touched and pleased I was when I received a package. It was a pair of 10-karat gold cufflinks. I have worn them ever since."

"You wouldn't be sentimental, Miss Arzner?"

"Yes, very."

Miss Arzner, who before becoming a director was said to be the best cutter (editing shots and tying them together into a complete continuity) in the business, believes that television is not very far away. And when it comes, she thinks that there will be a marriage between radio and the movies. That there can't be this great borrowing of talent back and forth, this constant mixture of the two without a final blending.

And she thinks that third-dimensional projection must follow. That color, being the third dimension of color (black and white), needs such a vehicle in projection before it will find itself in its real province.

On the salad now.

"Yes, I think that Garbo, without a doubt, is the greatest motion picture actress. And, incidentally, I have been on the MGM lot for a year and have not had one glimpse of her!"

She is very fond of Billie Burke and enjoys her depth of character. She loved working on *The Wild Party*, which skyrocketed Freddy March to stardom. It was her first talkie, and Freddy March was fun to work with. He thought it simply delightful that the director would permit herself to be such a grand audience for his antics.

Tea and cheese, and I was telling the director about my boss in Washington: "—and she has an intuition no one can touch."

"I'll tell you how I feel about intuition," she said. "I feel that it is the accumulation of one's highest intelligence and greatest experiences."

"And you don't believe in belittling that accumulation behind a name, a word that doesn't really express it?"

"No."

"I think in movies, the personality makes the actor. On the stage, it is just the other way around; the actor makes the personality."

A slim young man was sitting in a booth nearby.

"That is Gregg Toland. One of the best cameramen. Photographed *Nana*."

She called him over. It was easy to see that this artistic, sensitive young man was delighted to see her.

"Tell me about her," I said. "I can't get her to talk about herself."

He smiled and looked at her with great admiration in his eyes.

"She's marvelous to work for and with. It's the exacting quality that makes her great. She won't accept second best. She watches the myriad of little things that men forget. And she sees to it that they're done perfectly." He reached over and patted her hand. "Gee, it's swell to see you!"

She smiled that kindly smile at the man.

And then we went out into the night.

Yes, I'm sure that melody [that] occurs and reoccurs throughout the *Symphony in D Minor* belongs to Hollywood's only woman director—Dorothy Arzner.[1]

Note

1. Martin had several leftover quotations from her interview with Arzner and used them in other articles. She included Arzner's admiring commentary on actress Gale Sondergaard in "A Real 'It' Girl," *Washington Times*, December 24, 1937, and her advice on how not to break into Hollywood in "Jackie in Hollywood," *Washington Times*, January 8, 1938.

Starlight

Dorothy Arzner / ca. 1965

From Dorothy Arzner Papers, Library Special Collections, Young Research Library, UCLA.

[Arzner wrote the following undated essay while a filmmaking instructor at UCLA. Typed on UCLA Department of Theater Arts stationery, it was probably the text for her farewell address to her students and colleagues upon retirement from that institution. The identity of the astronomer mentioned in the piece is unknown, but given Arzner's characterization of his comments, he may have been a colleague of Edward Lorenz. Widely acknowledged for his contributions to chaos theory and the "butterfly effect" concept, Lorenz served in UCLA's Department of Meteorology during the 1954–55 academic year.]

Not long ago, I met a famous astronomer. He patiently tried to explain to me some of the principles that rule our stellar universe. It is not easy for an ordinary mind to tear itself away from the routine of everyday thinking and try to grasp cosmic affairs, such as the relationship between stars and planets. By way of demonstration, he dropped a pencil on his desk and said, "Look. By this action, I influence even the furthermost star of the universe. The vibrations I set up will spread and spread 'til they reach the outermost boundaries of all the solar systems, just as when a child throws a stone into a lake." And being somewhat of a philosopher as well, he added, "It is probably the same with our thoughts and actions. They set up vibrations in some subtle matter and are conveyed through the world in ever-widening circles, leaving an impression for good or for evil on every human mind that they touch in their course."

If this be true—and I have no knowledge at my disposal to prove that it is not—it places a tremendous responsibility on the individual for every thought, emotion, and action that emanates from him. Whether he knows it or not, he is a very powerful being who is, in every moment of his life, influencing the world and shaping its destiny.

We human beings have a tendency to blame everything and everybody but ourselves for what is wrong with ourselves and with the world. Evidently, we have no right to do so. The responsibility should be placed where it is due: at our own doorstep.

When the request came to me to "write something about the movies," I could not but help viewing the whole motion picture business in this light—call it "Starlight," if you like.

It is commonplace to say the movies have a great influence on life. It is so commonplace that it has nearly lost its meaning. Moving pictures are strong vibrations going out to a receptive humanity, producing a tendency in those who see them to feel, think, and act in the same vein. The actual realization of this fact is almost terrifying to any thinking person who works in the picture business. He knows that what he produces in a film is a real power sent out on its course through the world to work its way through human hearts and minds, influencing them for good or for evil, awakening them to essential values or lulling them to sleep by giving false pictures of the world and human relationship.

The moving picture, then, has a powerful part to play in the world for good or for bad, whether it knows it or not. It helped to make or unmake dictators, to create war or peace, hatred or love, brotherhood or exploitation.

In a film, there is not a move made or a word uttered, nor a feeling conveyed, that does not in some way make its imprint on human minds, hearts, and thoughts, and to some extent, help bring about just or unjust conditions in the world, whether social, [economic], political, or spiritual. After all, the individual problem is the world problem. The way the individual solves his problems determines the solution of the universal problems.

I can imagine that somewhere there is a gigantic hidden laboratory where the fate, of individuals as well as of nations, is continually being distilled. Every thought, feeling, and action eventually [find their] way into the huge retort of that great laboratory and become ingredients of a brew, which is the sum total of all human thought, feeling, and action. The quality of that brew determines the destiny of individuals, peoples, and nations.

I believe that moving pictures have a tremendous influence on that brew of destiny by way of their power to influence human minds and hearts.

The moving picture, and now TV, through the simultaneous appeal to mind, heart, and eye, has a greater power of suggestibility than either the press or the radio. What the eye sees in picture form leaves a deeper and more permanent imprint on the retina of the soul than the printed or spoken word.

If the Supreme Head of that great laboratory could take us movie workers by the hand and lead us into His hidden workshop and show us the part we play in the shaping of the world events, perhaps we should then be awakened to a new responsibility for every picture we sent out on its course around the world. We might, for a moment, pause in our work and consider whether the film picture we are making carries in it some element [that] could make for greater love, consideration, and understanding between human beings.

Have we the will, the understanding, the love to do it?

Dorothy Arzner 1970 Interview

Kevin Brownlow / 1970

From the Brownlow Collection, London.

[Kevin Brownlow interviewed Arzner at her home in La Quinta, California, on February 4, 1970. For this book, he graciously provided a surviving artifact from their two-hour conversation: an audio recording that covered about an hour's worth of their chat. The following transcript, prepared by the editor and approved by Brownlow, offers insights into Arzner's life and career not found in other conversations. It is, however, fragmentary in places. Among its missing components is Arzner's commentary on *Old Ironsides*, a film that represented a major turning point in her career. Fortunately, Brownlow was able to include a substantial number of her *Ironsides* comments in "The Epic: Silent," *Sunday Times* (London), October 4, 1970, and "An American Epic: *Old Ironsides*," *American Cinematographer*, August 1987. In addition, she spoke at length about her *Old Ironsides* experiences in Brownlow's follow-up 1977 interview, included in this book.

The transcription begins with Arzner's brief narrative on why she disliked giving interviews. She had mentioned to a reporter in 1936 that she received a special gift of gold cufflinks from her supervisor, Ruby Miller, during a Famous Players stenography department Christmas party in 1919. As she explained to Brownlow, the story that appeared in the newspaper was quite different.]

Dorothy Arzner: Everyone was giving everyone fabulous presents, and I was a stranger—the "new girl at school" and whatnot. Finally, at the end of the day, the head of the department I was typing scripts for brought me these cufflinks: plain little gold cufflinks with "DA" on them, and I thought that was so charming. I was so touched with them that I wore them forever. I used to wear blouses that didn't have buttons—now they all have buttons, so we don't have to worry. And so I wore these and just loved them. It was a sentimental thing, I suppose, but they also were very simple and plain and nice. Anyway, I told this story about this pair of cufflinks, and the story that came out in the press was that Miss Arzner had a hundred pair[s] of cufflinks and wore different ones every day. Well, you can imagine what that did to me, who was a fairly conservative person, that I had a hundred pair[s] of cufflinks and changed them every day. That finished me. "I don't want to have anything to do with people who interviewed me anymore," I tell them. It was just a certain honest little human story.

[*On* Fashions for Women, *her first complete film as director.*]

DA: I don't know why. There were just certain things about it that I remembered—that I was a little in advance. I remember I had one scene where [the Esther Ralston character] is quite sophisticated. Now, probably she isn't at all when I see it now, but I was very pleased because I was very young, and I thought I was doing a very sophisticated scene. But I was writing that and directing it and cutting it all at the same time, my first picture. I'd never told anyone how to do anything before. Of course, it was a great pleasure to me that it was a success.

Kevin Brownlow: Jumping ahead to the 1950s and 1960s, who did you have as students at UCLA?

DA: Coppola, who shot the last picture [for the directing workshop]. He was one of my students. He made a very interesting picture, too, for us. He built a whole concrete section of an overpass on the freeways and brought it into the studio in sections. Everyone thought he was crazy, and I supported him. When I read his treatment of his first picture, I said, "This boy can't miss." He had a really creative mind. Good writer—he was excellent. And then I had about five of them that have become cameramen.

KB: Oh, marvelous!

DA: And others doing lighting professionally now, for Disney. Two or three are with Disney. I get letters at Christmastime thanking me because when they go into the army, they can go into the photographic division instead of being a private there, going to Vietnam and being killed or shot. So, they're enormously grateful.

I was quite tough on them from the standpoint of really running [the directing workshop] like a studio and no nonsense. They went there on time, and they were out immediately. I never saw students work so hard. They'd start at noon because we couldn't really shoot until 4 o'clock in the afternoon. The men would stop building the sets, and then we would shoot until about 2:00 a.m.—from about 4:00 until 2:00 a.m.—and we'd have quiet. I didn't have anything but some old barracks that were there from the army to shoot in, but we built sets and had rafters for the lights and all the rest of it.

KB: How long did you do that for?

DA: I was there four or five years. First of all, I came just to lecture. I was asked to come because one of the professors was taking a sabbatical. I said, "I don't know anything about teaching." Arthur Ripley was the head of the department. He was a very fine man, really. He said, "Oh, just tell them what you know.

That's all I wanted you to do; tell them what you know," and I said, "I can't stand up and lecture." He said, "Well, they'll ask questions," which is true, so I started, and I did that for one semester.

Then in the second semester, I tried to have them write something and then work it with just a viewfinder and tell me how they were going to break it up and cut it and make scenes and have the students play the different parts so they could move it and know what composition is. I found that was impossible because they'd take the finder and go like that [*Arzner gestures*], different from the camera. So, we tried bringing a television camera in and seeing whether that would work, but we got so cluttered up with electronics and that sort of thing. Finally, I said, "I just don't want to go on unless we really make pictures. You have a camera right here and a few lights—now do it like matinee theater. Just no sets—furniture and drapes." So, they draped the whole thing, and we started that way, and then bit by bit the students began building little sets, and finally, we were ending up with real pictures with sets and furniture and everything in them, and a cast. They began casting professional actors from Hollywood, and the actors were delighted to be helpful to the students. So, they brought in professional actors from outside, cast any way they wanted, wherever they could get them, and we ended up winning awards.

KB: Do they still do this?

DA: Yes, they're still making them, although they've now gotten so far out with them. I went to one of the previews last year, and they're not really doing it with controlled lighting. They're outside shooting [their films] like documentaries much more, and if it isn't documentary, still so much of it is shot outside—and way out, as far as what they're telling.

KB: Also, the emphasis seems to me to be much more on film appreciation and criticism and watching films. I didn't realize they were still making them.

DA: They're still making them at UCLA, I know that. At least, I hope they are this year; they were last year. The training, I felt, was very important within a studio with light controlled, with everything controlled, not just shooting outdoors and take what you can get and have it like TV with whatever photography you get. I wanted them to learn how to light, and composition, and getting the whole thing under control. Then they can go off as far as they want. I used to say you could go way out, but at least learn what the controls are because they always looked down on Hollywood pictures. That was the establishment that they were coming into.

Yes, they have gone back. They're the ones that love the Mae West and all the older pictures. Before I left—the year I left, which was two years ago, I think—about two years ago,[1] they gathered as many of my pictures that they could and ran one every week on Friday afternoon for a festival. The place was jammed with the kids to see what I had, and it was fun for me to see them and hear their comments in the evening. I found they were very interested in these pictures that were made so far back. We had one of Clara Bow, *The Wild Party*, her first talking picture. They all seemed so dated to me, but I thought she was charming. I noticed Joan Crawford's picture that I made, called *The Bride Wore Red*. I didn't care for it at all when I made it, but when I see it on television, it's an awfully good television picture. She has a gentleness that you don't often see.

KB: Did she try to assert her performance?

DA: Yes, she's very strong anyway, and I suppose she's tried to look at herself playing these parts. *The Bride Wore Red* was from *The Girl from Trieste*, which was quite a story. I wanted to make it with Luise Rainer originally, but some way or other, Luise Rainer got in wrong with the studio. They put Joan Crawford in it, and I didn't want to make it with Joan but finally did.

[Break in the interview; Arzner presumably had been discussing *The Bride Wore Red's* costuming.]

... plastic clothes, and it's the women's clothes that make pictures just terribly dated. They come in with these long skirts down to their ankles today.

KB: You actually tried to pick them out. How could you do this? What about the costume department?

DA: You tell them what you want, and you work with the designer. Like Adrian, even. He'd make twenty designs, and I'd look and he'd say, "Now, you don't have to like any of them—I'll do some more for you." You choose whether you like them or not. You choose what you want them to wear—the kind of clothes you want them to wear. You work with the costume departments the same as you work with actors. The director really was the fellow that had authority. You also planned the sets that you wanted.

KB: That was unusual, though—wasn't it—at that time?

DA: It wasn't as unusual as you might think. I think every top director did it. I think Lubitsch and all of them really had a great deal of say in what they wanted. It was always a touch with Lubitsch, the new Lubitsch sets, everybody's palaces with doors.

KB: That's right.

DA: They all had different styles. Like *Craig's Wife*. I mean, I finally could get what I wanted. I took the art director to a house that had a Greek pediment because I wanted it like a Greek tragedy in *Craig's Wife*. Therefore, I had this very, very stark classic interior with black basalt on the mantelpiece instead of what was originally planned in the play with gold and *pois année* and all that sort of thing.

KB: Did you have a photographic eye when you were making pictures? Did you look through the viewfinder, or did you leave that up to the cameraman?

DA: No, I looked through the viewfinder always and always went through the whole scenes through the viewfinder for compositions.

KB: Do you believe in rehearsals?

DA: Yes, I certainly do, but I didn't in those days. In the early days, you rehearsed and shot immediately, and later, like *Craig's Wife*, I rehearsed the whole play and then had it all broken up, so they knew exactly where they were going from one scene to the other. The cameraman's with you and your whole company. I did that picture also because I wanted to make it. No one wanted me to make it, particularly Harry Cohn, and so I said I would give him an "A" picture for "B" picture money in addition to a star for him. He just laughed at me, more or less, but let me make it because I was making it for "B" picture money. I made it for $280,000. Of course, *Craig's Wife* did very well for everyone, especially Miss Russell.

KB: Is that your most successful picture financially?

DA: No, I don't think so. I wouldn't really know. I wouldn't know which one was most successful. In the early days, *Sarah and Son* with Ruth Chatterton was the most successful. It broke box office records at the Paramount Theatre in New York. I would say that was the most successful of its period, but you can't compare any of those to what pictures make now. As far as I was concerned, *Sarah and Son* did more.

And then, following up, was *Anybody's Woman*, which was the second starring picture for her, and she became known as the first lady of the screen. It also broke box office records at the Paramount Theatre. And then I was sort of the fair-haired girl director for a while. Salaries raised, and new contracts [were] written, and all the things that happen to you when you make a real hit for them.

KB: All the other woman directors had gone by then, hadn't they? They all faded out like Lois Weber.

DA: Yes, Lois Weber was the one before me—the only one I know of that was before me—and she really was a director on her own and made stars like Bessie Love.[2] I wouldn't consider that most that followed later really sustained as directors. There were a few that came and left after a picture.

KB: There were a few contemporaries of Lois Weber, but they lasted about one picture.

DA: I don't know them. So many have made one picture, and a lot of them have been made with their husbands—that sort of thing. I think Ida Lupino had her husband as producer. That's a help. [*Arzner chuckles*] I was out on a limb by myself most of the time.

KB: The details of how it all started because I love that story you told.

DA: I was in the ambulance corps during the First World War, believe it or not, and I was too young. I wanted to go overseas and drive an ambulance near the trenches or something. I was at that wild age. The commander was Commander Starkweather. They were grooming people for the Drake Section Sanitaire, a

French ambulance corps, and I was just too young. They just let me drive. I drove their car around. So when the war was over, I didn't want to go back to college. I was going to USC at the time, and I didn't want to go back after the war. We were only in for one year, you know. It was very quickly over after America got in. So, I remember I was having dinner with them one night, and I said, "Well, where do we go from here?" I remember they started saying Dorothy was a modern girl and she should be connected with a modern business—motion pictures—and I had been brought up practically next door to a theater. My father had restaurants that were always in connection with the Mason Opera House and the Grand Opera House here, which no one even knows about in Los Angeles hardly. I was rather bored with the idea of actors because I had seen so much of them. When I was little, they used to pick me up and toss me up in the air, and I used to hate it. So actors to me were just something I didn't want to have anything to do with.

Anyway, they insisted upon me going out and meeting William de Mille, so I remember the wife, Mrs. Starkweather, drove me out and dropped me off in front of the old Paramount studio, and I was yelling to her, "Don't leave me!" I knew that that appointment was made so in I went, and Mr. de Mille sat down. He later went to USC to teach. He was really quite a brain, like a professor, too. He looked at me and said, "Well, what would you like to do here?" and I said, "Oh, I don't know. I think I could be a set dresser," and he said, "What's the period of this furniture?" which was in his office, and I didn't know. He told me, and I'll never forget it. He said it was Franciscan, so I knew that was out as far as having any job given to me being a set designer, but he said, "I'll tell you—why don't you look around for a week, and I'll make it possible that you can go into the different departments." So I thought that's fine—see the inside of the studio and see the workings, so I did for a week in the studio. I talked to his secretary, and I walked on the Cecil DeMille set—he was making *Male and Female*. I can remember watching him, and I remember thinking, "You know, if you can do anything in this business, that's the thing to be because that's the fellow who tells everybody what to do. He's the big shot." I remember that thought just flashing through my mind, and I saw the cutting departments, and I talked with the secretary. She was a very experienced person. She talked to me and said, "Now, if you really want to come into the picture business, you should really start in typing scripts, because the script is the beginning of the picture and where you learn something about it." So after a week, I went back to William de Mille's office and thanked him very much and said, "I think I would like a job in the picture business." And he said, "Now, where would you like to start?" and I said, "I'd start at the bottom." He said, "Where do you think the bottom is?" I said, "Typing scripts," and with that, he said, "For that answer, I'll give you a job." So, he called the head of the stenographic department in and introduced me to her, and it was during the flu epidemic, too. I would never have gotten the job, I don't think, except that everybody was out with the flu.

She met me, and she took my name and number and telephone and the usual and said, "I'll call you when there's an opening." Two months went by, but in the meantime, a friend of mine from Westlake was working in a wholesale coffee house down on Main Street, and she said, "Oh, we need people down there. Don't you want to come down and take a job filing orders and working the switchboard in a wholesale coffee house?" I said, "Fine," because I was not wanting to go back to college. At any rate, I did go down, and I took the job. I got fifteen dollars a week, and I took the job. I filed, and these tough clerks are coming in and throwing this bunch of orders at me, but I was having a whale of a time because I had never worked. This was all fun.

I was working the switchboard one day when over the switchboard came a call from Paramount. Ruby Miller was the name, and she was very demanding, as I learned later when I took the job. You had to be letter-perfect in your typing, and I had only typed college notes with two fingers. At any rate, she said there's an opening and come out Monday morning, and I said, "How much?" She said, "Sixteen-fifty a week," so I thought that's about a dollar and a half a week more than I'm making. I went to Paramount, and I took the job and went in there Monday morning. She dropped this big bunch of stuff on my desk and the typewriter, introduced me around to the girls. There was another girl in the office—Mike Leahy, redheaded girl. She was a wonderful girl.

KB: Sidney Franklin worked with her.

DA: Mike Leahy. I think she did before she went to Paramount.

KB: Before she went there, yes.

DA: Or maybe afterward, I don't know.

KB: Seventeen years at Paramount.

DA: She was a wonderful girl. The first day I typed, there were so many mistakes that I didn't turn it in. I said, "Can I turn this in tomorrow morning?" and Miss Miller said "Yes" on my first day. I typed all night long, doing it over with two fingers, and did about twenty pages' typing in the next morning. I was a little better the next day but awfully slow because I knew I had to make it letter perfect. She wouldn't let you put an "e" over an "o" or anything like that. I was only about a third through when Mike Leahy, who was finished because she *typed*, came over and took almost all of my stuff. She started typing it up—putting my initials on it—and then put it back on my desk. That's the way I survived for the first week. With Mike Leahy, it was always as much as I would get done, and when she was finished, she would come over and take half of mine and do it. She really weathered me through the first week. By the time I typed all day long for a week, I began to build up speed. I could hold my own. So, I did that for about three months, and then it was Mike that told me about the next step to make—get a job as a script girl—and I think it was Mike that told me about the opening over with Nazimova. I did go over there, and apparently, William de Mille said to the head of the department, "What did you let her go for?" so I did one picture with Nazimova. They called me, and I came back and was a script girl at Paramount.

KB: What was the picture for Nazimova?

DA: *The Secret Doctor of Gaya*, it was called, but I don't know what it was released under. It wasn't a great success. Her husband was directing it and Mr. Herbert Blaché. It was so far back I can't . . . .

KB: Charles Bryant, wasn't it?

DA: Yes, Charles Bryant.

KB: What kind of a director was he?

DA: Well, he had an awful time. She was at the point where we'd all be called at nine o'clock, and she wouldn't come until four in the afternoon. She was a star and made it all difficult. I was too young to know what the difficulties were, but there were difficulties. A lot of incidents made it difficult. Set in India, you know—we had Indian extras and that sort of thing. But then I went back to Paramount and started again. From there on, I went bit by bit and became a cutter.

KB: Where's de Mille? Do you remember the films you worked on as script girl with him?

DA: I didn't work with him. The first picture I was the script girl on was for Donald Crisp.

KB: Donald Crisp, of course.

DA: *Six Best Cellars*.

KB: Bryant Washburn.

DA: Bryant Washburn. You really do know the back history, don't you?

KB: Well, you sent it to me, remember? [*Both laugh*]

DA: Oh, so you know? That's it.

KB: But then I remember that you were assisting the cutter on a picture—that first one.

DA: Well, I went in to watch her cut.

KB: Nan Heron.

DA: Nan Heron. She was very helpful. I think they were helpful and kind in those days. I guess they are now, too.

KB: No one had the feeling that you would like to take their job away from them?

DA: No, because the picture business was growing so fast, and I think they needed everyone in those days. I think it was harder later—now it's impossible. I don't know whether it would have been easy then. I just was very fortunate—I really was, all along—and I suppose I was a fairly agile person. But you have ideas as you see now. Young people are really outdoing the older people. You come in with fresh ideas. People were fine with Jim Cruze, who was just wonderful. I used to write the love scenes. He hated love scenes, you know; he was a real he-man. I used to write them out in detail. He'd say, "Why don't you do it?" and I said, "No, I will direct this scene when I'm a director," but he wasn't afraid of giving you credit. I didn't want credit until I became a director. I didn't take credit on *The Covered Wagon*. They put it on when it went into the modern museum.[3]

KB: Oh, that's how it happened.

DA: It wasn't on originally because I never wanted my name on the screen until I became a director. Even then, I made the mistake of not wanting it particularly, because I didn't want to be exploited. I saw so many people ruined by overexploitation, and I thought: this one woman director at Paramount—the first time Paramount has a woman director. If they overexploited me and you can't live up to it, they can ruin you with this. So, I think my name is a little tiny thing all mixed up down at the bottom of the Paramount Pictures title card. All I remember is that it said "Directed by Dorothy Arzner"—a little tiny thing—and it wasn't until later, after I made *Sarah and Son*, that I wanted a single card and 100 percent [of] everything that went with it, because then I had established myself to a certain degree. I think I was wise in the beginning.

KB: What made you go in and watch Nan Heron at work?

DA: She was the cutter of the first picture—of Donald Crisp's pictures. She was the cutter.

KB: Yes, but then what was . . . ?

DA: Well, I was interested in everything that was going on, really, so I did go in to watch her cut, and then she said, "I'll teach you how to cut." So she had me cut the next reel, and she watched me do it. Then, I went in on a Sunday and cut the next reel by myself and let her see it, if it was all right. From that time on, I was on my way as a cutter.

KB: Did you have a Moviola or any sort of viewer?

DA: You read the film. I used to. Bebe Daniels could tell you. I used to watch tears coming in Bebe's scenes and say, "Now, we can't cut that until a tear gets to," you know.[4] You'd go over every detail. I'd hate to go home at night and go to bed. I couldn't wait for the next morning to come to get back. I loved being a cutter. I loved cutting because you're by yourself with it at night, and you could do things that pleased everybody.

KB: I've been an editor myself for years, and quite often, my assistants would say, "How on earth did they do it in silent pictures?" I had the equipment, and I was trying and letting the film go through my hand so that you could see it moving, but I still can't work out how you could read film to be able to make the impeccable timing that those pictures had. It was one thing just cutting silent on a Moviola head, but another thing cutting in the hand, and I still never really understood unless you just did it.

DA: Well, you were on the set, too, so that you got into the rhythm of the picture. The script girl in those days in silent pictures kept script and cut the picture, both.

KB: What happened if it was on location, like *The Covered Wagon*?

DA: I cut *The Covered Wagon* and kept script all on location.

KB: All on location. I see.

DA: We had a whole thing set up, but it was so cold and so miserable that I didn't do much cutting there. I came back two weeks before the picture was finally finished and cut on a weekend. Then, when the shooting was finished, I had hundreds of thousands of feet of film to cut.

KB: What about action cuts? For instance, often in *The Covered Wagon*, you take a scene when Warren Kerrigan swings into the saddle in a close shot. Then you cut, and we're back in the mid-shot, and the action is as smooth as glass. What was the difficulty in matching this up—not so much so that he's in the right position, but to get the rhythm of the cut right?

DA: It's a feeling, I think. It's a feeling.

KB: Is it a matter of trial and error in the projection room? You'd see it in the projection room, bring it back, and cut it again?

DA: No, I remember very little of that. Of course, in silent pictures, you cut much more with the camera than you did with talking pictures. Not *The Covered Wagon*, though, because we had so much extraneous stuff—animals going across the river and all the rest of it. I was the same even later with talking pictures. I didn't shoot a lot of film you could fool around with. I used to cut with the camera pretty much, overlap some, and then go back and pick it up. Usually, I knew just where I wanted to cut to the close-ups. I think it's a feeling. I think it's knowing what you want to accent with the close-up and where you want to accent it.

KB: I'm sure it is.

DA: And I know that a lot of people would say, "When do you cut?" Especially at the university. They'd say to me, "When do you cut? Before they rise, during the rise, or after they've risen?" and I said all three—whatever it feels like. There's never a set way that you cut. It is a feeling, more or less, in a sense.

KB: It's a feeling, but it's a sense that has to be developed. This is the interesting thing.

DA: It is a sense that's developed, I think.

KB: How did you get it so soon? Because if you were doing Donald Crisp pictures, say, in 1920—was that it?

DA: Yes.

KB: Well, then, two or three years later, you were a top editor. Two years' experience even now wouldn't make an editor.

DA: I was directing in 1926.

KB: That makes it even more confusing, but it's really extraordinary how fast that you picked it up.

DA: I suppose just having a dramatic sense, more or less. I think you either have it or you haven't it. And I think it can be developed, too, but I guess I had it. I don't know. I don't really know.

KB: I think that's indicative of all the great people that are talented and didn't know. They just did it. It doesn't matter whether you know or not, so long as you can do it.

DA: Well, every picture I ever made was like the first picture I had ever made. If somebody told me I could get on a train and leave, I'd have been delighted the night before I started it. I still didn't know, and that was on every picture I ever made. I had a sense of what I wanted to do—it was all in the mind—but I didn't have it nailed down to know exactly what I was going to get.

KB: Did the responsibility scare you?

DA: It didn't the first time. I seemed to know I was going to be a director. The first picture, I was frightened. I had stage fright, there's no doubt about it, but I weathered it. I just went on doggedly. I whistled as I went into the studio to keep up my spirits, that sort of thing, but I got over it.

KB: Was there a lot of resentment from the male directors?

DA: I never found any. No. The only time that I found hesitancy was once in a while from a cameraman who thought that he wouldn't like to work with a woman director. When I knew that, or when I would hear of it, I would tell him, "Look, you don't have to. I can make it, and there won't be anything against you. I can change cameramen," and they would always come work for me and then afterward be delighted. I never found any problem, really, at all. I would hear rumors like Darryl Zanuck saying he wouldn't have a woman director, that sort of thing, but the people that worked with me—Gregg Toland. I loved him, and he loved working with me. Walter Mayo, who was Goldwyn's company manager and was my assistant director and company manager when I made *Nana*, said it was the happiest time in his life, and Billy Kaplan, who arranges most of the foreign films, or did, for Pan Berman. First of all, he was my property man, then I made him my assistant director. He said that was the happiest time of his life when he was with me.

KB: Why did you think there's never been a woman cameraman in this project?

DA: I think it's because there are enough men, and I think it is a man's world. There's no doubt about it. I don't think they want women directors. I don't know how I happened to get it, really. It just happened because they needed young directors, and I suppose things like *Blood and Sand*, where I helped out with that, and *Ironsides*, and that sort of thing.

KB: Could you tell me about the *Blood and Sand* thing? But before we get onto that, to keep the chronology straight, which was the first picture you were full editor on?

DA: I think I was full editor on the second picture I did.

KB: Was it a Donald Crisp film?

DA: I think it was a Donald Crisp film. I can't remember now—the very first one—but I was the cutter on the second one and script girl.

KB: Did you have assistant cutters?

DA: No.

KB: You had to put the trims away yourself?

DA: Yes.

KB: I think it sounds more and more incomprehensible. It really does. You would work as a script girl all day, then in the evening, you start cutting . . . .

DA: Cut, then you keep track of your trims up in the boxes. You had all these boxes.

KB: Did you have key numbers on the film?

DA: Yes.

KB: You did. Did you log it yourself?

DA: No.

KB: You didn't log it yourself?

DA: Because they were silent pictures. You had the edge numbers.

KB: But didn't you take edge numbers out of logbooks?

DA: No.

KB: Well, how did you know . . . ?

DA: By scene 1, 2, 3, 4, you put up in a box.

KB: Yes, but with the edge numbers on it. How did you know which edge number that related to if you haven't got a logbook, and you've torn off the front, and there you had . . . .

DA: The trim was in the box.

KB: The trim was in the box, but how did you know what this piece belonged to if it only has one edge number on it and nothing else? How do you know where it comes from if you haven't logged it?

DA: Because you should know the scenes well enough if you're the script girl on the set. [*Both laugh*] I used to be able to remember if somebody came in with their tie hanging out or something, or I'd walk on the set, record where things are, and something was moved, I'd know it moved. It's a memory. You have to have memory, too. You can't be without a memory and do that work in those days. Now they have script girls that take everything down. I never used my script girl when I had one. She was for either the laboratory or something else. I never used them. I knew what my scenes were, I knew what the film was, I knew what take was best before I looked at the rushes. I wouldn't have had to look at the rushes.

KB: In those days, did they have continuity sheets in which script girl types up the scene? What did you do as script girl?

DA: Just wrote notes on my script so that I would know the next day whether she was off or if she was on.

KB: Did you give documents to the cutting room at all?

DA: No, I was the cutter.

KB: I'm just trying to see how it differs from today.

DA: The silent pictures were very much simpler than today. Today it's very complicated in comparison, I think.

KB: So, the procedure . . . .

DA: It's very simple, more or less. The big problem was in big pictures, like, as I say, *The Covered Wagon* and *Ironsides*, *Blood and Sand*, which were silent pictures but had enormous amounts of film that you had to organize and dramatize and use as much as you could, wisely. Not have it too long or too short.

KB: Do you remember the titles of pictures that came before *Blood and Sand*? Any of those which you could recall, because if they didn't have your name on them, it makes it hard to find out what you did.

DA: Cutting?

KB: Yes.

[*Long pause*]

DA: I can't remember. I don't even remember the second one with Donald Crisp. I mean, I did a second one with Donald Crisp. I didn't cut too long, though, before I became a director. I went with Jim Cruze.

KB: How did the *Blood and Sand* thing occur? That was because you worked out a way . . . .

DA: Well, that's what happened in between. I was sent over to the Realart studio to head the editorial department. That's where I cut reams of it, all Bebe's pictures. Those are the pictures that I cut.

KB: Yes, of course.

DA: I must have been on the set. I don't know, but I cut an enormous number of pictures there. All of Wanda Hawley's and all of Bebe Daniels's, and I think Mary Miles Minter was there. Quite a number. I cut something like fifty-two pictures in a year. They'd come out four a month practically because they had four stars there. They'd make one a month with each one, so it was just a lot of pictures. Then I took charge of organizing the department so they could keep track of the negative also, and then the art department that had to illustrate the titles. I was in on the titling so I could know what kind of illustrations to guide the art department. So, I was the head of that editorial department at Realart

Studio when they called me back to do *Blood and Sand* because that was a big picture and because I had cut so many pictures over at Realart.

KB: What was the process? They were going to develop an elaborate process to matte in Valentino and the bull.

DA: Yes, they were. A Williams process it was called, I think.[5] They were going to try to work him in, some way or other—a double process, or maybe like a transparency idea. I suppose it was the beginning of the idea of doing process shots.

KB: Yes, it was a sort of traveling matte.

DA: I never saw it, and they didn't do it. There was a big convention of all the salesmen that came out to Paramount, and they had one of these big banquets. I assembled a big chunk of *Blood and Sand* to show them with the bullfighting and used the stock stuff and shot the Valentino stuff for it to fit into it to do this trailer. To show, so they could sell the picture ahead of time before the Williams process came through, and they were all so impressed. Then I cut all the bullfight stuff that way into *Blood and Sand* and Valentino doing the scenes—the close-ups.

KB: Was there a problem in those days about shooting an insert? It's so difficult nowadays, but could you just go and shoot an insert as an editor?

DA: No, no. I had to get the right script because I had to have Valentino and the bull. I had to have the whole company to be able to shoot.

KB: I see.

DA: But it's because I was going to make this trailer and said I needed to have some close-ups, and so they let me make these close-ups for the trailer. Then, because they were so impressed with it, then I could go on and do the film. They said we didn't have to use so many close-ups. I think we shot for a day.

KB: Would you explain? Because I found some production stills of that film being shot. Alvin Wyckoff is photographing it. He must have been the man you used because he was the photographer on the main film.

DA: Really?

KB: Yes, so that would explain it. It must be what you were doing.

DA: I think so. I don't really know because I can't remember. All I know is that Fred Niblo was the director. I remember Nita Naldi, but I don't remember the names of a lot of the other actors. Oh, Lila Lee was in the cast.

KB: And then you were showing it in the projection room.

DA: It was finished, and Jim Cruze was there. There were two projection rooms, small ones, and you had to go through one to get to the other. Suddenly I heard this voice say, "My God, who cut that?" and I thought that Jim was derogatory by the way he boomed out with it. I said, "I did," and he said, "Well, would you cut my next picture? I'm going to do *The Covered Wagon.*" I said, "I don't know, you'll have to ask the front office. If they say OK, it's OK with me, however." So we did. I decided to go with Jim Cruze.

KB: Was that a very tough location to cover?

DA: Very tough, really. It was about ninety miles from the railroad, and we broke all the oxen to the yoke. There had been tents, and it snowed, and there were lots of hardships. Alkali dust that deep that just cut into the women's faces. [*Arzner gestures to a collection of photographs*] The other picture in there that's of the group, and I'm sitting on the end, but I don't think you'd know it was me.

KB: Oh, really? Oh, dear. I keep finding somebody new in that group.

DA: Edwin Willat was taking pictures all the time in groups. Jim Cruze would give him about two minutes to get a still of the scene. Jim shot like a house afire, but he loved to finish at two o'clock in the afternoon—everybody'd go home—and then I'd go in and cut. The next morning, he'd say, "When can I see those rushes cut?" and I'd say, "They're ready." He used to love that.

KB: Karl Brown said that he didn't want to do *The Covered Wagon*. Did he mention this to you?

DA: I don't remember that.

KB: He wasn't too happy with the idea of doing a Western because Westerns in those days were just routine pictures.

DA: Karl Brown worked so hard. I can see him trailing off across the desert with that camera on his shoulder, keeping up with Jim Cruze. Everybody was geared at a high speed because he loved to shoot fast and make it continuous so that everybody could keep the mood and the whole thing.

KB: They didn't have too many takes.

DA: Very few.

KB: So, an early day and then dining.

DA: Very much so. I'm afraid I did the same thing.

KB: Did you learn anything else from Jim Cruze?

DA: I must have learned a lot. You can't help but learn all the time you're working with someone. I learned more from Jim Cruze than anyone—the style, I mean. I felt the one unforgivable sin was to bore an audience, so I used to always cut so that things moved, and I didn't drag scenes out or let people take a long time getting out of the door and that sort of thing. I think that all came from Jim Cruze.

KB: Can you remember any of the incidents that happened when you were on location on *The Covered Wagon*?

DA: Hundreds of them. I can remember so many different kinds. Some with the Indians moving in. We were very friendly with the Indians, but we had a problem with some of the girls we brought out from Hollywood. They were fascinated by the beautiful silver bracelets and ornaments, and the girls would all casually walk into the Indian tents. Then one night, an Indian decided to walk into the girls' tent. I heard these screams and whatnot, and the girls were going to tie up the Indian or chase him out of camp. I defended him. I said, "What can you expect?" I told Jim Cruze, "This is wrong. The girls have been walking in and out of his tent. What's wrong about the Indian walking in and out of theirs?"

He said, "By God, you're right."

That Indian was my friend forever. I can't tell you how much attention I got—the horse would be saddled up by Yakima Jim, who was an outlaw cowboy, part Indian. When it snowed one night, I heard this noise outside my tent, and I said, "Who's that?"

He said, "It's Yakima, tightening up your tent so it doesn't collapse with the snow."

He tightened Jim's tent up and mine, and the next morning all the tents were down but ours. [*Both laugh*] With the weight of the snow on the tents. So, of course, we made friends with the Indians.

I just remember a lot of personal things. One Saturday afternoon, everybody wanted to go into town. I suppose it was a Saturday afternoon, and I wanted to go too, so we all rode into town, which was not the ninety miles from the railroad town, but it was about six or seven miles into this little town. We went in there, and we had dinner, and it began to get dark, and it began to seem as though it was going to snow. So, I got on a horse and was going to ride back to camp before it started snowing when I heard the clop-clop of a horse in back of me and here was Yakima Jim behind me. He came up beside me and said, "Miss Dot, I saw you riding out of town, and I thought I'd better come along so that you get back safely to camp," and I said, "Fine." He really was a tough-looking wrangler. He was an outlaw cowboy who killed a couple people, and he looked just like they are supposed to look, dark and frightening.

Anyway, we rode along, and it snowed heavier and heavier, and pretty soon, there's no road to go by, and we rode and rode and rode, and colder and colder and more freezing. I said, "Do you think we're going towards the camp?"

He said, "The horses know how to go to camp."

Pretty soon, he pulled up his horse, and he pulled up my horse and reached over and stopped it, got off his horse, and said, "I have to take your boots off, Miss Dot."

This scared me to death. I was awfully young, awfully innocent—I was scared of anything. It looked like he might touch me, so I was just scared to death. Then, at that moment, when this fright rolled over me as he came over, he said, "Now, don't you be afraid of me. I just have to take your boots off so your feet don't freeze in them." With that, he pulled my boots off and rubbed my feet with snow and got them all red, put the boots back on both feet, got back on his horse, and we rode on. We finally saw the lights of camp, and Jim Cruze was fit to be tied because he was so worried about me. He felt they'd all get drunk, and I was with them. Anyway, I know he scolded a couple people for even letting me go with them, but I got back safely with Yakima Jim, an Indian who really took care. I suppose I'd have frozen feet if he hadn't. Things like that.

KB: Fascinating.

DA: I really learned that people are good, and it has to do with you a great deal—it must have. That's all I can put it up to—how clear you are. I wouldn't know otherwise because I certainly was exposed to everything, practically.

Warren Kerrigan's mother died while we were on *The Covered Wagon*, and he had been going on. We had to go in the snowstorm again. It was really the wrong time of year out there. I rode all night in the snowstorm into town. He didn't get the train. We waited all day long, and then, into the next late afternoon, we did get the train. I had just gone to bed from two nights of no sleep and shooting the night before. For about three days and nights, I hadn't slept. Somebody rapped on my door and said, "Helen De Rosa," who was a girl that was on the picture, "has broken her leg, and they're bringing her in." So, I got up, and they brought her in. As they started to undo her leg to look at it—the doctor in that room in this little railroad hotel—I felt sick to my stomach, and I remember getting out of the room. I remember seeing this old fellow down the hall, and I headed toward him and just grabbed him by the shirt and out I went. Just completely. I just fainted, and I had never fainted in my life. I had on a polo coat over a pair of pajamas—I'd been in bed, you see—and the next thing I knew, my head was on the polo coat, and they had taken a decanter of water—one of those big bottles of water—and thrown [it] all over me to bring me to. And as I came to, I said the usual thing—"Where am I?"—and he said, "Oh, that's alright, little lady, you just fainted," and I said, "Oh, how disgusting."

I remember staggering back to my room after that and getting into bed and saying, "Wake me up for breakfast," because this was late at night when they brought her in. I didn't wake up until the next night, so dinner. I came to, finally. Helen De Rosa had had her leg put in splints and everything was alright, but I remember going down into the dining room and all these old fellows—whiskered railroad men—looking at me and smiling, saying, "How do you feel?" I said, "Oh, fine—fine." And I did; all I needed was sleep. I was there alone practically because Helen De Rosa went on the train that night into Los Angeles with her broken leg, and I was alone in that funny little railroad town.

So then I was to go back the next day. After dinner there, I found that this woman that was the one prostitute in town had heated rocks and put them in sacks in the bottom of the car so I would be kept warm while I traveled back during the ninety miles in the snowstorm. She had this amazing face that was weather-beaten. I said, "Oh, you're so kind," and she said, "Why shouldn't I be kind to a lady?" Evidently, the men had gotten her to do this so that I would be taken care of back in the car because we didn't have heat in the cars in those days. All we had was a little oil stove that Ernie Torrence used to carry around with him everywhere he went. He would go calling on you in your tent and bring his own oil stove to set up. He had the hot water bottle, and we're making scenes, and he'd carry it around on his stomach until he came. He was awfully good—he really was a wonderful person.

KB: He was Scottish, wasn't he?

DA: Yes, and everybody was suffering [from dysentery]. I avoided it because my grandfather was a miner, and I remember he said, "If you ever go out on the desert, don't drink the water. Drink milk, but don't drink the water." I didn't, and I was about the only one to escape. The others all looked green; they were sick for days out there.

KB: The idea that a gigantic location like this with Indians and . . . .

DA: We had five tribes of Indians, and we had cowboys . . . .

KB: How was it organized? How was it kept under control?

DA: Vernon Keays was Jim Cruze's assistant director, a marvelous assistant. He knocked himself out day and night. Everybody did. When we were delayed by the snow, even Paramount wanted us to come back and finish the picture on the Lasky lot. I remember Jim Cruze telling them, "You'll have to come and get us!" He knew that really was real enough, and that picture—I don't think you could shoot the wagon train any better today than when it was shot. It was so real—it looks like the desert. I remember he talked to the whole company. He said, "We may not be paid." To a man, everybody said, "Let's stay." There was a wonderful spirit in those days—the pioneering spirit is what it was.

Jim was a wonderful man to a company. He demanded work, and he wouldn't tolerate anyone who cried or complained, but on the other hand, he never demanded of me like some directors did where you have to wait on them. He carried his own script. All he'd do is ask questions about a scene—what was next, or how it was, or whatever. He expected you to do your job completely, but not wait on him like a handmaiden.

Notes

1. Arzner retired from UCLA in 1965, not 1968 as she implied here.
2. Weber never worked with Bessie Love. Arzner probably meant Billie Dove, who starred in two Weber films in the mid-1920s.
3. Paramount donated a copy of *The Covered Wagon* to the Museum of Modern Art Film Library in November 1935.

4. In a 1967 letter to Brownlow, Arzner expressed a similar sentiment: "I was young and enthusiastic. Yes, I could read film even to teardrops. Good young eyes, and an enormous interest. Also knew the script backwards and was on the set as much as possible, watching the action." Letter to Kevin Brownlow, April 25, 1967, Brownlow Collection, London.

5. In the early 1920s, American cinematographer Frank Williams had perfected a double matting process that allowed filmmakers to create composite images consisting of actors in the foreground and separately filmed locations in the background.

Approaching the Art of Arzner

Francine Parker / 1973

From *"Action!": The Magazine of the Directors Guild of America* 8, no. 4 (July–Aug. 1973).

There can be no doubt about it: woman has a different point of view on life. And the world does take on a rather startling and surprising look when observed through the eyes of a skilled, talented, hard-working, learned, and thoroughly unintimidated female. It is essential to comprehend this point in order to assess the amazing artistry of Dorothy Arzner. That artistry encompassed outlandish wit, dazzling characterizations, warmth, humanness, meticulous imagery, technical virtuosity, as well as a spectacular command of the language and mechanics of the motion picture. And, in its day, top box-office draw.

A cinematographer friend and I visited Dorothy Arzner early this year at her home near Palm Desert. She was waiting for us, waving from the deep, flat lawn fronting her house. After a minute of freshening up, she drove us to a lively restaurant where we lunched under a cool umbrella near the pool and asked frantic questions of her between sips of tame Bloody Marys, bites of fresh bread, and huge chunks of a frighteningly bottomless salad.

What would she be like, this "woman director" or "lady director," as she is invariably called in film texts? Small, vibrant, gentle, devilish, very pretty, her eyes a sparkly blue and gleefully electric, her voice soft and slow and warm, no put-on, very much unremote, though perhaps too modest for a one-time "Top Ten" Hollywood director.

Arzner is the only director to have directed these strong personalities: Clara Bow, Ruth Chatterton, Claudette Colbert, Esther Ralston, Nancy Carroll, Sylvia Sidney, Katharine Hepburn, Rosalind Russell, Joan Crawford, Anna Sten, Lucille Ball, Maureen O'Hara, Merle Oberon, plus such male performers as Fredric March, Charles Buddy Rogers, Paul Lukas, Clive Brook, William Powell, as well as the then-bit players: Cary Grant, Ginger Rogers, Frances Dee.

Her collaborators were stars in their own right. One was Harry Fischbeck, whose "deep-focus photography" on D. W. Griffith's *Sorrows of Satan* was, according to historian Kevin Brownlow, "not to be duplicated again until Orson Welles and Gregg Toland made *Citizen Kane*." Fischbeck worked brilliantly with Arzner on her *Working Girls* (1931)—a real sleeper of a movie, which the studio told Arzner they would prefer to forget was ever made. Another coworker was Gregg Toland, whose glittering photography crowned Arzner's *Nana* (1934). Playwright-screenwriter Zoë Akins, with whom Arzner worked long and continuously. And Robert Wise, who edited her *Dance, Girl, Dance* (1940). Starring Lucille Ball and Maureen O'Hara, *Dance, Girl, Dance* received much latter-day acclaim at the Woman's Event in Edinburgh last year, and later in London at the British Film Institute's Woman's Film Festival.

Arzner was "the only editor from the entire silent period to be officially remembered," according to historian Brownlow. And not only because of her tour-de-force cutting of the bull-fight sequence in Valentino's *Blood and Sand* (1922), extensive sections of which were shot by her as well. When she cut that sequence of *Blood and Sand*, she had already moved up from script supervisor to full charge of the editing department at Realart, a subsidiary of Paramount.

Arzner's swift and distinctive style resulted in her editing thirty-two features in one year for Realart, as well as training new cutters and participating in production conferences. After her cutting of James Cruze's *The Covered Wagon* (1924), she and Cruze worked out the action for the epic *Old Ironsides* (1925), which she edited, wrote, and in some small measure, shot. The slim, young girl, in her boyish white trousers and sweater, was a familiar figure among the two thousand men during the long months of harsh and difficult location shooting.

Arzner directed Paramount's first talkie, *The Wild Party* (1929), with Clara Bow and Fredric March. Clara Bow does her first screen talking in a wacky, warm, highly styled romantic comedy about the twenties' flappers and emancipated co-eds. As Stella, she is the power behind a group called "the hard-boiled maidens." Much to the frustration of the college authorities, they arrange all-night parties, raid the local speakeasies and nearby men's colleges. As is usual in Arzner, the relationships between women are intriguingly explored, adding depth to our understanding of the relationships between women and men. The romance between Clara Bow, the student, and her professor, Fredric March, is delicate and touching—more so contrasted against the film's background of near high-camp.

Arzner's *Sarah and Son* (Ruth Chatterton, Clive Brook, 1930) broke box office records at New York's Paramount Theatre. That film, together with Arzner's *Anybody's Woman* (1930), led the press to characterize Ruth Chatterton as "The First Lady of the Screen." Dorothy Arzner's films often topped the list of Paramount's box office winners.

Dorothy Arzner was born in San Francisco and grew up in Los Angeles. Her father, Louis Arzner, owned a famous Hollywood restaurant known as the

Hoffman Café, a small place with dark paneled walls and dim lights. The kind of restaurant where people stayed after dinner and talked until two o'clock in the morning. It was a rendezvous for the pioneers of the motion picture industry. In the center of the Hoffman was a round table, around which gathered D. W. Griffith, Bill Hart, James Cruze, Mack Sennett, Charlie Chaplin, Erich von Stroheim, Hal Roach, and others. Dorothy Arzner said that her friends always predicted that she would end up working in pictures because she loved actors. "Goodness," she told me, "I didn't love them. I was afraid of them. They were always tossing me up in the air."

She grew up in the atmosphere of the Hoffman, went to Westlake School and then to USC to study medicine. When World War I broke out, she became an ambulance driver and delivered messages for the Intelligence Department. There she met William de Mille, who offered her a job in the industry when she left the service. She was assigned to the Story Department as a typist, but she didn't know how to type. With the help of another girl in the office, she pulled her way through. She felt she got a real motion picture education as a typist: "The script is the blueprint of the structure."

The young, friendly, long-haired waiter who had evidently served her similar lunches leaned over to ask, "Miss Arzner, when are you going to write your life story?"

"Never," she said.

"Did you really know all these people you talk about? What did you actually do?"

"She's a famous director," I said.

"Really? A *director*?" said the young man.

"A director. Like Frank Capra," I explained.

"No, not as big as Capra," Dorothy Arzner added.

But I remembered seeing a very old magazine article with individual headshots of Hollywood's then-star directors: Lubitsch, LeRoy, Capra, Vidor, Lloyd, Cukor, Mamoulian, Dieterle, DeMille, Boleslawski—and Arzner.

When Samuel Goldwyn sought to make a star out of Anna Sten in *Nana*, he reportedly said, "Get me Dorothy Arzner!" She undertook the film, but she claims she would have directed it much differently if she had been allowed more latitude. The Arzner touch is unmistakably there: the comic counterposing of scenes; the effective "small moments"; the flamboyant peripheral characters; the breathtaking beauty. The *Variety* critic noted that "[t]he Dorothy Arzner style of direction recalls the Von Sternberg-Mamoulian technique." The film won two European awards for direction and played to full houses as much as ten years later in Rome.

Miss Arzner told us that she had won another interesting award in 1928. At an International Festival of Women's Films in London, she had won first prize for her directorial assignment, *Fashions for Women* (1927), Esther Ralston's first starring film. She was pleased that a theater critic, New York *Times*'s Brooks Atkinson, made the comment: "If fashion films are to be made, let Dorothy Arzner make them."

When she was given this first assignment as director—after unrelenting persistence on her part—they handed her a French farce, told her to make a script out of it and "be ready to shoot in two weeks." She had four original scenarios to her credit, one of them Columbia's first picture to be shown in a first-run house. Her enthusiasm to have a whole feature to herself knew no bounds. She had the script ready to shoot in two weeks, cleanly shot thirty setups on her first day, and finished ahead of schedule. A newspaper review was headed: "*Fashions for Women*—Triumph for Star and Woman Director." The 1928 edition of the Swiss publication *Close-Up* commented: "Dorothy Arzner, in her so far brief career as a director, has already won an established reputation and a following of discriminating admirers . . . and promises to become an increasingly important factor in the evolution of cinema technique."

We talked on, probing old memories. How Jesse Lasky had called her "a dreaming young schoolgirl" for urging Paramount to make sound and color motion pictures. How fussy she was about scripts—her insistence that script choices be in her contract. How flattered she was that William Wellman called her after seeing *Craig's Wife* to say, "I wish I had made that!" How she would work straight through on every aspect of her films, on their minutest details. How much she enjoyed teaching at the Pasadena Playhouse and UCLA. Her philosophy was clear: maintain conscious control of your medium, nothing random. To "entertain" to her means "to take over," to enter someone else's mind with your own statement. No meandering camera, no purposelessness masquerading as style, no diffusion disguised as profundity or poetry.

Dorothy Arzner is particularly proud of *Craig's Wife*, the George Kelly play she brought to the screen. It was shot at Columbia without Harry Cohn's blessings, although she brought it in for only $150,000. He thought it wouldn't sell because it didn't have a happy ending. Kelly disagreed with Arzner's interpretation of the play. Although she used Kelly's words, shooting it in the right order as if it were a play, she managed to get a different meaning out of it. Kelly admitted after seeing it that it was damn good, though not his play at all. The Rosalind Russell characterization of Harriet Craig, a woman who sacrifices everything and everybody to ensure her own material security, evokes understanding—not disdain.

We discussed sound with her, its treatment being one of her hallmarks. We were impressed by her innovative use of the juxtaposition of sound and image; her eloquent overlappings and segues; her early use also of continuously running theme music—*Working Girls* (1931), *Merrily We Go To Hell* (1932); her handling of the original Rodgers and Hart theme song with lyrics in *Nana* (1934); the interesting silent *Manhattan Cocktail* (1928) with Nancy Carroll, which had a theme song, score, and effects, but no dialogue. In *The Wild Party*, the mikes bothered her, she said. They were stationary, and the actors had to keep moving to be near them. At the end of the first day's shooting, she told her sound man to bring in a fish-pole and "we'll attach a mike to that." It worked.

Some critics might dismiss Arzner's works as social comedies—valuable only as period studies of female psychology. Others might find her work more interesting thematically than stylistically. One critic remarked that in her work, a "reversal of some common traits in films directed by men takes place. Scenes involving women are generally complex, thoughtful and multi-dimensional, whereas her male characters are relatively barren." After studying Arzner films, I have found this to be untrue. The only "reversal" one sees is that her women are multidimensional, placing all the characters on an even footing. Fredric March gives a multifaceted performance as Jerry opposite Sylvia Sidney's Joan in *Merrily We Go to Hell*. So do Paul Lukas and Buddy Rogers in *Working Girls*, Clive Brook in *Anybody's Woman*.

The humanistic aspect of Arzner is the essence of her art; even her peripheral characters are brushstroked in with startling detail. Her concentration is mainly on actors and their varying rhythms and colors (she *never* used a dialogue coach). The stark reality combines with a certain lyricism, which she evokes from their performances. She is a master of comic business, as in the hilarious *Anybody's Woman* and the wedding ring sequence in *Merrily We Go to Hell*. Sometimes a farcical sequence will go on and on, becoming unbearably funny until one realizes the human pain it juxtaposes; sometimes, there are passing interludes or one-line zingers, provoking postponed chuckles.

Her flair for the zany, both structurally and visually, however, is combined with an extraordinary realization of technical detail in establishing illusions of special backgrounds and milieus. The English atmosphere in *Christopher Strong*, directed by Arzner in 1933, stirred English novelist Gilbert Frankau to remark: "I attended the premiere here in London with fear and trembling of Hollywood's lack of authentic atmosphere, but came away feeling the picture had been made in England." Remarking on Katharine Hepburn's performance, another critic several years later observed that "she was directed to a terrific quietness and intensity which I think she has never since reached. There wasn't any emotional flutter about her."

Arzner was known for her clarity of vision and definition of detail before launching her shooting schedule, as well as for her flexibility during shooting. This showed up as much when she did something wrong ("They expected me to alibi all my faults, but I was known for just admitting my mistakes and then incorporating them") as in her lack of conflict with her collaborators: editors, cinematographers, art directors, performers. Jean Renoir said it best: "The more you help your partners to express themselves, the more you express yourself."

As did Lois Weber and Alice Guy-Blaché before her, Dorothy Arzner believes that "woman's dramatic sense is invaluable in the motion picture industry."

"I was just interested in life," she told us. "I don't know how I made it."

The Best Love Story on the Screen

Charles Higham / 1974

From *Kate: The Life of Katharine Hepburn*, by Charles Higham (New York: Norton, 1975). Title supplied by the editor.

[Though Katharine Hepburn claimed in her 1991 autobiography *Me: Stories of My Life* that *Christopher Strong* "was fun to do" and that she and Arzner "had a good time working together," the women famously clashed while making the celebrated 1933 RKO film. Their fraught relationship was at the top of Hollywood chronicler Charles Higham's list of subjects to discuss with Arzner for his in-progress Hepburn biography. Higham, who by coincidence was the godson of *Christopher Strong* novelist Gilbert Frankau, used only two paragraphs from his 1974 Arzner interview for his book *Kate: The Life of Katharine Hepburn*. In these paragraphs reproduced below, Arzner talked mainly about her up-and-down relationship with Hepburn while shooting two *Christopher Strong* scenes during the winter of 1932–33.]

Miss Arzner says, "I remember one night I was working on a shot of a truck and a motorcycle colliding. The actual collision would have been too difficult, so we had to have the drivers barely miss each other, then cut to give an impression of an impact. Hepburn was watching, and each time the drivers came closer and closer to hitting, she'd cry out, 'That's it!' She was concerned for the safety of the players—she always stood up for the small people on the picture, the underdogs. After the fourth time, she yelled out, 'You can't get any closer than that!' She was *directing*, you see. And when I ordered another take, she said to me sharply, 'I'd heard you are a cruel woman. Now I know it!'"

Miss Arzner adds, "Kate wasn't someone you could mold easily, that you could control. She was extremely strong-willed. Her *tone* was all wrong; I had to soften her constantly. But sometimes she was wonderful. There was a scene in a boat on a lake that she played to perfection. She was in the boat with her married lover, and she said, 'Do you love me, Chris?' and he replied, 'Call it love if you like.' I wanted the scene played without any emotion at all. I canceled a whole morning's work because I just couldn't make the scene 'play,' and finally, I decided it had to be two people looking just dead ahead, two people who couldn't express any emotion—just a monotonous emptiness. At first, she played the scene headlong, but when I told her to look blank, she did, and her voice went wonderfully flat and toneless. She and Colin Clive played it superbly—people said it was the best love story on the screen."

Dorothy Arzner Interview

Gerald Peary and Karyn Kay, with Joseph McBride / 1974

From *Cinema*, no. 34 (1974).

The following interview was conducted over several months by mail between Wisconsin and California. Questions were posed, answers supplied, then more questions surfaced from the previous answers. Dorothy Arzner personally read over the final print and made corrections and additional comments, so hopefully, in the best sense of the term, this ends as an "authorized interview."

Because Ms. Arzner is busily at work completing an ambitious historical novel (based on the early settling of Los Angeles), she found it impossible to detail adequately her film career. Very generously, she allowed a personal visit to her California desert home for additional information. The addendum to the interview is based upon conversations during that meeting (with thanks to Joseph McBride for his questions on that occasion).

Question: How did you decide on a film career?

Dorothy Arzner: I had been around the theater and actors all my life. My father, Louis Arzner, owned a famous Hollywood restaurant next to a theater. I saw most of the fine plays that came there—with Maude Adams, Sarah Bernhardt, David Warfield, etc., etc., ad infinitum. D. W. Griffith, Mary Pickford, Douglas Fairbanks, Mack Sennett, and all of the early movie and stage actors came to my dad's restaurant for dinner. I had no personal interest in actors because they were too familiar to me.

I went to the University of Southern California and focused on the idea of becoming a doctor. But with a few summer months in the office of a fine surgeon and meeting with the sick, I decided that was not what I wanted. I wanted to be like Jesus—"Heal the sick and raise the dead," instantly, without surgery, pills, etc.

All thoughts of university and degrees in medicine were abandoned. Even though I was an "A" student and had a fairly extensive education—I had taken courses in the history of art and architecture—I became a so-called "drop-out."

Since I was not continuing in my chosen career, I only thought of work to do and independence from taking money from my dad.

This was after the World War, and everything was starting to bounce—even the infant picture studios. An appointment was made for me to meet William de Mille. He was told I was an intelligent girl. There had been a serious flu epidemic, so workers were needed. It was possible for even inexperienced people to have an opportunity if they showed signs of ability or knowledge.

Q: Could you describe this meeting?

DA: There I was standing before William de Mille saying, "I think I'd like a job in the movies." William de Mille: "Where do you think you'd like to start?" Answer: "I might be able to dress sets." Question: "What is the period of this furniture?"—meaning his office furniture. I did not know the answer, but I'll never forget it—"Franciscan." He continued: "Maybe you'd better look around for a week and talk to my secretary. She'll show you around the different departments."

That sounded interesting enough to me. I watched the four companies that were working, particularly that of Cecil DeMille. And I remember making the observation, "If one was going to be in this movie business, one should be a director because he was the one who told everyone else what to do. In fact, he was the 'whole works.'"

However, after I finished a week of observation, William de Mille's secretary told me that typing scripts would enlighten me to what the film to be was all about. It was the blueprint for the picture. All the departments, including the director's, were grounded in the script. So I turned up at the end of the week in William de Mille's office. He asked, "Now, where do you think you'd like to start?" I answered, "At the bottom." He looked penetratingly serious as a schoolteacher might, then barked, "Where do you think the bottom is?!" I meekly answered, "Typing scripts." "For that, I'll give you a job."

I was introduced to the head of the Typing Department. I was told I'd be given the first opening, but I had my doubts. Weeks went by. I took a job in a wholesale coffeehouse, filling orders and working the switchboard. It was through that switchboard that the call came from Ruby Miller, the Typing Department head. I was making twelve dollars a week. I said, "What's the salary?" "Fifteen dollars a week for three months, then sixteen-fifty." So for three dollars more a week, I accepted the movie job. And that is how I started at Paramount, then called the Famous Players-Lasky Corporation.

Q: How did you become a cutter and editor?

DA: At the end of six months, I went from holding script to cutter, and a good cutter is also an editor, working in conjunction with the director and producer, noting the audience reaction when preview time comes. I was assigned to Realart

Studio, a subsidiary of Paramount. I cut and edited fifty-two pictures while chief editor there. I also supervised and trained negative cutters and splicers.

Q: Did Realart have its own stages and crews independent of Paramount? What kinds of films were made there?

DA: Realart Studio was equipped fully—cameramen, set designers, writers, and I was the only editor. It was a small studio with four companies and four stars: Bebe Daniels, Marguerite Clark, Wanda Hawley, and Mary Miles Minter. One picture a week was started there and finished in four weeks. It would be eight reels when finished and called a "program picture." In those days, pictures played for a week in theaters, and the cost of the ticket was thirty to fifty cents. At the end of the week, there was another picture.

So much for Realart Studio. I was recalled to the parent company, Paramount, to cut and edit *Blood and Sand* with Valentino as star, with Lila Lee and Nita Naldi. Fred Niblo was the director. June Mathis was the writer, having gained much fame and authority from guiding and writing *The Four Horsemen of the Apocalypse* to enormous success. It was a "Big Picture"—hundreds of thousands of feet of film, twenty-three reels in the first tight cut, finally brought down to twelve.

Q: What were the physical circumstances in editing at this time?

DA: There were no Moviolas or machinery. Everything was done by hand. The film was read and cut over an 8-by-10-inch box set in the table, covered with frosted glass and a light bulb underneath. The film pieces were placed over a small, sprocketed plate, overlapped, and scraped about 1/16th-inch, snipped with glue, and pressed by hand.

Q: Were scenes shot simultaneously from several angles to help your editing?

DA: No, films were shot normally with one camera, except for large, spectacular scenes.

Q: Do you feel that editors were paid decent wages before unionization?

DA: For the time, I was paid very well. I never had any complaints. If you were a good editor, you asked a reasonable rate.

Q: Had you done any shooting on *Blood and Sand*?

DA: Yes, I filmed some shots for the bullfights.

Q: Were there special instructions in editing Valentino's scenes so as to preserve the glamor?

DA: There were no special instructions. The glamor was all on the film, put there by the writer and director, both of superior experience.

Q: What other movies were made with James Cruze?

DA: Then came *The Covered Wagon*, another "supercolossal" picture made eighty-five miles from a railroad in the "wilds of Utah." We used five tribes of Indians, and oxen were broken to the yoke. I stayed with Cruze through several pictures (*Ruggles of Red Gap*, with Eddy Horton, *Merton of the Movies*, and a number of others) until I left to write scripts for independent companies, like Harry Cohn's Columbia. Then Cruze asked me to work on *Ironsides*, another "big picture." He wanted me to write the shooting script, stay on the deck of the ship with him, keep the script, cut, and edit—all of which I did for more salary.

Q: Could you talk a little about Cruze, a director known today almost only by name?

DA: It would take too long to tell you about James Cruze. He was one of the "big directors," but he didn't exploit himself. He saved Paramount from bankruptcy, and he was one of the finest, most generous men I knew in the motion picture business. He had no prejudices. He valued my ability and told people I was his right arm.

Q: Were you about to walk out on Paramount to direct pictures at a minor studio when given your directorial chance in 1927?

DA: Yes. I was going to leave Paramount after *Ironsides*. I had been writing scripts for Columbia, then considered a "poverty row" company. Harry Cohn made pictures for eight and ten thousand dollars, and I was writing scripts for five hundred dollars apiece. But I had told Jack Bachman, Cohn's production man, that the next script I wanted to direct or "no deal." When I finished *Ironsides*, I had an offer to write and direct a film for Columbia.

It was then I closed out my salary at Paramount and was about to leave for Columbia. It was late in the afternoon. I decided I should say goodbye to someone after seven years and much work: B. P. Schulberg. I had previously written a shooting script for Ben Schulberg when he had a small independent company. He had been short of cash and couldn't pay, so I told him to take it and pay me when he could, which he did later. It was "bread on the waters" because soon after, he was made production head of Paramount when we were about to start *Ironsides*.

But Mr. Schulberg's secretary told me he was in conference. So I went out to my car in the parking lot, had my hand on the door latch, when I decided after so many years I was going to say goodbye to someone important and not just leave unnoticed and forgotten. The ego took over. I had a feeling of high good humor.

So I returned and asked the secretary if she minded if I waited for the conference to be over. She did mind. Mr. Schulberg would not see anyone. It was late then, and he had told her not to make any more appointments. Just about then, Walter Wanger passed in the hall. He was head of Paramount's New York studio on Long Island. And as he passed, I called out, "Oh, you'll do!" He responded, "What's that?" And I told him I was leaving Paramount after seven years, and I wanted to say goodbye to someone *important*.

"Come into my office, Dorothy." I followed him, and when he sat down behind his desk, I put out my hand and said, "Really, I didn't want a thing, just wanted to say goodbye to someone important. I'm leaving to direct." He turned and picked up the intercom and said, "Ben—Dorothy's in my office and says she's leaving." I heard Ben Schulberg say, "Tell her I'll be right in." Which he was—in about three minutes.

"What do you mean you're leaving?" "I've finished *Ironsides*. I've closed out my salary, and I'm leaving." "We don't want you to leave. There's always a place in the scenario department for you." "I don't want to go into the scenario department. I'm going to direct for a small company." "What company?" he asked. "I won't tell you because you'd probably spoil it for me." "Now Dorothy, you go into our scenario department and later, we'll think about directing." "No, I know I'd never get out of there." "What would you say if I told you that you could direct here?" "Please don't fool me, just let me go. I'm going to direct at Columbia." "You're going to direct here for Paramount." "*Not unless* I can be on a set in two weeks with an 'A' picture. I'd rather do a picture for a small company and have my own way than do a 'B' picture for Paramount."

With that he left, saying, "Wait here." He was back in a few moments with a play in his hand. "Here. It's a French farce called *The Best Dressed Woman in Paris*. Start writing the script and get yourself on the set in two weeks. New York is sending Esther Ralston out to be starred. She has made such a hit in *Peter Pan*, and it will be up to you."

So, there I was, a writer-director. It was announced in the papers the following day or so: "Lasky Names Woman Director."

Q: What was your directing training prior to *Fashions for Women*?

DA: I had not directed anything before. In fact, I hadn't told anyone to do anything before. I had observed several directors on the set in the three years that I held script and edited: Donald Crisp, Jim Cruze, Cecil DeMille, Fred Niblo, Herbert Blaché, and Nazimova. I kept script on one Nazimova picture, *The Secret Doctor of Gaya*, directed by the husband of the "directress" Madam Blaché, but I don't recall meeting her.

Q: Who championed your cause at Paramount? Adolph Zukor? Were you given trouble because you were a woman?

DA: Ben Schulberg, Jim Cruze, Walter Wanger. Adolph Zukor was in New York, where the pictures were distributed and had little to do with the making of movies. No one gave me trouble because I was a woman. Men were more helpful than women.

Q: Could you talk about Esther Ralston, star of *Fashions for Women*, but a forgotten star today? Was she the same type as Clara Bow, another of your leads?

DA: Esther Ralston was not the same type as Clara Bow—just the opposite. She was blonde, tall, and more of a showgirl type—very beautiful. Clara was a redheaded gamine, full of life and vitality with the heart of a child.

Q: The aggressive character that Ralston played in *Fashions for Women*, Lola, seems like the kind of character of many of your women. Do you agree?

DA: No, I do not think Esther as Lola was like other women in my pictures. You would have to see Nancy Carroll, Clara Bow, Katharine Hepburn, Ruth Chatterton, Anna Sten in *Nana*, Merle Oberon in *First Comes Courage*.

Q: You made the first movies with Ruth Chatterton. Wasn't she an unlikely movie star—a bit older and more mature than most leading ladies?

DA: Ruth Chatterton was a star in the theater. When talkies came to Paramount, they signed the stage actresses as many of the silent stars fell by the wayside. She was a good actress.

Q: Did you affect her career?

DA: Yes, I certainly affected it. When I made Ruth Chatterton's first motion picture at Paramount, *Sarah and Son*, it broke all box office records at the Paramount Theatre in New York. Chatterton became known to the press as "The First Lady of the Screen."

Q: Why did Ruth Chatterton move over to Warner Bros.?

DA: Warners offered her everything an actress could desire—choice of story, director, cameraman, etc., including a salary greater than Paramount.

Q: You made a series of Paramount pictures with Fredric March. Was this coincidence, or did you ask to work together again and again?

DA: I took Fredric March from the stage in *The Royal Family* and cast him in *The Wild Party*. I guess my pictures gave him a good start, and I liked his work, so I cast him as the lead in *Sarah and Son*, *Merrily We Go to Hell*, and *Honor Among Lovers*.

Q: In 1930, you began making movies with Robert Milton. Could you explain the nature of your collaboration?

DA: Robert Milton was a fine stage director, but he didn't know the camera's limitations or its expansions. Because I did know the technique so well, I was asked to help him. I codirected *Behind the Make-Up*, then I was called in to complete *The Constant Wife*, which he had started with Ruth Chatterton. I don't believe I took screen credit on it. I merely helped with technical work. He directed the performances. I blocked the scenes for camera and editing.

Q: Didn't you direct one part of *Paramount on Parade*? What was the idea behind this extravaganza?

DA: "The Vagabond King" [i.e., "The Gallows Song"] was the part I directed. *Paramount on Parade* was an innovative-type picture made mainly to exploit Paramount and its directors and stars and to show off the studio.

Paramount was the greatest studio, with more theaters and more big pictures than any others until the Depression. Its Hollywood plant was one block square, on Sunset Boulevard and Vine.

Q: Were you given a choice of technical crew when directing at Paramount?

DA: Yes, I had the cameramen, assistants, costume and set designers I liked best. A director had his or her crew that stayed from one picture to another. I made my assistant cameraman, Charles Lang, my first cameraman. Adrian and Howard Greer did clothes for me.

Q: *Honor Among Lovers* was one of the first Ginger Rogers films. Did you discover her? Was her famous "stage mother" found on the set during shooting?

DA: Ginger Rogers was a star in *Girl Crazy* in the theater. I saw her and liked her and requested her for a small part in *Honor Among Lovers*. Paramount gave me about everything I wanted after *Sarah and Son* and *Anybody's Woman*, so I imagine they offered her much money. She could also continue playing in *Girl Crazy* at the same time. I never saw her mother.

Q: *Honor Among Lovers* ends with Julia, the married woman, going on an ocean voyage with a man not her husband. Was this unorthodox ending your choice? Was there pressure to have Julia finish the movie in the arms of her husband?

DA: I collaborated in the writing of *Honor Among Lovers*, which I made for Paramount in New York. As audiences were ready for more sophistication, it was considered the smartest high comedy at the time.

No, there was no pressure regarding the script. I had very little interference with my pictures. Sometimes there were differences in casting, sets, or costumes, but usually, I had my way. You see, I was not dependent on the movies for my living, so I was always ready to give the picture over to some other director if I couldn't make it the way I saw it. Right or wrong. I believe this was why I sustained so long—twenty years.

Q: Why the title *Merrily We Go to Hell*?

DA: The movie was made during the overboard drinking era during Prohibition. Freddy March played a drunken reporter with whom a socialite, Sylvia Sidney, fell in love. The title was his philosophy. He made Sylvia laugh when she was bored with the social life of her class. You would have to know the times to judge "why the title?"

Q: You were at Paramount at the same time as Marlene Dietrich and Mae West. Did you ever wish to make a movie with either of them?

DA: Yes, I always wanted to make a picture with Marlene. There was a wonderful script called *Stepdaughters of War*. I'd worked on it for months for Chatterton, but when she signed with Warners, it had to be called off. Much later, we were planning it again with Dietrich. It was to be a big antiwar picture showing the tragedies of war and how war makes women hard and masculine. When the World War broke out with Nazi Germany, it was called off again.

Q: Could you describe your contract at Paramount? Did you have special clauses giving you control over certain phases of production?

DA: I was under contract to Paramount for three years at a time, paid by the week. I ended with a two-year contract, including choice of story. I never had to worry about control over phases of the production. The departments were geared to give a director what he wanted if he knew exactly what he wanted.

Q: Why then did you leave Paramount?

DA: Paramount changed by 1932. When I left, there was a complete change of executives. In fact, they were so fearful of the success of *Merrily We Go to Hell* that they spoke of shelving it. I begged them to release it, I was so sure of its success. A year later, they were asking me, "Make another *Merrily We Go to Hell*," but by that time, I wanted to freelance.

Q: You were working already on *Christopher Strong*?

DA: Yes, David Selznick asked me to do a film at RKO, which he headed at the time. It was to be an Ann Harding picture, but she was taken out due to contractual difficulties. So I chose to have Katharine Hepburn from seeing her about the studio. She had given a good performance in *Bill of Divorcement*, but now she was about to be relegated to a Tarzan-type picture. I walked over to the set. She was up a tree with a leopard skin on! She had a marvelous figure, and talking to her, I felt she was the very modern type I wanted for *Christopher Strong*.

Q: Did you pay special attention to directing Billie Burke in this movie? It seems the best acting performance of her career. In fact, you seem more interested in all the women characters than in Christopher Strong. Is this true?

DA: Yes, I did pay special attention to getting a performance from Billie Burke. But I was more interested in Christopher Strong, played by Colin Clive, than in any of the women characters. He was a man "on the cross." He loved his wife, and he fell in love with the aviatrix. He was on a rack. I was really more sympathetic with him, but no one seemed to pick that up. Of course, not too many women are sympathetic about the torture the situation might give to a man of upright character.

Q: What was your relationship with *Christopher Strong*'s scriptwriter, Zoë Akins, who had also written *Sarah and Son*, *Anybody's Woman*, and *Working Girls* for you at Paramount in 1931? What did Slavko Vorkapich contribute to the movie?

DA: My collaboration with Zoë Akins was very close. I thought her a fine writer. Vorkapich did the montage of the around-the-world flight when Cynthia (Katharine Hepburn) was met by Chris in San Francisco, and their affair was consummated. Incidentally, *Christopher Strong*'s story was not based on Amelia Earhart. It came from an English novel based upon the life of Amy Lowell, who did make the around-the-world flight and also broke the altitude record in her time.

Q: Why do you think Cynthia killed herself? Did you consider other endings?

DA: No, there was no other ending. Cynthia killed herself because she was about to have an illegitimate child. The picture was set in England. We had not accepted so easily the idea of an illegitimate child. In the boat scene, she asked, "Do you love me, Chris?" His answer: "Call it love, if you like." This was from a tortured man who deeply loved his wife and child but fell in love with the vital, young, and daring aviatrix.

Q: Wasn't there a moment when Cynthia tried to save her own life by putting the oxygen mask back on her face after she had ripped it off?

DA: No, Cynthia did not try to save her life. If you remember, she looked back over the whole affair seen through superimpositions as she flew to break the altitude record. Suicide was a definite decision.

Q: How would you evaluate this movie?

DA: *Christopher Strong* was one of the favorites of my pictures at the time, although I was always so critical of my own works that I could hardly consider any one a favorite. I always saw too many flaws. I was grateful, however, when they were considered so successful.

Q: Some sources have credited you with making an RKO film, *The Lost Squadron*, usually listed as directed by George Archainbaud. Did you work on this film?

DA: No, I had nothing to do with George Archainbaud or *The Lost Squadron*.

Q: All articles about your career say that you were the only woman director in Hollywood at this time. But another woman, Wanda Tuchock, codirected a movie called *Finishing School* at RKO in 1933. Were you aware of this? Did you know her?

DA: I vaguely remember Wanda Tuchock was publicized as a woman director, but I paid so little attention to what anyone else was doing. I never was interested in anyone else's personal life. I was focused on my own work and my own life.

Q: How did you become involved with *Nana* at Goldwyn Studio? How was Anna Sten picked to play the lead? Were you satisfied with the completed film?

DA: Goldwyn chose me to do *Nana* because, when he returned from a trip to Europe, he saw *Christopher Strong* and thought it the best picture of the year. He picked Anna Sten, wanting a star to vie with Dietrich and Garbo. It wasn't that I would like to have shot *Nana* differently. I wanted a more important script. But Goldwyn wouldn't accept any script at all until he finally handed me about the fiftieth attempt.

Q: Why did you choose Rosalind Russell for the lead in *Craig's Wife*?

DA: I did not want an actress the audience loved. They would hate me for making her Mrs. Craig. Rosalind Russell was a bit player at MGM, brilliant, clipped, and unknown to movie audiences. She was what I wanted.

Q: Was *Craig's Wife* an expensive picture to produce? Was it profitable for Columbia?

DA: No, *Craig's Wife* was not a high-budget picture. To make, I told Harry Cohn I would give him an "A" picture for "B" picture money. He fell for that. It was not one of the biggest successes when it was released. But it got such fine press that, over the long run, it was released several times and stood high on Columbia's Box Office list.

Q: Were you also producer of *Craig's Wife*?

DA: I was not the producer, although the whole production was designed by me. Outside of the development of the script, enormously protected from Harry Cohn's interference, Eddie Chodrov was the supervising producer.

Q: Did the playwright, George Kelly, involve himself in the production? Didn't you differ with him on interpretation?

DA: George Kelly had nothing to do with making the picture. I did try to be as faithful to his play as possible, except that I made it from a different point of view. I imagined Mr. Craig was dominated somewhat by his mother and therefore fell in love with a woman stronger than he. I thought Mr. Craig should be down on his knees with gratitude because Mrs. Craig made a man of him.

When I told Kelly this, he rose to his six-foot height and said, "That is *not my* play. Walter Craig was a sweet guy, and Mrs. Craig was an SOB." He left. That was the only contact I had with Kelly.

■ ■ ■

Dorothy Arzner journeyed to MGM after *Craig's Wife*, excited to make a film from an unpublished Ferenc Molnar play called *The Girl from Trieste*. It was about a former prostitute—a victim of "economic exploitation," to quote Arzner—trying to go straight. The movie was to star Luise Rainer. MGM, however, replaced Rainer with Joan Crawford, and *The Girl from Trieste* was rewritten as the lighter, frothier *The Bride Wore Red*. (It seems possible that Crawford had requested MGM to put her into the Arzner picture at this time, [in] 1937. She admired *Craig's Wife* enormously, so much so that she starred in *Harriet Craig*, another remake of the project, at Columbia in 1950.) Despite making a lifetime friend of Joan Crawford, Arzner was disappointed by the rewrite and uncomfortable working in the MGM factory. Mammoth sets were constructed for *The Bride Wore Red*, which Arzner was ordered to use. She remembers Joan Crawford decked out in a lavish red gown, even though the picture was shot in black and white. Altogether, Arzner considers *The Bride Wore Red* rather synthetic, not a favorite of her movies.

Arzner was nowhere in sight when *Dance, Girl, Dance* was begun by another RKO director. This was a personal project of Erich Pommer, the former head of Germany's famed UFA Studio, then in exile in Hollywood. As producer, Pommer had conceived, cast, and started shooting *Dance, Girl, Dance*, but everyone involved was unhappy and confused. After a week, Pommer removed the original director and brought in Dorothy Arzner to take charge. She reworked the script and sharply defined the central conflict as a clash between the artistic, spiritual aspirations of Maureen O'Hara and the commercial, huckster, gold-digging of Lucille Ball. She decided to base Ball's character of Bubbles on the real-life "Texas" Guinan, whom Arzner had spotted waving out of her taxi window to everyone in New York, [saying,] "Hi, I'm 'Texas' Guinan!"

Dorothy Arzner's contributions to the war effort were a series of short films for the WACs and also the training of four women to cut and edit these movies. Arzner had great fun making these shorts, for her actors were the Samuel Goldwyn stock company, including some of her old *Nana* cast. These documentaries were never shown in theaters nor in general release but were restricted to WAC training situations—*How to Groom Oneself*, etc. Apparently, they were successful, for the government offered Dorothy Arzner an appointment as Major. She turned it down because, as she says, "I never wanted to be in the Army."

She returned to Columbia after seven years' absence for *First Comes Courage*, the story of anti-Nazi resistance and the Norwegian underground. The screenplay was based on *The Commandos* by Elliott Arnold, and unlike many directors, Arzner read the novel before beginning the movie. She employed a favorite editor on the project, Viola Lawrence, also responsible for *Craig's Wife*, and she cast several German expatriates in the major roles. Reinhold Schünzel was reunited with Carl Esmond nine years after they had made a movie together in prewar Germany, *English Wedding*, with Esmond as star and Schünzel as director. There was no second unit work on *First Comes Courage* nor on any movie which Arzner can remember except in a bit of *Sarah and Son*. Arzner directed herself all the location photography, the army maneuvers, the scene inside a submarine, the frightening fistfight in which the battling actors fall between a terrified horse and a potentially lethal pitchfork. (She still shudders to remember the danger in shooting this last sequence.) The final scenes of the movie were filmed by another director when Arzner contracted pneumonia with a week to go and remained terribly sick for almost a year. At recovery, Arzner made a brave decision, one that she has stuck out for thirty years. She told herself that she had "had it" directing movies, and she left Hollywood forever in 1943.

Occasionally, in the ensuing years, Arzner has become involved in some kind of project. She began the first filmmaking course at the Pasadena Playhouse on a nonexistent budget, instructing her students with a single camera and tape recorder. She made over fifty Pepsi commercials for her old friend Joan Crawford, and she taught filmmaking at UCLA for four years in the 1960s.

The few movies which Dorothy Arzner sees today are old pictures on television or at the College of the Desert near her home. Her ties with the industry absolutely are cut. When she shows old photographs of her swank Hollywood estate, sold long ago, she laughs to herself about her youthful affectations. "I was a famous Hollywood director then." There is no doubt that she is totally content with her desert anonymity, the fresh air, and her fifty beautiful rosebushes in place of the subterranean growth of Los Angeles living.

Film Director Dorothy Arzner: Tribute to an Unsung Pioneer

Mary Murphy / 1975

From *Los Angeles Times*, Jan. 24, 1975.

A tiny woman in a white pantsuit and soft white shoes [that] look like baby booties opens the door. Her hair is slicked back into a ducktail, exactly as it has been since she was fifteen, but now the vibrant brown color has been shaded honey blonde, and the roots are graying.

If you had read faded clips on Dorothy Arzner, pioneer film editor-writer-director from 1923 to 1943, you would know she was said to resemble Napoleon when she directed, hands clasped behind her back, legs spread apart. And that she was short, stocky, and boyish, with a quiet executive manner.

You also would remember that she was said to be a strict disciplinarian, that Katharine Hepburn once called her "cruel," and that Arzner threatened to walk off almost every picture in power plays, which she always won. She was a breed unto her own who fought the battles of being the first successful woman director with such giants as Louis B. Mayer, Samuel Goldwyn, and Harry Cohn.

What is missing from these descriptions is any hint of Arzner's warmth or vision, any sense of the fiery enthusiasm beneath the stern manner. The face that looks so harsh in setside photographs is soft and likable in person.

Ten years ago, Arzner went into self-imposed seclusion to a spot in the desert where she used to get away on weekends along with her friends Gable, Garbo, DeMille, and Swanson. She wanted anonymity and refused all interview and photo requests. Films were no longer part of her life. The closest she got to showbiz was going to a drive-in for a hot dog and Coke and watching whatever happened to be playing that night.

She then, more than anyone else, understands the harsh and bitter irony of the tribute being paid her by Hollywood Saturday night—thirty-one years after she made her last film.

Significantly, it is not men turned repentant but women in search of their history who are sponsoring the film retrospective at the Directors Guild. Arzner herself will participate in a panel discussion with directors William Wellman, Robert Wise, and Francis Ford Coppola. Coppola she remembers as her most promising student when she taught film at UCLA.

Dorothy Arzner, whose name is as obscure as John Ford's is famous, directed the first talking picture for Paramount in 1929. *The Wild Party* starring Clara Bow is the story of a college girl's love for her professor (Fredric March), which explores with great sensitivity the code of loyalty and camaraderie among girls in a dorm.

Arzner is credited as the director who saved Katharine Hepburn from Tarzan movies when she picked the unknown actress for her first starring role in *Christopher Strong* (1933). Arzner says Hepburn was "modern, hard and witty" and just right for the role of the "contemporary" woman torn between her lover and her career as a flyer. Although Hepburn gives an uneven performance, we nevertheless can see the superwoman of the future.

When Arzner presented the script of *Craig's Wife* to Harry Cohn, he threw it across the room, yelling, "It stinks." The problem with *Craig's Wife*, according to Arzner, is that "men saw the woman as an SOB, and Cohn, like everyone else those days, wanted his heroines to be virginal and sweet. Basically, he just didn't understand it."

Arzner has a vision of the film separate from that of Cohn or *Wife* playwright George Kelly. They saw Mrs. Craig is a selfish bitch, while Arzner saw her as a woman who is ultimately regenerated. She urged Rosalind Russell, who had been groomed as a comedienne, to play the part. Russell thought it would ruin her career and offered to give up a year's salary to get out of the deal. The film made Russell a star and earned her an Academy Award nomination.

As a director of twenty features, Dorothy Arzner changed the image of women on screen. In the wild and experimental days after the transition to sound, Arzner captured with unique force the emotional reality of women alone and in relationships with friends, lovers, roommates, and rivals. Her women were full characters.

In 1940, she made her most blatantly feminist film, *Dance, Girl, Dance*, starring Maureen O'Hara as a ballerina and Lucille Ball as a burlesque queen. In the struggle for success, Ball exploits O'Hara. It is only at the end of the film that Ball realizes both have been exploited. The film has become a cause célèbre and has been shown in the Edinburgh and British women's film festivals the past two years.

Arzner says she merely wanted to "capture life with a camera. I shot the way I thought the mind would wish to progress—from far away to close up. No medium-range shots and closeups of the whole cast as they do today.

"I edited in the camera as I went along, and I never let anyone else tell me how to direct. My philosophy is that to be a director you cannot be subject to anyone, even the head of the studio. I threatened to quit each time I didn't get my way, but no one ever let me walk out. I had a loving father, so I wasn't dependent on the job, and in that way, I was able to be more independent than men with four children. I watched Cohn and Mayer abuse men like they were slaves. It was savage, but they had to take it."

Arzner said she hated the tension and the pressures. "Unlike the leaders of the women's movement today, it was not my nature. I had no defenses. I would rather walk away."

She did, in 1943.

The clips will tell you that Arzner retired after *First Comes Courage* because she contracted pneumonia and almost died. "I was sick for a year, the only time in my life," she says. But there is more to her departure than illness.

In typical Arzner style, she lets the information slip out on a casual tour of the sixty-five rosebushes [that] grace the yard behind her spotless Spanish-style home. It comes up during a discussion of Charlie Chaplin.

"Yes, it was so unfortunate that he was blackballed, but then we were all blackballed at some time," she said.

Arzner was not a radical. Whatever special perceptions she had were contained in work and not in a platform of rhetoric. Eventually, her vision of women and how they should be portrayed on screen and treated in the studio clashed with the dictates of Louis B. Mayer, whom she calls "the great dictator."

"He sent me two or three scripts. One had Rosalind Russell playing three parts. It was silly. Then I did *The Girl from Trieste* [i.e., *The Bride Wore Red*], which turned out to be synthetic and plastic. I refused to do the next two or three scripts, and I was suspended. Mayer put out the word that I was difficult, and you know how producers talk to each other. I think that was the reason I left."

From directing, Arzner went to teaching film at the Pasadena Playhouse and then at UCLA.

"She was a remarkable woman," says Katharine Hepburn. "She just did what she wanted, working along quietly, and nobody thought a damn about it. Of course, looking back, it seems queer as the dickens but not so then. Ladies just did a lot of things without talking about them. That was the difference."

Arzner says she has lived an "enormously full life, in fact, many different lives, and I have no regrets. I'm an odd person. I've always been too independent to subject myself to anyone. My life has been pretty much in my own hands.

"I've loved my work, and now I love the quiet.

"My wish is to remain anonymous in my community, not to have my neighbors whisper about me because I was famous. That was my other life."

Famous Filmmaker Is No Feminist

John Hussar / 1975

From *Desert Sun* (Palm Springs, CA), Aug. 6, 1975.

[All ellipses in this article appear in the original text.]

She was snipping at some sculptured red and pink roses in the backyard of her home [that] has a slight likeness to the old Paramount studio in Hollywood.

She wore a casual white pantsuit, and her honey-brown hair was trimmed ducktail style like it was many years ago when some said she looked like Napoleon.

The sweet gondola smile and friendly grasped handshake erased the preconceived images of Dorothy Arzner as the disciplinarian pioneer film editor-writer-director from 1923 to 1942.

She was a first in one of the most competitive struggle-to-the-top businesses.

When she was recently honored by the Directors Guild of America for her overlooked talents and "innovative" accomplishments in pictures, Frank Capra, in a telegram, said this of Ms. Arzner: "Two generations before the feminists of today's liberated women, Dorothy Arzner stood tall among men in men's most competitive adventures, film directing. Dorothy, we at the Directors Guild love you as a woman, but tonight we admire you and salute you as one of our greatest pioneer film directors."

The lavish praise heaped upon Ms. Arzner earlier this year in Los Angeles almost came thirty-two years too late, after she had completed her last picture and "retired."

But from all accounts, it wasn't too late for Ms. Arzner to appear at the tribute, which showed several of her films featuring *Christopher Strong*. In a recent interview in her home, which nestles quietly in the Cove area in back of the La Quinta Hotel, Ms. Arzner said she even balked, at first, at the tribute.

"I don't like tributes, they're phony. Give me a roast!"

But there is some hesitancy in her voice when she says that. She is skimming through the book of stills they gave her at the tribute categorizing her career.

She confessed she had no stills of her own from any picture, nor does she keep any of her scripts. "I tore off each page as I shot it." Her memorabilia [are] limited, to say the least.

She describes herself as a dedicated woman who "really had no other ambition but to become a film director," even though she attended medical school for two years in Los Angeles.

The San Francisco native said she was never "an organizational director" that populated the studio scene in Hollywood in its prime adolescence.

"And neither was Francis an organizational director," she continued while discussing her debut as an instructor at UCLA after she shook Hollywood from her livelihood.

"Francis" is Francis Ford Coppola, who was one of her UCLA students. "I told him he was going to be an ambitious, talented director one day . . . and he certainly is an outlaw."

Dorothy, too, is an outlaw of sorts. She makes no bones about the heads she had to crack in controlling all her films from start to finish.

"I walked out of my first film [*Fashions for Women* in 1927] at Paramount . . . ." And there were very few power plays she didn't win over the years: "'Get yourself another boy,' I use to tell them," she laughed.

And her admirers, men and women, remember that she became the first successful woman director in competition with such other picture pioneers as Harry Cohn, Louis B. Mayer, and Samuel Goldwyn.

She started at Paramount in the script-typing secretarial pool or "at the bottom," as she called it shortly after World War I.

In 1922, she was promoted to cutter in the film editing room at a time when all editing was snip and paste. A few months later, she became head of the editing department at Realart, a subsidiary of Paramount. Two years later, she started writing for the screen and finally made her directing debut in 1926 with *Fashions for Women*.

In 1929, she directed Paramount's first talking picture, *The Wild Party*, starring Clara Bow and "Freddy" March.

In the later years, she had completed twenty films (including four silent) from start to putting the music and ready to be sent to the theater.

"'The secret to my success," she added, "is staying power . . . you don't fool around."

Ms. Arzner's pictures have always been acclaimed for their strong and detailed portrayals of women.

One critic says of her: "She refuses to let her heroines get away with being simply sweet and virtuous; they were always more complex than that."

That statement virtually describes Arzner, who admits to having had to "bend a lot of minds" in having complete control of her pictures, even when it meant "getting her own point of view across."

She made a point of getting her view across in *Craig's Wife*. (An "A" movie made for "B" money for Cohn for Columbia studios.)

The picture starred a relatively unknown bit player at MGM by the name of Rosalind Russell—the actress's first claim to stardom.

The point of view discussion erupted between Ms. Arzner and George Kelly, the playwright.

"I did try to be as faithful to his play as possible, except that I imagined Mr. Craig was dominated somewhat by his mother and therefore fell in love with a woman stronger than he. I thought Mr. Craig should be down on his knees with gratitude because Mrs. Craig made a man of him.

"When I told Kelly about this, he rose up to his great height and said, 'That is not my play. Walter Craig was a sweet guy, and Mrs. Craig was an SOB.' That was the only contact I had with Kelly," Ms. Arzner laughed.

The woman director, who insists she is not an active feminist and thinks "men are basically weaker than women," continued making pictures showing women to be spirited human beings like the heroine in *Christopher Strong* starring Katharine Hepburn.

It was also Arzner that started Lucille Ball on her road to becoming one of the world's favorite comediennes in *Dance, Girl, Dance* with Maureen O'Hara as the commercial, huckster, gold-digging Bubbles, which was taken from the real-life "Texas" Guinan Ms. Arzner once spotted in New York.

In pre-World War II times, Ms. Arzner was shooting *First Comes Courage* when she became horribly sick with pneumonia. Even after the almost-finished picture was delayed for one year, the illness continued, and she said she had "had it" with Hollywood forever.

In later years, she started the filmmaking course at the Pasadena Playhouse, using one camera and one tape recorder. In the early sixties, she made over fifty Pepsi commercials for her old friend and coworker, Joan Crawford. She also taught the filmmaking class at UCLA "like a studio would" during the first four years of the 1960s.

But, as she said, the years rolled on, and she retired from moviemaking. "I no longer have an interest in pictures . . . and no regrets.

"And," she added, "I had had enough. Twenty years of directing is, I think, about enough."

But there are still the rosebushes and the screenplay on the early California families to be finished.

Interview with Director Dorothy Arzner

Kevin Brownlow / 1977

From the Brownlow Collection, London.

[Kevin Brownlow conducted his second interview with Arzner on June 5, 1977, at her home in La Quinta. He and colleague David Gill had intended to include interview extracts in their Thames Television documentary series *Hollywood: A Celebration of the American Silent Film*, but Arzner's refusal to be filmed forced them to alter their plans. She did agree to be recorded on audio tape, and Brownlow kindly made its transcript available for this book. He and the editor restored material that had been cut from a previously published version and lightly edited other sections of the transcript for clarity.]

Kevin Brownlow: Your first contact with picture people occurred at a very early age. Can you tell us about that?

Dorothy Arzner: Yes, it was at Paramount when I was a typist. I got a job as a typist with William de Mille giving me the job. It's a long story. Do you want long stories?

KB: I want an even earlier one. It was much, much earlier. You first met the great Mr. Griffith and other people in a . . . .

DA: Oh, in my father's restaurant, yes. They had a round table, and D. W. Griffith came in with Mary Pickford and Tom Moore and Owen Moore and all of them. I don't remember all of them, but I remember my dad telling me that Griffith always brought his company in there to eat until they finished the picture, and it was sold, and then he paid his bill. But he said he always paid his bill, and so I remember seeing them, that's all. I don't know how old I was—pretty young, going to school—and I remember seeing *Intolerance*. I think it was the first time I ever visited a set. [It was] the scene where they were pouring lead down upon the attacking side. Griffith was doing the real thing almost, having them pouring hot lead down onto the enemy. It was very exciting.[1]

KB: A bit before that, though, can you tell us that lovely story about Wilton Lackaye?

DA: They weren't motion picture people—they were stage actors. It was the Grand Opera House, which was the first theater in Los Angeles that my father had a restaurant in connection with. I used to go to the theater, which ran sort of blood and thunder plays, and Wilton Lackaye was the heavy. He would come into the restaurant, and I was little, and he picked me up and threw me up in the air, and I'd come down whacking at him. I hated it because they always thought of little girls—four or five years old—as something to pick up and toss about, and I didn't like it.

KB: When you finally made contact with Paramount, Mr. de Mille—William de Mille—challenged your ambition as a set dresser?

DA: That's right. I was introduced by a rather important woman that he knew personally, who was gathering young people to drive ambulances and of course, I applied. I wanted to go to France and drive an ambulance on the front line. I was too young to join the Red Cross, so I applied to her for this Los Angeles Emergency Drivers [program], which was training for the Drake Section Sanitaire. Then, when the war was over, I drove for the commander, and the commander's wife invited me to dinner.

I was saying, "Where do I go from here?" I didn't want to go back to the university. I was going to USC—I was two years at USC—and I didn't want to go back to school.[2] I'd had a taste of being out in the world, so I said, "Where do I go from here?" and she spoke up and said, "Dorothy's a modern girl. I think she should be in a modern business, the motion picture business." Apparently, she was a motion picture buff. I mean, she was very enthusiastic about motion pictures. She thought they were the coming thing, so she arranged an introduction for me and said, "Now, you have an appointment with William de Mille, and I'll drive you out." She drove me there and dropped me off and left me, and I can remember standing in the middle of Vine Street yelling at her, "Don't leave me!" But anyway, I went in because the appointment was made, and that's when I met William de Mille. He said, "Well, what would you like to do?" I said, "Well, I don't know, but I think I could dress sets," and he said, "What's the period of this furniture?" in his office, and I didn't know. He said, "It's Franciscan," so I will never forget what Franciscan furniture is.

Then later, he told me to look around for a week, which I did, and he said, "Why don't you talk to my secretary?" I talked with her, but I looked around first, and the first set I was interested in was Cecil DeMille's. He was making *Male and Female*, I believe. I can't remember all the actors in it, but I remember sitting there, seeing, and saying to myself, "Gee, he's the whole works. That's the thing to be if you're going to be in this business—be the director and tell everybody what to do," and that's all. I just made that observation, and then I talked to William de Mille's secretary, Mildred Bell, and she told me the thing to do is to start typing scripts because that was the blueprint of motion pictures. In other words, that's the thing where you really could see [the planned film] and then look at it and think what you would do with it and all the rest of it, so I typed scripts for three months. But very quickly, I was ambitious to get out of typing scripts, and I went over to the Nazimova company later and held scripts on the set for Nazimova, and that was an experience. Finally, I called back, and the head of the stenography department told me William de Mille had apparently said, "What did you let her go for?" I felt, "Well, that's good—I can go back," so I went back to Paramount, and I held script on the set. Donald Crisp was the director on the first one we were making. It was during Prohibition. The first picture, I remember, was called *The Six Best Cellars*, where they had that home brew, and everything started exploding in the basement. It was a comedy. I can't remember what the story was, but it was with Donald Crisp, who was the director.

KB: And this brought you into the cutting room?

DA: Yes, it was Donald Crisp. I think it was that picture. I don't remember just what picture it was, but Nan Heron was his cutter. I was interested in learning, so she let me watch her cut the first reel, and then she watched me cut the second reel. I went in there on a Sunday. We used to only have five reels to these program pictures, and I went into the studio on Sunday and worked all day long, cutting the next reel myself, and showed it to her. I saw that if you made mistakes, you could correct them; you could get reprints. I saw that it wasn't any great tragedy if I made an error, so I cut the whole reel on Sunday and showed it to her. She thought it was just fine, and from then on, I was a cutter. It was very quick.

KB: What was your attitude to editing?

DA: I loved editing, just loved it. Nobody could bother you, and you could do things with the actors. You could cut them off if they were no good, and you could cut off their long draggy exits and cut to the other side into something else so that you'd get them out of the room. I remember I used to love to do things to the film that usually the director liked because he worried about certain things and, if you could correct them, well, it was just fine. I loved editing, and I did quite a number before I got to the point of *The Covered Wagon*. That was the big thing that began to have attention given to me as a top editor.

KB: But *Blood and Sand* just brought your attention to . . . ?

DA: *Blood and Sand* was the first [big film]; it was before *Covered Wagon*. I devised a method to show the bullfights. We were waiting for a process, and they were having a convention of salesmen at Paramount, a big banquet, and they wanted to show *Blood and Sand*. So I went in and said I think I could cut the bullfights in if they'd let me have a bull tied to a stake, and if Valentino would be willing to cooperate, then I could match it into the Madrid bull arena [sequence], which I did. Valentino was wonderful. He thought it was such a good idea. They could show the picture then intact to the salesmen. It was an expensive picture, and they were anxious to have the salesmen see it. It had something like three or four bullfights in it, and also [Valentino's character, Juan Gallardo] was killed in one—he was gored by the bull in the end—and I had him in the Madrid arena stuff, and I just matched frames.

KB: I think it needs a slight explanation for the audience, to explain that it was stock footage.

DA: It was stock footage from Madrid. I remember the first night I looked at it all because it was the real thing then—the horses really were gored—and I was ill to my stomach watching this stuff. After a while, I could look at it without any reaction, but then I had to start selecting what I could use. Also, I had to match the costumes with Valentino wearing the costume that would match. I'd show him the film and tell him just how far he could go, and we'd have the cowboys out there with the bull tied to a stake, and the bull would lunge. Valentino was marvelous. He'd lunge out, and I'd cut to the long shot of the Madrid arena where this matched perfectly so that today, if you look at *Blood and Sand*, that's the way it is. There was nothing more done. It was left like that, and they called off their fifty-thousand-dollar process.

KB: And James Cruze saw that?

DA: Yes. We had two projection rooms side by side, and you had to walk through one to go to the other, and he was walking through the back when I was running *Blood and Sand*. I can remember him saying, "My God, who cut that?" and I modestly said, "I suppose I did." He said, "Would you cut *The Covered Wagon* for me? I'm about to do an epic picture," and I said, "Well, if you arrange it, of course. It doesn't matter who I cut for," so he did. That's how I went with him on *The Covered Wagon*.

KB: What was the spirit on location for *The Covered Wagon*?

DA: It was a very tough location. We were eighty-five miles from the railroad in the wilds of Utah, living in tents at the wrong time of year, too—it was February. The snows came, and we had to clear snow to get some of our shots towards the end. There was deep alkali dust, about two feet deep. It just cut into your face terribly. There was a lot of hardship to it. We had five tribes of Indians and cowboys and oxen broken to the yoke and hundreds of horses. The whole wagon train was out there in the middle of the wilds of Utah.

KB: There was one occasion when Cruze tried to get everybody to stay on?

DA: Oh, yes. Because we ran into the snow and it was difficult to shoot, Paramount sent word that he should come back and shoot it on the Lasky lot. That's when he stood up with all the company in the countryside and said if they'd stay with him, why, he'd be able to finish the picture and see that they'd be paid. Maybe they wouldn't be paid, but they all were willing to stay whether we were paid or not. We wanted to see the picture through. We'd been through so much and he'd been so great. He was really a fine man in every way, except that he drank a quart of liquor every night. But it never affected his work because he never drank in the daytime. I never saw him drunk, really.

KB: Can you tell us about the assistant on that picture?

DA: Vernon Keays was the assistant. He was an excellent assistant and worked hard. I don't remember much—I was just with Jim Cruze pretty much—but I know that Vernon Keays managed very difficult things, handling all the crew and the Indians.

KB: And the cameraman?

DA: Karl Brown was the cameraman, and I can still see him pick that camera up and almost run from one shot to another. He was strong—how he did it, I don't know—and just lasted through the day. Everybody would be exhausted. It's hard work, but he was unusually good, and I don't ever remember a shot that wasn't good. He was an excellent cameraman.

We had a lot of cameras there, and when we put things like all the animals across the lake, which was supposed to be the Platte River, why, there were lots of cameras on it and the same way with the starting of the train. It was so thrilling to me when we finally gathered that long train and saw Charlie Ogle, who was the older man that led the whole train, when he gave the word and the crack of the whip to start that train, and you saw it slowly pull through this deep alkali dust. It was very thrilling to see it move because it took so many hours to line it up.

I don't know how many wagons we had. It was a great line almost beyond the horizon, and then we had teams of animals behind, the oxen and the horses and men on horseback and all the rest of it. When you moved that line, it was a thrilling thing. When that word went out to start the train, we had lots of cameras on that. Also, cameras [focused] on the wheels that showed the alkali dust that it was going through. All that cutting was interesting to me, and I could dramatize that thing that I had such an emotional feeling about when I saw it.

You see, in those days, the cutter was on the set with the director; he was the right hand. I even used to line up the scenes to shoot—you know, "shoot this one first and that one second"—because I knew the order that they should be shot in. I had thousands of feet of film—I don't know, 250,000 feet of film, I think—to cut down to ten reels, reams of film to go through. Jim Cruze shot very fast. If he was just doing an ordinary scene of a picture, he would cut right with the camera. That's what I learned from him, and so I did the same. Nobody could ever do anything with my film; there wasn't a lot of extraneous film. Of course, with pictures like *The Covered Wagon* there was, but mostly just shots that would fit into the starting of the train or else to the swimming of the animals across the lake and those things. Otherwise, when he did the dramatic scenes, he cut with the camera. They hardly sat down until he picked them up the next minute, you know, just into the seat, practically. Sometimes you'd wish you had a couple of frames more, but your mind covered the space.

KB: *Get Your Man*—can you tell us that marvelous story about the waxworks?

DA: That's the one episode in *Get Your Man* that I liked, and I can't remember too much what the story was. It was set in France, and it was Madame Tussauds waxworks.[3] That was the whole comedy of Buddy Rogers and Clara Bow visiting the waxworks and being frightened of the skeletons and the famous murderers. We did most of the famous groups that were in Madame Tussauds. Marion Morgan, who was Marion Morgan, the dancer, used her dancers, and there were no wax figures at all; they were all live figures. I did the Coronation of Napoleon, which was a big group, and then we had one bust of the Spanish Infanta. I don't know whether you're interested in that story about Schulberg betting five hundred dollars that that was wax. I had the Spanish Infanta, which was one of the dancers, and just used the bust. Clara Bow went up and touched her eyeball and Ben Schulberg, who was the producer at Paramount at that time, bet five hundred dollars that that was a wax figure. The whole staff came down after seeing the rushes and asked where the Spanish Infanta was, and I said, "Right over there." She was sitting on a high stool laughing and talking to Buddy Rogers, and so he said, "You've just lost me five hundred dollars!"

Anyway, the scene that I liked showed Buddy Rogers and Clara Bow locked in the waxworks that night. They didn't get out by the time it was locked up, and so they finally sat down on a bench. It was late at night, so during the time that we were lighting the set, they were in the position that I'd asked them to be or at least to be together. They both went sound asleep and ended up in each other's arms. They were [a] boy and girl in love with each other, and they were sound asleep when I started to shoot the scene of them being awakened, and I made everyone be quiet. When the old nearsighted janitor came around and flicked them with his duster, thinking to dust them off as he dusted all the wax figures in the morning, they woke up from it. They looked very sleepy, both of them. It was just right. It was just marvelous because they had been asleep for about an hour.

KB: You gave us the impression, though, that they had actually fallen asleep while you were shooting it?

DA: Yes, they had! They had actually fallen asleep because it would take us quite a while to light sets and that sort of thing. I had a very slow cameraman at the time, too, that didn't light very fast. It seemed to me we were always working at night until midnight. There were not any guilds or unions at that time to stop us, so we were always working to get out of the set and certainly to get out of a big set like the waxworks.

KB: What do you think Clara Bow's quality was?

DA: Clara Bow's quality was like a gamine's. She was full of life and energy and moved quickly and darted around, almost. She was attractive to all the boys; she always had men around her. When I took her to be in a picture, I said, "Now, I don't want a lot of men around here, and I don't want any nonsense going on," and so she used to sit in her dressing room and have the door wide open and say, "See, there's no one in here." That's the sort of thing she did, and she was charming.

I can remember one night we were shooting the last scene of a picture. I think it was *Get Your Man*. I know it was about four in the morning, and they had separate rooms in a hotel. I said, "Now you come together, meet in the middle, and then we fade out," and they and the whole crew burst into laughter, saying, "Now you meet in the middle and fade out." Clara Bow rushed up and threw her arms around me and said, "She doesn't know what she said," [and to me,] "Anytime you say anything like that, the crew will make a double meaning out of it—something to laugh at." Anyway, that's the sort of person she was. She was so good, really, and I feel everyone took advantage of her, except I don't think I did. She was marvelous. She could cry in a scene and, if you felt the scene wasn't going quite right, she could put the tears back in again. She was a marvelous silent actress, full of animation and full of projection of her thinking and emotions through the screen. Then I made her first talking picture, which was very difficult for her, because to be able to be aware of the pantomime that she was so accustomed to and then have to have words to remember, she just stuttered. We had quite a time in the beginning.

KB: In silent pictures, when you were directing her, did she tend to improvise, or did she tend to give you the same performance on each take?

DA: I can't remember. I just know she was awfully good and very obedient to do the scene exactly as you asked. I don't ever remember having any controversy with her wanting to do it another way than I'd asked and, whichever way she did it, she was so right. She just automatically was a natural because the whole thing was emotional with her, and she understood the emotional content of the scene, so there was never any quarrel. She did it her way. I never gave people specific line readings and intonation. I just gave them the spirit of the line and what I wanted to get in spirit, mostly. I'd help that way, all the way through my directing. I don't remember ever giving anyone a reading, except that I had John Boles study with the coach for *Craig's Wife* because I felt that he needed to have some coaching.

KB: Do you think that Clara Bow set fashion, or do you think she reflected it?

DA: Well, I think she was the outstanding flaming youth, and she *was* flaming. I mean, she was so alive it was like a dancing flame, and she just projected through the screen with such life quality. Elinor Glyn gave her the name of the "It" girl. Then she had sex attached to her and all the rest of it, but I think that she was the one that really made it popular, the first flaming youth.

KB: Can you tell us the saga of *Old Ironsides*?

DA: Yes. It's kind of a sad story in some ways because it was—I can't think of the man's first name. Carr was his last name.

KB: *Harry.*

DA: Harry Carr was the one that brought the idea to do *Old Ironsides*. We were doing the American history story with Stephen Decatur [who] was the leader who commanded *Ironsides*. You saw the whole layering and the keel of the ship, and that he was just a boy, and his father's shop that designed *Ironsides*, and then later he commanded it. Later, as I think history tells us, Lord Nelson said he freed the seas of piracy. But in the meantime, *What Price Glory?* was such a success in New York [and its coauthor] Laurence Stallings had evidently got talking to Jesse Lasky. He sold him the idea that we were just making an old-fashioned picture [and that Decatur and the Marines] weren't the heroes; it was the merchant boys—the merchant ships that were the heroes. He went into this symbology of the merchant ship being the heroine and the *Ironsides* being the hero, and he sold Lasky a bill of goods. So they changed the whole story, and Carr was dismissed. We started making the *Ironsides* that got released, which was the story of just a farm boy who was taken onto a merchant ship and fell in love with the daughter of the man that commanded the merchant ship. And then the meeting up with *Ironsides*, the big ship, and the war between the Tripolitans and *Ironsides*.[4] So, the whole story to me was no longer American history.

On *Covered Wagon*, everything sort of worked for us, and everything went along; even though the weather was bad and the hardships were hard, everything worked. But on *Ironsides*, everything went against us from the first day that we looked for locations. We were in a terrible storm, almost all went down, and then we were always having days we couldn't shoot. It would take four or five hours to line up all the ships, and then the wind would come along and blow them all haywire. It was a man-killing job to even get the picture and of course, finally we got into the trough of the sea, and all the masts crashed over our heads, so we had to go against history and show *Ironsides* as though it had had its masts blown. Then, in blowing the masts to cover that, three men were killed, and Jim Cruze was held for murder.[5]

KB: How did that happen?

DA: He ordered the men go up to dress the masts, and the shots went off to blow the masts too soon. The powdermen, I guess. I don't know. I shouldn't say how it happened. It was an accident, and I wasn't present. That was the last day's shooting, and I had gone. And the first thing Jim Cruze said when he came back to Hollywood was, "If you'd been there, it wouldn't have happened," because I was always saving people.

The first time we went out on *Ironsides*, we were passing the *Virginia*, the battleship, and we had a broadside loaded, so that we, the motion picture company, could fire a broadside as we passed and salute the *Virginia*. We had all these twelve-year-old boys as powder monkeys, and I said to Jim, "Don't have them so close to those guns, Jim." He was busy getting the shot going and it had to go off just at the right time, and he practically said, "Don't bother me." I tugged at his coat again and said, "Please move those little boys back from the guns." He finally did yell out, "All you boys get back!" and so they did move back, and just then, they blew the gun out—all the breeches blew out, which is the rear end of the cannons that were made at Paramount Studios. They all blew out, and there were piles of suitcases behind them, and there wasn't a little piece of cloth left intact. It would have just blown those boys to pieces, and from then on, almost anything I said to Jim, Jim would say, "Come on, Dot, let's see." I'd say, "You can't shoot today, the weather's too awful," and he'd say, "Well, come on, we're going out to find out." I'd have to go out with him in this tugboat, and we'd be under the ocean and waves rolling over us. I remember a big wave hit us, and I'd say, "You see? We can't shoot today," and he said, "I think you're right. Well, then, let's turn around and go back." So, we didn't shoot that day.

It was just one hardship after another of getting a sea picture, and we had no motors on the square rig sailing vessels. We brought all the old sailors from square riggers from around the East Coast and up in Oregon—every place we could gather them. We had them, and when they were out with us, they started deserting every day.

Finally, we ended up with the cowboys from *The Covered Wagon* manning the ship. They did it better than the sailors. They just learned by being around. Jim Cruze always had a whole bunch of them that were loyal to his Western pictures. He made a lot of Western pictures, and so he had them on the picture and the first thing we knew, they could haul down the sails. We did keep a few of the sailors—there was one fantastic Scandinavian man that could just jump four and five feet. We had 210-foot masts, and he could jump from one to the other and roll up the sail and all the rest of it. It was fantastic what some of these Scandinavians could do on a square rig sailing vessel. We were terribly impressed with it. We had a lot of interesting incidents on that picture.

KB: Tell me the story of being rescued by Art Bridges.

DA: We were out on the *Esther*, which was the merchant ship, and we hit this storm. The superstructure was being broken off and washing away and the sand ballast . . . the ship was leaking. We were out on the other side of Catalina Island in the storm, sixty-five-mile-an-hour winds, and we were lost at sea. The captain wanted to head out to sea, and Jim Cruze ordered him to go back to San Pedro. The old captains believed that, in a storm, you go out where it's safe, not near the coast, but Jim wasn't going for that. He wanted to get back to San Pedro. Well, we just didn't get back. We kept being washed toward Point Dume, and I think we were there all day and all night and the next day and into the night.

Art Bridges, who was the tugboat captain that had always been around with us, pushing the boats, [was] looking for us, and finally, about dawn, he saw us there and picked us up—threw a rope on us—and hauled us. Just as we were getting into San Pedro, being hauled by him, he ran out of diesel fuel, so then we were in trouble. So, they burned mops. The navy was sitting in San Pedro, and they burned mops on the deck, and we blew a distress signal, but you couldn't hear it in the storm. I remember we were just going nearer and nearer to [Dead Man's Island]. They finally blew it up. It was a dangerous spot. They finally took it out of the entrance into San Pedro harbor, but we were going right towards it.[6] You could almost reach out, like towards that window, and I remember Jim Cruze saying, "Now, when we hit, you go up the bowsprit and you'll drop off onto the island." Just then came the great big old red stacker that the navy had sent to us, and they threw a line to us and saved us. I remember Wally Beery saying, "Well, I was all prepared to tie Dot to a hatch cover," and Jim Cruze said, "Don't ever tie her to anything, she's better off by herself than tied." He had to cover, so it means people were always concerned about what was going to happen to me, or they were thinking of me at least. But we had Duke Kahanamoku on the set,[7] and he was always alert to see that I didn't fall into the ocean and drown. I fell in once between the two ships, and he just reached over and grabbed me up and set me back on the shore.

KB: How did Cruze get off the murder rap that he was on?

DA: I don't really know because I wasn't in on too much that he did. I know that Paramount didn't stand behind him too strong. I think they finally proved it was an accident. The only thing was that he naturally ordered the men up on the yardarm, and when the things went off just too soon, they weren't quite in a safe position. They were supposed to be in a safe position for the yardarms to be blown, and they hadn't quite gotten there when the dynamite went off. It was loaded into the mast, and they fell about two hundred feet to their death. A couple of them. I think there were two men killed. I saw Jim Cruze grow gray on that picture; having black hair, he was white almost by the time he'd done it.

Every night I used to say, "What am I doing, giving my life for a motion picture?" I kept arguing that I shouldn't do it, it was foolish, and then the next morning there'd be a rap on the door, you see, because I'd also have a nice room always close to where Jim Cruze was, and he'd come by and rap on the door and say, "Dot, come on to breakfast," and out you'd go and start every day. Every night you'd say, "What am I doing, giving my life for a movie?"

KB: And when the picture was released, was it a hit?

DA: Not quite, not as much as they would have liked to have. I don't know why, but later it became successful. It made quite a lot of money later, but it would have been much better if it had been American history. It was just a little offbeat by being with Laurence Stallings's modern view of a story for *Ironsides*.

KB: Didn't this have a special screen process?

DA: Yes. When *Ironsides* came in full sail toward the barge where we were shooting, [the image] suddenly enlarged to the great big Magnascope, but that had been done in *Wings*, and then we came along and used the same thing.[8] It was pretty handsome—that shot was beautiful—and there was nothing more thrilling than being on that boat in full sail because it was carrying 210-foot masts on the hull—it should only carry 180 feet—and you felt you were just flying. It was top-heavy, and it would get this roll and still went pretty fast for this big boat. It was a very thrilling ride. We always thought it was dangerous at every minute.

KB: And then you're about to leave Paramount, and you get a break.

DA: That was after *Ironsides*. I had written a script for Harry Cohn, and then I'd said I wouldn't write another one unless he'd let me direct it because I did write scripts that could be shot. I put down close-ups, medium shots, and told exactly what the camera should cover, so it was a shooting script, and so he wanted me to do another one. I said I would only do it if I could direct it, so he says, "There's no reason why you can't direct one, so do the next one."

I went back to Paramount to close out my salary from *Ironsides*, and that, to me, has always been an unusual incident because there was no one there except Ben Schulberg. It was late in the afternoon, and I'd finished everything—cleaned up everything—and I decided that I should like to say goodbye to Mr. Schulberg. The secretary wouldn't let me see him. He was in conference, and I said, "Well, then, I don't mind waiting," and she said, "No, there's no use waiting. He has a dinner engagement, and he's going right out after that, and he wanted no more appointments." So I remember saying, "You don't mind if I sit here, do you?" She said, "Yes, I do," so I remember going out to my car and having my hand on my car door and saying to myself, "No, I'm going to go back. I have been here for twelve years and leaving, and I should say goodbye to somebody important." So I went back in again, and she said, "Are you back?" I said, "Yes, I'll just really wait and see if I can't catch him as he goes out. I just want to spend one second with him." She still said no.

Just then, Walter Wanger went by the hall, and I said, "Oh, you'll do." He now was quite a big shot in the eastern studio. He was out visiting, and I knew he was an important man at Paramount. He said, "Well, Dorothy, come on into my office," and I went in and put my hand out and said, "I just want to say goodbye to somebody important—and you're important enough—because I'm leaving." With that, he picked up the phone and called Ben in this conference, whatever he was in, and said, "Ben, Dorothy's in my office, and she says she's leaving." I'm sure he said, "I'll be right in," and with that, he was in Walter Wanger's office in about two minutes. He said, "What do you mean, you're leaving?" I said, "Just that—I'm leaving. I'm leaving to direct," and he said, "Where are you going to direct?" I said, "I won't tell you because you'll ruin it. It's a Poverty Row company." It was Harry Cohn's company, and he'd been making pictures for about twelve thousand dollars or something like that. At any rate, I said, "No, I won't tell you," and he said, "Well, what if I said that you could direct here?" But then he said, "Come into our scenario department, and then we'll think about you directing," and I said, "Nope, if I can get into the scenario department, I'll never get out of it." He said, "Well, what do you want to do then?" I said, "I want to be out on a set in two weeks directing an 'A' picture with an important star, otherwise let me go," and with that, he jumped up and went into his office and brought back this French farce which was called *The Best Dressed Woman in Paris* and said, "Here, get yourself on the set in two weeks." Well, I didn't—it took three weeks. I nearly killed myself writing the script and shooting and cutting everything, casting and fashion shows and everything else. I was just unconscious, practically, but I got through it.

KB: And the release title was . . . ?

DA: *Fashions for Women*, supposed to be *The Best Dressed Woman in Paris*. Esther Ralston was a little cigarette girl, and the famous best-dressed woman in Paris had decided to go off and marry and deserted these two couturiers that were the ones that gave this fashion show every year. So, they had to have someone. It was [in the tradition of the] Cinderella stories that we always had, and so it was this little cigarette girl, Esther Ralston, who was a beautiful girl. She played Dearest in *Peter Pan*, if you remember.

KB: You had another story about *Old Ironsides*?

DA: Well, it was another unusual thing because, as I was walking down the pier the last week or two of *Old Ironsides*, I was with the property man who had practically saved my life many times on *Ironsides*, and I said to him, "I know I'm going to be a director as soon as this picture is finished." I did know it inside me, and he knew I was going to become a director, which was rather fantastic. I knew it inside me, and I had made the statement as we were walking along over in Catalina on the pier about two weeks before we finished *Ironsides*.

KB: Now, you were going to talk about your anxiety not to be overexploited.

DA: That was in the beginning, when I was going to become a director. I asked that I not have my name big. I just wanted it small down at the bottom, about the same size as where it said "A Paramount Picture." I didn't want the idea that they were going to make something of me being the only woman director that Paramount had. I had seen them overexploit people like Lila Lee and actresses that were trying to take the place of Mary Pickford. I felt that if you overexploit any of these things, an audience backs away from you. I wanted to have my pictures stand up along with the men's pictures and be box office successes without any idea that a woman had made it. Just let the picture stand on its own.

KB: How much resentment did you encounter?

DA: I don't really remember any resentment, except when someone appealed to Darryl Zanuck for me to direct a picture at Fox.[9] He said, "I don't want a woman director," so that's the only thing. I don't think Warner Bros. particularly wanted to deal with a woman director either, but I did not find resentment. I would find a little bit of them telling me afterwards that they were worried about coming on the set with me—either a cameraman or an assistant. I had an assistant once that was worried about coming on the picture with a woman director, and then he said afterwards, "You certainly knew your business, so I forgot very quickly what my feelings were in the beginning." After all, the director at Paramount was—no doubt about it at Paramount—the director was authority. Therefore, you weren't very aware [that the crew] may have had feelings and they may have resented me, but I never was aware of it.

In fact, I wasn't aware of very much outside of what my own job was. I told you the story of Adolph Zukor coming on the set, asking me a question, when I was doing Clara Bow pictures. I thought he was a visitor, and I started telling him all about the movies and then, as he left, my assistant came up and said, "Did you know who you were talking to?" and I said, "I haven't the slightest idea who I was talking to." He said, "It's just Adolph Zukor who pays your salary," and I didn't know. I never was interested in patronizing important people. I only dealt with the person who hired me and when they hired me. I figured they were the ones, the only ones, I went to. Ben Schulberg had made me a director, so he was the only one I was really aware of.

KB: How did you cope with the coming of sound?

DA: It was difficult, but it was just something you took in your stride and you did it. Because we were in booths, we couldn't move, and the sound man would say, "There's hums in the system." We really had great difficulties with sound in the beginning, but as I said, making pictures was difficult anyway, so one difficulty was not much different than another one. You just took them in your stride and solved them as you went along. That's how it happened on the first one with Clara

Bow because she was so confined by the microphones that hung there, and then you couldn't say anything till you got over to the other one they hung over there. They just had these things hanging on spots where the scenes were supposed to be played. In other words, your soundman was laying out your choreography of the scenes. That bothered me because I used to like people talking and moving, and so I remember saying to my property man, "Do you have a fish pole?" He said, "Yes," and I said, "Well, you bring your fish pole and ladder tomorrow and hang that thing on it and we will make some moving shots." That was the beginning at Paramount of the moving microphones, which we did, and it worked. Of course, the poor sound man, who was an expert from MIT, just nearly had a fit. He said, "It's gonna click," and I said, "Well, tape it up so it doesn't click." This was the whole thing of motion pictures in those days; you solved problems. Once, Esther Ralston was half-fainting or something, and she had to be dragged off the scene. She was so heavy that nobody could do it gracefully, so we did it with a roller skate—a board on a skate—and they picked her up and just dragged her off. She had a lovely dress that covered everything. We had to devise these things.

KB: When you saw the first sound film in the theater, what were your feelings?

DA: Well, it came about so gradually, because the first—I think it was Warner Bros. with their first picture—what was it? *City Lights*, was it? The first sound picture that Warners made?

KB: *The Jazz Singer*?

DA: Well, *The Jazz Singer* was the first big one, but there was one made after.

KB: *Lights of New York*.

DA: *Lights of New York* or some such thing, and I went east and also heard the sound device,[10] and that's when I was assigned to do *Glorifying the American Girl*. I came back to Paramount, saying, "We must have that sound device and color—sound and color—to do *Glorifying the American Girl*," and that's when they gave me the absent treatment for a few months because I was a dreaming schoolgirl and wanted to change the business. Paramount didn't want to come into sound because they had too much invested in theaters. They had the majority of theaters, and it would have cost a fortune for them to change over to sound, which they finally had to do, but they didn't want to. They were the last ones to come into sound of the big studios.

I didn't want to do *Glorifying the American Girl* without sound and color, especially the Follies show I wanted, if nothing more than because we were doing parts of the picture in sound and color in the beginning. So I was taken off the picture, and somebody else made it in the east, and it was a flop. I was pleased it was a flop because it exonerated me as far as knowing what I was doing. I really had quite a great story for it, *Glorifying the American Girl*.

KB: So, you approved of sound as soon as you . . . ?

DA: Yes, I was the youngest director. I was so young that I was already into things that were coming, just like youth is today. They know more about what's going to happen than we do, than I do, certainly. I'm still hanging onto the past somewhere—not very much, but we aren't pioneers anymore, which we were then. We were pioneers and wanting to be and eager for whatever was new, because I know that, even with my first picture, I wanted to do what would be transparencies [i.e., rear-screen projection], but they told me it couldn't be done. I wanted to have the clothes that would be like yachting clothes and be able to have the background with them at sea and just have the wheel of a yacht and have men and women with yachting clothes. I wanted to do a fashion show that was very modern, but that was all way beyond. I was always known as a dreaming schoolgirl that wanted to do things that were impossible to do but later were done, could be done, but I was reaching all the time for something unusual. That's why I was able to do the Cretan legend, which I did—Theseus and the Golden Thread that led them out of the labyrinth—and the waxworks.[11] I always had something unusual in my pictures if I could catch it because that was the way that I knew I could draw attention to my pictures.

KB: Looking back at the silent era, do you think anything was lost when sound came in?

DA: I felt there was when sound came in, and I don't know now whether it was or not. I don't suppose so. Sound is progress, but there were wonderful silent pictures at the time. Josef von Sternberg's picture of the doorman who earlier had been a great general was a wonderful silent picture.[12] There were wonderful silent pictures, and Murnau's pictures were great. I remember just thinking that you couldn't touch those pictures with sound because sound began to confine us so. Now with tape and all the rest of it, it isn't quite as limiting as it was in the beginning of sound. We all thought that sound would ruin pictures in the beginning because the cameras were in a booth, and we'd just had all kinds of difficulties handling it, but later, great flexibility came about. We learned how to cut sound and all the rest.

Notes

1. The filming of *Intolerance* occurred between October 1915 and April 1916, so Arzner would have been in her late teens when she witnessed this scene from the film's Babylonian story. According to an *Intolerance* title card, the Babylonians were pouring hot oil, not lead, down on Cyrus's attacking troops.

2. Arzner informed a 1940 federal census taker that she completed only one year of college. It is possible, though, that she started a second year at USC but dropped out before finishing it.

3. Madame Tussauds is not mentioned by name in the film.
4. Arzner was referring to the First Barbary War (1801–5) that pitted the US and Sweden against Tripoli and three other north African "Barbary States." Now Libya's largest city, Tripoli was then a semi-autonomous province within the Ottoman Empire.
5. According to San Pedro newspaper accounts, the explosion killed Charles Davis and injured five other sailors. Three men seriously wounded by the blast filed lawsuits against Famous Players-Lasky and Cruze, as did Davis's widow. See "Cannon Explodes Aboard Frigate 'Constitution' Off Catalina," *San Pedro Daily News*, June 28, 1926; "Suits for Damages at Movie Ship Wreck are Filed in Courts," *San Pedro Daily News*, January 7, 1927.
6. Arzner had erroneously identified the site of the near-collision as Point Dume, a promontory about fifty miles northwest of San Pedro. The hazardous rock outcropping in San Pedro harbor was in fact Dead Man's Island. Charles Farrell, who played the Commodore in *Old Ironsides*, confirmed the point that the ship "almost wrecked on Dead Man's Island" during the film's production; see Mary Chapman, "The Kid from Cape Cod," *Motion Picture Classic*, July 1926. Arzner remembered correctly, though, that the islet had been demolished. In 1928, the federal government began eliminating it with dynamite, dredgers, and steam shovels to improve access to the harbor.
7. Duke Kahanamoku, a native Hawaiian who won medals in swimming at the 1912, 1920, and 1924 Olympic games, played a pirate captain in *Old Ironsides*.
8. Developed by Lorenzo Del Riccio, the Magnascope projection process employed image magnification and screen masking and was used mainly for the presentation of large-scale action scenes.
9. The "someone" was Jesse Lasky, who had been ousted from Paramount in 1932 and, as an independent producer, signed Arzner to direct *The Captive Bride* for Fox two years later. This film was unrealized.
10. Arzner presumably meant Warners' sound-on-disk Vitaphone apparatus.
11. Arzner was referring to two different sequences that she directed: the prologue to the now-lost *Manhattan Cocktail* (1928) and *Get Your Man*'s wax museum segment, discussed at length in the interview. Though *Manhattan Cocktail* was mainly a modern-day tale of small-town folks seeking success on Broadway, Arzner based its opening sequence on something quite different: the Greek legend of Theseus and the Minotaur. For a review that details this sequence, see Welford Beaton, "Delighted to Give This Little Girl a Big Hand," *Film Spectator*, October 20, 1928.
12. Arzner may have conflated F. W. Murnau's *The Last Laugh/Der letze Mann* (1924) with Josef von Sternberg's *The Last Command* (1928). Emil Jannings starred as a doorman in the former film and an ex-general in the latter.

Dorothy Arzner

Boze Hadleigh / 1978

From *Hollywood Lesbians: From Garbo to Foster*, by Boze Hadleigh (Riverdale, NY: Riverdale Avenue Books, 2016).

[Boze Hadleigh conducted the following interview with Arzner by telephone in 1978. All ellipses appear in the original text.]

Boze Hadleigh: I believe you directed three silent movies? . . . Unlike several directors, you survived the transition from silence to sound. Why?

Dorothy Arzner: I was always concerned with the technical side of things, so the newer technology didn't throw me.

BH: It's said you were the one who encouraged Paramount to follow Warner's lead and try talking pictures.

DA: I may not have been the only one urging them to do it, but I may have been one of the most persistent advocates of sound.

BH: You were a rather new director. Was that a factor in your survival [in talkies]?

DA: It may have been a reason for more experienced directors and older ones who didn't make the transition. They were used to directing without sound, so they would lean towards postponing something new like that.

BH: Were you always mechanically inclined?

DA: I was.

BH: Did you play with dolls or trucks or something else as a child?

DA: [*Slight laughter*] Just about everything except dolls.

BH: In my research, I came upon a newspaper article from the 1930s that said, "Hollywood's Only Woman Director Never Bellows Orders Herself." That was the headline. Do you recall that?

DA: I think so. It likely said that men wouldn't allow or appreciate a woman giving orders. That that was why I was the only woman director in town.

BH: "Woman" is a noun, yet people will say woman director or woman doctor, when it should be female director, etc.

DA: "Female" is both a noun and an adjective.

BH: Of course it would be better if they just said director and doctor, right?

DA: Correct. But you're right in your observation. They say male model, not man model, which sounds awkward. They don't seem to mind if *woman doctor* or *lady doctor* sounds awkward.

BH: You may not have bellowed orders, but I've seen photos of you using a megaphone on the set....

DA: To amplify my voice. I didn't want to shout.

BH: You didn't have one of those voices that carries?

DA: I sometimes wished I had. Like newspaper vendors—boys.

BH: Did you feel much pressure—more pressure than was put on a man—to deliver a hit movie?

DA: There was pressure to deliver on time and within budget, and the assumption that if it wasn't popular, it might be the last one.

BH: In various long-ago interviews, you made a point of stating that you weren't financially dependent on directing.

DA: I wasn't boasting about wealth. I was saying in a roundabout way that I wasn't prepared to stay in pictures if I had to cave in to demands and interference [that] I felt were unfair.

BH: May I read a quote? You told one Francine Parker, "My philosophy is that to be a director, you cannot be subject to anyone, even the head of the studio. I threatened to quit each time I didn't get my way, but no one ever let me walk out."[1]

DA: That's me, word for word. [*Snickers*]

BH: You were ahead of your time in terms of the power and respect you asked for as a director. Directors weren't celebrities then.

DA: Not celebrities—hired help. I should have stuck around until the *auteur* phenomenon. [*Chuckles*]

BH: You were born too soon.

DA: In a way, I was.

BH: But someone had to be the first, and it was you. Do you think you were "difficult"? I mean, we know *they* were.

DA: Sometimes I was. They often were. Thank you.

BH: With your philosophy of directing, weren't you on an inevitable collision course with patriarchal Hollywood?

DA: It was likely just a question of time and their exploiting the occasion.

BH: You said no one ever let you walk out. Until Harry Cohn on *First Comes Courage*, that is....

DA: That's right.

BH: With only one week of filming to go?

DA: Something like that.

BH: The official reason was pneumonia or ill health?

DA: Yah . . . Hollywood protects you until about five minutes after the door's slammed behind you.

BH: Were you let go, or did you walk out or . . . ?

DA: Nothing's that simple . . . . The result was the same.

BH: It was also Harry Cohn of Columbia who ended the directorial career of gay director James Whale. You were both replaced by Charles Vidor.

DA: [*Pause*] Whale was a very good director. A real individualist.

BH: British and flamboyant. And he dared live openly with another man—he wouldn't get a wife. Do you think it boiled down to that? Or was he, to some degree, difficult or antagonistic?

DA: I think the first set of circumstances did him in. How demanding he was, I don't know. It might have been a reason, but I'm doubtful. He did very well by Universal, commercially and artistically. He could have done the same for Columbia, which could have used him.

BH: Don't you think that a gay director or female director was more vulnerable than a heterosexual male director who might have been more demanding or delivered fewer hits but was permitted to stay the course?

DA: What I've heard for an awfully long time is that a woman has to be twice as good as a man to be regarded comparably. It's true for any minority group.

BH: Including, still, women—who aren't a minority.

DA: Yes, even more particularly in today's films. There are a few more women directors, but they haven't lasted as long as I did. They work less often. One money-loser, only one, and it's likely the end . . . . Even the stars are all men. The few women in them—

BH: Excuse me for interrupting with one of your own—pertinent here—quotes. A few years back, you told the *New York Times*, "When men do put women in pictures, they make them so darned sappy, weeping all over the place, that it's disgusting."

DA: I haven't had cause to revise my opinion. And you?

BH: Sappy and weak. The fire and resistance of a Davis or a Crawford or a Stanwyck are missing in most actresses. Mostly now, they're just girlfriends.

DA: You haven't asked about censorship and the [Motion Picture Production] Code. When I do speak with film students and scholars, they point out its shortcomings. Correctly. But most forget or don't realize that the Code at least forced women on screen to *do*.

BH: In other words, the girlfriends and the mistresses and even prostitutes had to go out and get careers?

DA: Just so. If women couldn't be depicted as erotic or use their charms to make a living, they had to get jobs and become career girls.

BH: But only until they married at fadeout.

DA: At fadeout, there had to be a man and woman, newly joined or about to be, with a future full of traditional gender roles.

BH: Patriarchy.

DA: Yes. No variations.

BH: And a future brimming with children.

DA: "Be fruitful and multiply." It was the corollary to the motion picture's message of encouraging male-female pairs.

BH: Notice how often in films then or now, the villain is single, while the hero always has a girlfriend or wife.

DA: Both, lately. Also notice that any woman on her own is threatening or even villainous. If she is a villain, she must be extirpated.

BH: Extirpated?

DA: Destroyed.

BH: What a nonviolent way of saying it! [*Both chuckle*]

DA: Then but also now, and maybe even more so now, older women who aren't grannies are too often made out villains or semivillains.

BH: There is rather a contempt in American culture for older women.

DA: Occasional admiration but usually contempt.

BH: In countless movies of the thirties and forties, the woman who's a threat—even if she's Bette Davis, who always put up a fight—is eventually neutralized by a man who proposes.

DA: He proposes, she says yes to his terms. It's submission.

BH: Have you read *The Female Eunuch*?

DA: No. But it's a thought-provoking title. It's often done to women.

BH: They're castrated of their power and sexuality?

DA: Even physically. Female circumcision in sub-Saharan Africa is a tradition almost never described in our country.

BH: It should be. Also the fact of slavery in Saudi Arabia—Black slaves—and such facts as women there can't vote or drive.

DA: In Saudi Arabia?

BH: Yes. Did you mind never working with Bette Davis? She'd have been ideal for you.

DA: I liked her screen persona. I never knew her as a person. You said her characters often put up a fight. That's what women loved her for. She was feisty, and it was a fantasy for them. Of course, when she didn't give in, she was . . . bumped off. Got shot, typically.

BH: No actress got shot more often than Bette Davis.

DA: It's as if in the current pictures, somebody declared that the battle of the sexes is over and that the men won. The women don't put up a fight anymore. They don't even fight a man's sexual advances for their own sake.

BH: Do you think this is a backlash against women's rights?

DA: Whatever it is, the men who write the films are now allowed, or for all I know encouraged, to degrade the women on the screen.

BH: And to trivialize them. Is it true you almost worked with Garbo? Can you describe the project?

DA: It never took place. It was shelved . . . . Louis B. Mayer was the deciding factor. It would have been done under Irving Thalberg, but he passed away.

BH: Do you think Mayer, who must have sensed Garbo's real sexuality and that of the women around her, wanted Garbo directed—and therefore supposedly controlled—by men only?

DA: Mayer knew that I was independent. Yes, he wanted Garbo directed by men. Men he could control.

BH: You were also set to direct Dietrich . . . .

DA: She'd hoped to do a picture about war from a woman's point of view. War had broken out with Germany. The title would have been *Stepdaughters of War*.

BH: We think of Dietrich as such a clotheshorse and glamour queen. Did she want to transcend that?

DA: Yes, however, they wouldn't kill the goose who laid their golden eggs.

BH: Even when she was no longer box office and older?

DA: They're always more likely to repeat a formula that's often or occasionally successful than to try something entirely new . . . . Marlene was lucky enough, or unlucky, to stay beautiful throughout her career. She'll be the last to wither.

BH: Did you have a crush on her? [*No reply*] So many women and men did and do.

DA: I think so. I agree.

BH: Were you assigned to direct so many actresses because of your gender?

DA: They would avoid me for Westerns or action pictures. If it was a love story, then they thought of me. The studios' A-scripts often eluded me. I would be given an actress's first starring assignment—not quite an A-picture in terms of prestige, but unequivocally not a B-picture. If the actress became a star, they got someone else to direct her.

BH: Why?

DA: They wouldn't trust a woman with an A-1 budget.

BH: I read that for your first movie, you insisted on a big-budget project. Is that true?

DA: I let Walter Wanger know that I would rather do an A-picture at Columbia, which was then a second-tier studio, than a B-picture at Paramount.

BH: So they were prepared to humor your desire to direct, but only with a minor project?

DA: I backed them into a corner. I wasn't about to do it their way. I had years of experience and results behind me. I didn't want to have to start all over again, at the bottom—where they might have kept me, out of bigotry.

BH: It's almost surprising to younger people that such an illustrious career as yours began with your being a secretary.

DA: Do set the record aright—I was a typewriter. Or a "typist" now. Scripts, on a typewriter. The machine was called a typewriter, so was the girl who used it. That one machine created more opportunities for women than any other I can think of.

BH: Is it true that before you, talkies would use stationary microphones, and the actors had to remain in place while reciting their lines?

DA: In that era, pictures were much closer to the stage. Locations, expansive movement, and so forth were the exception.

BH: Had you ever wanted to be an actress?

DA: I thought I would like the results of being an actress, the rewards. I never thought highly of what actresses continually have to go through.

BH: Is it true Clara Bow initially resisted being directed by a woman?

DA: That wasn't very exceptional. [*Chuckles softly*] Clara was devoted to flirtations with men. In her opinion, the more men on the set, the merrier.

BH: Do most actresses like to flirt with their director?

DA: Sooner or later most do it, if only for the crew.

BH: Or their own protection?

DA: If she's not a big star, it is a farsighted tactic.

BH: Why do you think so many films from the early 1930s are all but forgotten?

DA: Well, motion pictures reached their maturity in the latter 1930s. In style, technology, and format. Early talkies are now often regarded as quaint or archaic. They were also shorter, closer to one hour, which makes them too short for television broadcast, even with the myriad commercials they pad them with.

BH: Your movies have been revived at art houses, museums, and on campus, but are rarely seen on TV.

DA: That's the way it is.

BH: And it's not just the films. Various major stars of the early thirties are almost anonymous now. One of them whom you directed was Ruth Chatterton.

DA: In *Anybody's Woman*.

BH: Your film together turned her into "The First Lady of the Screen." It was a very transitory title.

DA: One never knows, at the time, who is going to endure and who isn't. Or why.

BH: You boosted Rosalind Russell from supporting player to star.

DA: I saw the star quality in her before anyone else did.

BH: Might one reason be that she wasn't conventionally feminine? Some thought her a bit masculine.

DA: I like masculine qualities in people . . . I could tell that she had substance.

BH: The vehicle with which you made Russell a star was *Craig's Wife*. Is it really your favorite of your films?

DA: It's as good as any of them. I found the relationships interesting. The wife and her husband, and even more significantly, the woman and her house.

BH: George Kelly won several awards for the play *Craig's Wife*. I suppose partly because it warned women to value their husbands above materialism and even the biggest, most immaculate house?

DA: [*Chuckles*] There is another psychological thread in that story. She doesn't trust men because her father abandoned her mother and his daughter when she was a child. She wants a perfect life, so that nothing can go wrong.

BH: She's a control freak.

DA: It's more evident in the remake. It was less subtle than my film.

BH: The remake, *Harriet Craig*, was more woman-centered and star-centered, as the title implies. I think it's one of the most interesting things Joan Crawford ever did.

DA: Great acting.

BH: Wonderful characterization. Many people say she was really playing herself—as actresses tend to do, once they're older and surer of themselves.

DA: Joan was a friend of mine, a good friend [*firmly*].

BH: Post-Hollywood, you directed over fifty Pepsi commercials for her, didn't you?

DA: I had more control over them than I did with my pictures, not omitting the one I did with Joan.

BH: Why do you think *Bride* is less remembered than many other Joan Crawford movies?

DA: It has its following, but . . . I couldn't say. She did so many pictures. Most of the early ones are out of sight and out of mind. Film buffs think of Joan in 1940s pictures or some of her 1960s horror entries.

BH: Like *What Ever Happened to Baby Jane?* Do you think there really was a big feud between Crawford and Davis?

DA: Publicity, I think. Mostly publicity.

BH: Hollywood publicity would rather have us believe that two stars hate each other than love each other, wouldn't it?

DA: Miss Davis had no such desire for Joan.

BH: I didn't mean them in particular. Um, why do you think it's said that 1939 was the greatest year for Hollywood films?

DA: I have my doubts as to any magic attaching to that year. Several good ones were made in 1939. There were some mediocre 1939 pictures, too. One was *The Day the Bookies Wept.* To name just one.

BH: Which women in film do you admire?

DA: I'd have to think too hard to come up with a logical answer.

BH: Then what women out of film do you admire?

DA: I admire women who lead. Leaders . . . Golda Meir, very much. I've also followed with interest the careers of two other Asian leaders—India's Indira Gandhi and Sirimavo Bandaranaike of Ceylon. These are the first three women to lead nations. Bandaranaike was the first.

BH: And the least known. A Buddhist, a Hindu, and a Jew. Do you think the USA will ever have a female leader?

DA: In which century? I cannot predict the future.

BH: What do you think of the word "gay" for someone who's primarily homosexual?

DA: I think it is preferable to "homosexual," because human beings are much more than sexual response. In that sense, "lesbian" will serve. "Gay" sounds a bit flippant.

BH: How about some of the older terms, like "Uranian"?

DA: I knew a man who often used that word, and his listeners often thought he meant Ukrainian.

BH: Do you think that homosexual women should be called lesbians or gay women? Although the latter sounds like a 1930s movie title.

DA: It does. [*Chuckles*] I feel that the terminology isn't the key. Whatever term is used, outsiders' bigotry will result in animadversions.

BH: In criticism?

DA: Criticisms.

BH: It's more important what a group of people think of themselves than what they call themselves. But to call everyone a heterosexual or homosexual isn't right or correct.

DA: When a rape is committed, the newscast does not refer to the man as a heterosexual nor as a heterosexual rapist.

BH: No, yet if somewhere a woman shot her female companion, they'd call her an alleged lesbian murderer.

DA: Or murderess.

BH: Do you think Harry Cohn was the worst mogul?

DA: Louis B. Mayer was equally . . . the same caliber of man. He had more power, ergo, he was worse. It's the degree of power.

BH: Do you agree that the major difference between a Hitler or Stalin and a fanatical TV evangelist is the amount of power they've been given?

DA: I would say so. It is a good point, that people give such men any power they have.

BH: People and, nowadays, the media. Did you really have a clause in your Columbia contract saying you didn't have to attend meetings aboard Harry Cohn's yacht?

DA: One of my contracts had a clause to that effect.

BH: Would he have understood that it had to do with your presumably not wanting to mix work with socializing, or would he resent it because a woman didn't want to board his yacht?

DA: It's likely he resented it all around. But I wasn't going to work under those conditions.

BH: Do you think he took your film away out of revenge? Or what really happened?

DA: The true reason I retired from Hollywood may forever remain a secret, and I'd rather it does.

BH: All right. You discovered another big star of the 1930s, Sylvia Sidney....

DA: *Merrily We Go to Hell* was her first starring role, and it was a very big success. You've probably not heard of it. Miss Sidney is at another plateau of her long career, in featured parts now . . . I saw that she was frail-looking but had a lot of mettle. In most of her pictures, she suffered, and she survived.

BH: She's been described as the prototypical "silently suffering Jewish actress," whatever that means.

DA: People weren't open about their faith then.

BH: Not if it wasn't the majority one. You also directed Katharine Hepburn in her first starring role.

DA: I directed Hepburn in her first vehicle . . . I get asked about that picture [*Christopher Strong*] a lot. More often than I can comprehend. It's your turn now.

BH: Why, if it's about an aviatrix, as they still call a female flyer, is the movie titled after the male character she falls in love with?

DA: I didn't write it, but a male name was thought to have more widespread appeal. Unless the female lead was a famous star.

BH: Like Joan Crawford in *Johnny Guitar*? Westerns, a male genre. At least they called her Oscar winner *Mildred Pierce*.

DA: Joan's last picture was called *Trog*, after a caveman.... Her death last year was a great loss; I lost a good girlfriend, and we all lost a woman who defined the word "star."

BH: I know. I was in Spain when it happened, in a tour group, and all the American women over forty reacted with disbelief that she had died.

DA: She was one of the few legends. Joan began in silent pictures, which most audiences aren't aware of.

BH: Yes. But back to *Christopher Strong*. Do you think it was intentional for Hepburn's character to seem so butch in the first part of the film before she falls in love with the married man and then kills herself after he impregnates her? And do you think such a plot would hold up today?

DA: Zoë Akins wrote the script, and she was rather brazen in some of her themes. I think she wanted for the heroine to be very much surprised that she too could fall in love. I think also that Hepburn stamped her individuality on the part, making her seem aggressively independent and, at that time, shocking to some people.

BH: Many filmgoers found Hepburn an acquired taste. What about the plot, which starts out so hopefully and then descends into typical misogyny?

DA: I think the picture is remembered for Katharine Hepburn. It was not an outstanding success, but it's better known than some of my pictures that were, due to Hepburn and due to it being the first picture that she carried.

BH: I understand there was some coolness between you on the set, and you each called each other "Miss."

DA: That was not atypical of the times. "Miss" this and "Mister" that. American informality hadn't yet taken over from English manners and ways of speaking. After Miss Hepburn was reminded by the front office who was directing the picture, we got along quite well.

BH: But you didn't socialize in the thirties and forties.

DA: She had her circle of friends. I had mine.

BH: I've read speculation that the reason you were friends with Crawford but not Hepburn is that Crawford had a definitely heterosexual image, whereas Hepburn did not, though she later tried to straighten it out—as it were—via her alcoholic pal Spencer Tracy.

DA: [*Long pause*] Interesting.

BH: What did you do after *First Comes Courage*?

DA: I made training films for the Women's Army Corps during the war. I did television commercials—you've already referred to that. And I taught. I found that very pleasant.

BH: You began the first film course at the Pasadena Playhouse?

DA: Mmm. And I taught at the university in Los Angeles. Then I retired.

BH: In the fifties and sixties, did you ever think you'd be rediscovered?

DA: I didn't give it much thought.

BH: Why do you think Ida Lupino seems forever to be apologizing for having been a director?

DA: [*Laughs*] Well, she didn't set out to become one. I did. She was a prevailing actress who got into directing by default.

BH: Why are directors who are women so quick to insist they don't really give orders to men? What do they fear—unpopularity?

DA: That will change. It's most likely changed some in Israel and India and Ceylon. The example of women in positions of authority will make men more used to sharing their power. The power that women had agreed to give them.

BH: The monopoly is ending. May we briefly discuss another female director? She directed only two movies. One is *Maedchen in Uniform*, the most famous lesbian-themed film.

DA: Leontine Sagan. Very good picture. She was brought to Hollywood. You know the story? She had to flee Germany because of the Nazis. She directed a picture in England. She came to the United States, and here she wasn't given her promised assignment.

BH: I heard that Mayer opposed the lesbian theme of *Maedchen* and the fact that it had no men in it.

DA: Neither did the 1939 Metro-Goldwyn-Mayer picture, *The Women*.

BH: Directed by a man. Or did *Maedchen* have any men in it? I saw it so long ago. Did Sagan's Hollywood career, or career-that-never-was, fall victim to local homophobia?

DA: I don't know the whole story. But that seems to be the crux of the matter. She made a name for herself in theater, however. I believe she went and founded the National Theatre of South Africa.

BH: I hope I don't offend you by reading a quote from Leontine Sagan. She said, "What could Dorothy Arzner lose if she came out, in her retirement, and admitted to lesbianism?"

DA: [*Long pause*] I think our connection is bad.

BH: I wouldn't say it's bad.

DA: This is a good final question for you.

BH: I didn't mean to give offense. I just wondered what your response would be to her question.

DA: To her challenge, it sounds more like. But I too have a question—has Miss Sagan ever "come out" herself?

BH: I don't know.

DA: I doubt she has. If I'm not mistaken, she had a husband. I never did that. So she's hardly in a position to give advice or issue challenges.

BH: If she is, or was, lesbian and did marry a man, you're right, she's not in a position—

DA: Especially publicly. It's rather shocking to me that she would address me indirectly and publicly.

BH: I understand you object to being called a feminist or lesbian director.

DA: I am not a director. I'm retired. And whatever I may have been in my private life, it didn't pertain to my work, at the time, in motion pictures. You wouldn't call a woman a Democrat director? I would not.

BH: I would call her a director who is a Democrat, a feminist—hopefully—and a lesbian.

DA: That makes more sense. But now you'll have to excuse me.

BH: I hope you'll excuse me. It's been a privilege, and thank you for your time.

DA: Thank you for your interest.

Note

1. This quotation appears in Mary Murphy's interview, not Francine Parker's. Both are included in this book.

Appendix: The Unfinished Autobiography of Dorothy Arzner

Dorothy Arzner / 1955

From David Soren, *Art, Popular Culture and the Classical Ideal in the 1930s* (Baltimore: Midnight Marquee Press, 2010). Lightly revised by the editor.

[Arzner began developing an autobiography in 1955 but dropped the project after discussing her experiences through about 1920, declaring in the unfinished document's final sentence that "I cannot cover the rest of my biography." It is unclear why she stopped, though she may have belatedly realized that, if she continued with her autobiography's focus on domestic relationships, she would have to cover a topic that she had shielded from public view for decades: her life with Marion Morgan, whom she met in 1921.

Based directly on Arzner's original typescript, the following document restores material cut from or altered in the version published in 2010. It also includes fresh annotations based on information from census records, city directories, and the like. Arzner wrote it in a very impressionistic and conversational style, often employing sentence fragments instead of complete sentences. She also tended to write in massive page-long paragraphs. This version includes paragraph breaks where it seemed appropriate and silent corrections for noun-verb agreements, obvious misspellings, and missing or misused punctuation marks.]

Part I

It was San Francisco, the first year of the twentieth century. That, in itself, has a certain significance. Whether it is dramatists who have dramatized San Francisco or San Francisco that dramatizes lives, I do not know; but many of the people in my world who have been born there have a particular individuality that dramatizes itself one way or another. Most of them have a deep love for that city, particularly the ones who were there before the thirties. It holds rich memories and an excitement.

Even young people, while sitting at the cocktail tables on the top of the Mark Hopkins Hotel, will comment on the beauty that surrounds them. The cocktails become secondary to the beauty of the two heroic bridges that span the bay—the Twin Peaks, with their heads in the mist, and the Golden Gate, truly golden as the great gold disc of the sun seems to splash its way down into the sea. Perhaps in one's blood, there is an electronic connective with the place of one's birth. Perhaps it's the big city of the gold-mining days that stirs us with a desire to blaze trails. Perhaps it's the realization of a dream—the dream of a man named Fair, who had a vision.[1] He saw one of the most beautiful cities in the world—San Francisco.

There was a hill overlooking the waterfront town; they called it Knob Hill. Fair, the Virginia City gold miner, built his home on top of that hill, and three other associates did the same. His home is now replaced by the famous Fairmont Hotel. Across the street, the Mark Hopkins Hotel replaces the home that was there. On the third corner, one of the great mansions remains. This is no structure of useless Victorian cupolas. It is a solid, classical structure built of dark red terra cotta blocks of stone with the finest plate glass shining from large square windows, letting in the sun and light and giving a wide view of the sky and sea about. A graceful green-bronze fence rail surrounds the grounds, possibly designed and wrought by an Italian artist. A covered entrance lends dignity to a beautiful door, and just inside are marble halls and a grand marble staircase. This is no structure to be replaced by so-called modern architecture—this is as fine as one could wish for today. It has nobility. There is an excitement in the realization that a piece of architecture still stands that holds, in its form, the life and culture of the nineties in the West.

Snatches of stories have been told to me of flamboyant women and aristocratic sons, too warm-blooded for the conventions of the East. A hotel was named The Palace Hotel. I saw victorias [horse-drawn carriages] drive into the courtyard of that hotel. The courtyard now is a large dining room—still beautiful—and has an air about it of a palace courtyard. The ladies riding in the victorias wore large hats—tipped just a bit with a large, tied ostrich plume falling across the crown and down on one side of their face. The men wore frock coats and derbies or top hats. It seemed that every man wore a mustache—it was a sign that he was no longer a boy, I guess. The living moving pictures did seem gay. Beautiful horses pranced as they turned into the court. Within were red velvet and crystal chandeliers flickering a lovely yellow light. Even electricity was not so steady then. The wealthy of the gold rush were having their day. Virginia City—the Yukon—and from the East—all kinds of people poured into San Francisco. Trade started to boom with the Far East. Meetings and separations to seek more life and more and more life. Life clanked with the horse and cable car bells; it twinkled with theater and café marquees. It moaned with the steamboat whistles and laughed a little too loud with the ladies of the "Gay Nineties," now grown older. It crept in with the fog and roared in with the January storms off the Pacific.

In the midst of this melee and the beginning of a new century, the god Janus put into the records the birth of Dorothy Emma Arzner, born in San Francisco, California, USA.[2]

Father—born in Karlsruhe, Württemberg, Germany.

Mother—born in Glasgow, Scotland.

In 1942, when all Americans had to prove their birthright as American citizens, there was no proof that I had been born. The record had been destroyed in the devastating fire and earthquake of April 18, 1906. My pride of birthplace was now being tested by questions. My last name, originally Artzner, was German. I had earlier responded when I heard the phrase "a citizen of the world." I liked the phrase. I liked the idea of belonging to the whole instead of being a limited person. However, school records and a bank record satisfied the inquiries—had I been in America for more than twenty years? All was well. I was not a German enemy. But I cherished the idea that I was a citizen of the world.

My father was an immigrant boy of fourteen when he came to this country, alone, without relatives or friends. "Fabulous America!" had reached across the world to become a boy's goal. To get to America was his ambition. There he could make money and be independent—make his own way. It took him thirty days to cross the Atlantic. He arrived in America with twenty dollars.

My mother was one of eight orphaned children born in Glasgow, Scotland. Her older brother John had come to America, and as he earned the money dressing working tools in the shipyards, he brought them one by one to this country.

My brother, David, was four years older than I.

This was the small family pattern into which I was born, a kind of "behind the scene[s]" reality of life related to the show that was going on out front. No red velvet or crystal chandelier—just a simple wooden cottage halfway up one of the hills, very similar to many others that stood in a row.[3] These were small examples of Victorian architecture. Bay windows bulging from the parlor and wooden balls on dowel sticks for the decorative arches. Colored glass around the door windows and a fancy hand-turning bell. A long flight of wooden steps led up to the first-floor entrance door above a basement. These houses are still standing in San Francisco, only the basements have been converted to garages.

What is left of my first five years of personal experience are bits and pieces. No recollection of having a body—just a mind recording brief snatches of moving pictures that later took on significance and within me a depth of feeling toward them. I dramatized them. I tied them to later events. I saw them as beginnings of later crises.

When I was born, my brother did not like having a little sister. He wanted a brother. He must have made it quite evident since I was told of it many times. I've wondered to what extent this had a bearing on my becoming a tomboy because that was what I became in action as I stood at the end of a long hall, and a baseball came flying at me. I either caught it, or it went through me. Later my brother was so very proud of his little sister's superior ability that he would show me off by having older boys take turns at hurling their swiftest pitches at me, and I can recall the sound of that solid thud as the ball came to a dead stop in my catcher's mitt, too big for my little hand, but somehow one can learn to handle inadequate situations.

There was something about my mother that was always exciting. I think it was the natural love of a child for its mother personified by being left alone a lot without her. She was small and had dark, curly hair. Not at all the popular type of the day—large, full-bosomed blondes. As always, "gentlemen preferred blondes" then, too.

There must have been an emotional content that made her approach so vivid. I can hear the rustle of taffeta coming down that long hall—it was black taffeta with ruffles on the bottom. That sound brought joy. The picture of black taffeta was probably all I saw from my point of view on the floor. I don't remember her face, actually. I have a photograph or two but no recollection of the likeness to my mother. My mother became an ideal made of the fabric of a child's longings. She was warm and emotional one moment, and the next, we would be left alone for hours. I remember one time looking into the contents of a store window with my mother by my side and the next moment, when I looked about, she had disappeared. A panic rushed over me; I was lost! Only to find that she had moved around the corner to another window.

I can hear a song my mother used to sing as she stood in a little clothes closet selecting a dress to wear:

All I want is fifty thousand dollars
Sealskins to protect me from the rain
Vanderbilt and Pierpont to escort me—

(I can write the notes of the melody if I were near a piano.)

There, memory of the following words stops short—but the melody continues to finish the fourth-line phrase. With much research, I have not been able to find that song. It seems to me to tell so much of the times. Fifty thousand dollars was a fortune. Sealskins were the luxury fur, and Pierpont Morgan and Vanderbilt were the millionaires of the day.[4]

At night, jumping up and down in the middle of the bed with my brother and singing:

Yankee Doodle went to town
A ridin' on a pony
Stuck a feather in his crown
And called it maca-ro-ni.

Hilarious laughter—then prayers.

Now I lay me down to sleep
I pray the Lord my soul to keep
God Bless Papa. God Bless Mama
God Bless Davey and me.

Street scenes looking out the window.

A Chinese man in black coolie [sic] suit and large straw hat with two large, heavy baskets, three feet deep and a foot and a half across, filled with vegetables and hanging from the ends of a pole arched across his shoulders. He moved with short steps that gave the impression of running. I remember feeling it was too heavy for his frail little body.

Next, a black, curly-haired Italian vendor, swinging up the street, with a stocking cap pulled to one side and singing lustily his wares: white plaster casts sticking out above the basket he carried rakishly on one shoulder. I remember these rather awful bits of sculpture sitting on pedestals in the parlor of many houses.

The tamale man was always a pleasant sight. He came along at night when darkness outside seemed a bit formidable. First his voice calling, "Tamales—nice hot tamales!" It was the little bright flickering light from his charcoal burner swinging by that gave off warmth and life.

The messenger boy, with dark blue uniform suit and a square patent leather visored cap, seemed to be a theatrical bicycle performer. He went by balancing a huge tray of food, covered with a white napkin, on his cap with both hands on the handlebars; at least he never hung onto the tray. Just when he came to be the symbol of clandestine suppers, I do not know, but he did.

The dark, black figure of the lamplighter. His movement was never hurried. He lit the lamp at the corner with a long stick that turned the gas key and also carried the lighted match. He became a work of art in that golden light. With unhurried rhythm, he crossed the street to the next lamppost.

All seemed orderly and intent upon their very individual enterprise until the Chinese laundry wagon would pass. Then there was commotion! Dogs barked— boys shouted, "Chink—Chink—China man [sic]. Go back where you came from!" and rocks were thrown at him. The excited Chinaman with [a] long queue flying stood up in his one horse-covered wagon and whipped his bony horse into a gallop through the shower of rocks—he, yelling in high-pitched voice, Chinese swear words and pointing at the boys as he disappeared down the street. I had been told a legend that if a Chinaman pointed his long finger at you, you would turn to stone, so there was always a scampering for cover on my part.

Now the beginning of drama. I seemed to be the observer of myself and the incidents. I was lying on a double bed, crying lustily as a bottle crashed into a mirror above a sideboard covered with glasses. My mother had thrown that bottle.

A little girl sitting between pointed standards of an iron rail fence watching older girls at play. I played baseball, and this seemed to separate me from them.

Sticking my head between the wooden rondels of a decorative fence rail, trying to get into where some other children were playing. My head got caught so that I could go no further nor back out again. I remembered the fearsome thought that I would have to stay there forever or have my head cut off.

Playing with shiny green mottled tile that was scattered about in the process of being a new fireplace mantle; also, repairs were being made in the basement to house a very large billiard table. The billiard table was the indication of prosperity coming into the home such as the cocktail bar in present-day homes.

I can see the great beer wagons loaded with kegs being hauled up the cobblestoned hills and every sorrel muscle bulging from the magnificent horses of great bulk.

The clanking of bells from the fire engines. I rushed to the window to see the fire horses as they passed. They, too, were great shiny animals putting forth every effort from their great hearts for speed.

I climbed on the edge of my doll's bed then up on a ledge of the wainscoting, but I slipped and smashed the doll's head in. The doll was blonde and brown-eyed and my biggest and best doll. Oh, I had dolls. Naturally, I was given them, I was a little girl; but they were just things that had to be taken care of. I hauled them with me for many years, but always they sat in corners neglected.

I only remember one Christmas during those first years. "It was the night before Christmas and not a creature was stirring" when suddenly, from my darkened room into the light from the hall, I saw the fleeing figure of my brother with my little black stocking in his hand. I had hung it at the foot of my bed. In that instant, I knew Santa Claus was a fake. I don't remember when I believed that he was real. I only remember the moment of full realization that he was not real.

Eavesdropping on quarreling words between my papa and mama. Nothing violent, just words of dissention. Long days of being left alone and left with other people: a tobacconist and his wife. I used to love to watch him roll the large leaves into cigars and cut the ends. Sometimes he would let me push the cutter. There was a life-size wooden Indian outside.

A strange family with strange children. I met one many years later; she was a fortuneteller from cards. All I can remember is my reaction to dirt and disorder.

A piece of flannel was given to me as a handkerchief—that bothered me most of all. I was crying for my mother, which I did the whole time I was there. Then one evening, she appeared like a dream princess, and I was saved from the ogres and villains. As I look back, probably the only villain was dirt and a kind of disorder that exists with too many children and not enough money.

I was also left with a policeman's wife. A little precise woman with a tight black dress buttoned up the front to her neck and black rushing about the collar. Everything seemed black and rigid. On the wall was a picture of her dead husband, a formidable man in uniform, and a wreath of brown "immortal leaves" hung 'round it. Death seemed to be in the house. She was kind, but I didn't like the pictures I saw.

I also remember a large colored picture of my brother on a white easel. He was about five years old and had long, golden curls to his shoulders. He was dressed in a black velvet Lord Fauntleroy suit with a large white collar and a ruffle on it. That picture was the bane of his existence, even though he had long since had them cut. It was the style for little boys to have long curls if they had them. It must have come from the aping of the English aristocrats.

Now my brother and I seem to exist in a house alone.

The parlor satin cushions and a sick kitten lying on one of them while we watched it breathe its last breath.

Playing train with the parlor chairs in a row.

A wooden chute—greased runners—a wooden box—and me in it. One slide—and I was thrown on my face as it landed at the bottom, and the scene blacks out of my memory.

Storm outside—we were alone again—another glass door, to the basement. Tagging behind my brother—he was struggling to get the door open against the storm when a gust of wind slammed it shut on his arm, which broke it. Neighbors running in. Doctor called. Watching—waiting for the doctor. Then splashing through the mud down the street, I saw the familiar one-horse shay.

Such relief! Such great, kind friends—the doctors of those days. The one-horse shay on a rainy day was unmistakably a doctor.

That break in my brother's arm seems to have been the beginning of what later was a frailty—broken several times playing baseball and football; it undermined his strength.

A trip downtown with my father—this was an unusual occurrence. As we entered the lobby of the Palace Hotel, I saw my mother sitting in the corner. I thought she looked beautiful. She was dressed in a sealskin jacket and wearing violets. I rushed toward her—my face was crushed into the violets and fur. She started to cry, and so did I. Then a pulling apart. That was the last time I saw my mother, except for one brief glimpse a few years later. I was five years old. Now my brother and I were "children of divorce."

Part II

There was no problem readjusting to a new environment. Evidently, everyone was kind and made an effort to entertain a lonely little girl. At least there were people about, and that seemed to be interesting. There were five in my uncle's family—my brother and I added made seven.

The house was a white Victorian wooden house. One floor sitting above a basement. The front—a lawn with a white picket fence around it and a gate that led to the front entrance. But it was a view from the rear that seems to have been my approach. I believe it was through the back gate that one came from the railroad station. Everything must have been within walking distance because I have no recollection of vehicles, only bicycles, and walking on wooden sidewalks.

There was a long stair against the rear of the house that led to a little landing and a back screen door that led into the kitchen. The kitchen was dining room and kitchen and living room combined. Though there were a front parlor and a back parlor along one side and three bedrooms and a bath with a galvanized iron tub on the opposite side. In the front parlor was an upright piano, and on it was the first piece of sheet music I had ever seen. It was "The Rose of Killarney," and a colored picture of a lady's face in a large red rose on the cover. In the back parlor was an organ, a formal dining table [that] was never used except for Sunday dinners, and in a bay window was a couch where I eventually slept.

The backyard was fenced with a gate at the rear. A chicken house with chickens. A large windmill with a water tank, where I used to make mud pies, and the base served as a counter from which to sell mud pies to my aunt.

There was the outhouse with two boards for a walk from the house that led to it from the rear stairs. I remember the board in the house was new, and there were two big holes in it and one little one made especially for me. Also hanging on the wall was Montgomery Ward's catalog.

The detail of the period is familiar to most, so I will not go into it all. Oil lamps to be cleaned every day. All hot water was heated on a wood stove. Three meals to cook—chickens to be fed and all the rest of the household drudgery that a woman had to assume. The Saturday night bath was a real routine—hauling water to the bathroom and heating it on the wood stove was a chore.

My uncle was a tall typical Scotchman. Handsome, ruddy, with curly iron-gray hair and a rather large head that sat erect on his shoulders. My aunt Lena was small, thin, and frail. A gentle little woman with all the signs of hard work imprinted on her face and form. She wore gray gingham dresses that buttoned to the neck and long sleeves. Her hair was pulled back into a tight knot at her neck. Her face was sweet but thin and lined. I remember sitting on her lap and, being a healthy, plump little girl, I would say, "Here, I'll give you some of my cheeks," and I'd pull at my cheeks and place it imaginatively onto hers. I can see her sad, sweet smile. I would be up in the morning with her, making the mash for the chickens, and soon I was also helping with the making of butter, pushing a plunger up and down in a tall wooden bucket. There was an older boy, Willie, who was away all week in San Francisco working and Johnny, a younger boy about fourteen, who went to school and worked at night in the telegraph office. Polly, the girl, was fourteen and starting in high school.[5]

When I first arrived, I was to sleep with my cousin Polly. She would wait until the lights were out and then start telling ghost stories until I would cry with fright. Aunt Lena would scold her, but it did no good. Finally, they set up the couch in the back parlor, and there I slept in peace. I remember liking that little place to myself. My cousin Polly evidently was not too happy having me usurp her privacy and used this method of revenge. I guess I tagged about after her because there is an incident that stands out vividly. She was sitting before a mirror, brushing her hair, and the next thing I knew, I turned and found that she had disappeared. I looked all over for her. Then, when I finally found her back sitting before the mirror and asked where had been, she said, "Why, didn't you see me? I turned into a little flea and was sitting on the curtain there." That was frightening to me. I guess I believed her, and it was frightening.

This period in my life seems to have so many firsts in it. The first time I was accused of a lie. My cousin Polly and I each had been given what was called a "tick tack toes." If you squeezed the metal bug, it gave off a *tick-tack* sound. Mine seemed to go out of commission and wouldn't work at times, then would work. My cousin lost hers, and mine seemed to be working at the time. I was accused of having taken hers. To my knowledge, I had not taken it. But my kind aunt made a point of the fact that my cousin said I had lied. I remember the effect on me of my aunt thinking that I had lied. My best friend had gone against me. My best friend had called me a liar! I remember sticking fast to the fact that I had not taken my cousin's toy, that the one I had was mine. I was crying copiously. And the impression left was that I had been unjustly accused. I was made to give mine to my cousin. This injustice stayed for years.

Many times, I have wondered about that incident. Knowing how unaware children are of these rights and wrongs and how eager to have what they want—I hope it was true that I had not lied. Though whether I had lied or not is of little significance unless I knew what was a lie and what was the truth and then went against the truth. And I would only ask that from a more mature person than a five-year-old. Especially when we know how much subterfuge and untruth seems [*sic*] to be rampant in the world. The statement of simple fact is very rare. Perhaps Mr. Shakespeare comes nearer the truth: "If you believe it, it's true."[6]

Another first. My uncle and a friend of his that lived across a field used to play cribbage in the evening. He, too, was a Scotchman, a friend from "the old country." He seemed to be a very well-educated man because he was so interested in teaching me things. I learned to tell the time from a clock that hung on the wall. I learned the name of cards. I learned to play casino. I was also told wonderful stories about castles and knights in armor and queens and kings and princes and princesses all rather tied up with those little square cards that were so important to the evening's entertainment.

I found out that things that did not look hot could burn. My aunt was placing the lamps in a row on the table, and because the glass upright shade over the wick looked so slick, I put my little hands around it and with instant, excruciating pain I had seared the palms of my hands. I went around for days all done up in bandages. This was the first time I remember being hurt very badly.

I had my sixth birthday, and that meant I could go to school for the first time. There was always much to do about curling my hair on rags for Sunday and lovely clean white dresses and ribbons and bows. I guess my mother had established the curls. From pictures, both my brother and I dressed and looked like the wealthy children of the era. My father also was by now known to be reasonably successful. He paid for everything we had and gave us most everything we wanted.

My recollection of that first day in school was mainly associated with having learned to raise my hand before speaking. Because I remember gales of laughter at the dinner table when I raised my hand to speak from habit so quickly impressed during the day. Also, we were told to raise our hand with two fingers up when we wanted to go "out."

My brother did not play a very important part in my life during this period. There are pictures of him with larger boys with baseball mitts, so I was no longer included in his baseball playing—he now had boys to play with. I was busy having my sweet little aunt for a companion. Being given little pieces of pie dough and filling to mold a little individual pie for myself. Making mud pies and having my aunt come by the counter as a buyer of them.

Then there was a little boy I played with—Willie Parrot. He used to haul me everywhere on my tricycle. He had a little harness, and I drove him.

I also had a black kitten I was very fond of. One day my aunt had made a berry pie, and it had strips of dough on top—very fancy. Guess she baked it for a special occasion. She put it out on a little shelf to cool. The next thing I knew, she flew out of the kitchen door with a coal shovel, and I saw that shovel go flying down the stairs after the black cat. It missed him. But in spite of the top of the pie having been eaten off, I was shocked at the violence. She was so mild and gentle and kind and long-suffering. I had such a love of that little kitten. I remember defending him. But it was too much for her. Now as I look back, she well deserved some outlet.

Uncle Johnny was a good man when he was sober, but on Saturday night, he would hold back some of his pay and Sunday night, after being away most of the day, he would come home actually roaring drunk. We could hear him coming, singing usually, at the top of his voice and sometimes falling into the honeysuckle house. A kind of little shady summerhouse formed by thick honeysuckle vines. Other times he would be in the house. He was very funny to all of the children—full of wit and loud laughter. Tossing nickels and dimes about for us. But my poor little aunt saw no humor and only suffered deeply. She would have to get him to bed. He did not always want to do what she wanted him to do, and he would throw her off with a deadening thud against the wall or the door. His language was not what it should be at those times, and I'm sure she was fighting to protect the children from exposure to his drunken outbursts. Monday morning, all would be as usual. But these violent Sunday nights became kind of nightmares.

There was a story about my uncle. There was a rolltop desk in the back parlor, and it was the place of valuable possessions. I had a little diamond ring my father had given me for Christmas, and I remember there was a little secret drawer that I could put it in when I was not wearing it. Also, in another one, the savings were kept. There were no banks near. One banked any great amount in San Francisco. But here, all my aunt's savings were kept in that desk.

This story of my uncle happened before I went to live with them. It seems my aunt had the four children, and all were little. One day, Uncle Johnny did not come home. She discovered the savings had been taken from the desk and only a small amount left. Weeks passed—and when she had become desperate, not knowing what to do for money, a letter came from him saying he was in Scotland. I have always thought about him a lot. He had a good mind. He had pride and was one of the finest toolmen in the shipyards. After I grew up and was walking beside him, he used to remark that I stepped out like an aristocrat. That was revelatory to me. He longed for a life beyond just laboring. I think in desperation, after years of laboring for others, he decided he would close his mind to all responsibility and leap into freedom from it all for a "fling." He did—but it was hard on my aunt and evidently something that was not to be easily forgiven. But he returned after his trip and settled down to the hard work he'd always known, "dressing tools."

One day, my aunt was busy getting all dressed up. This was unusual for her. The house was all in order and so quiet. There was an air of strangeness about it all. She never went out. I had never seen her in a black suit and a hat and veil and her hair dressed a little bit by being curled in front but the same simple knot in back. She informed me she was going to San Francisco for a week—for me to be a good girl and she would be back soon. But this seemed a tragedy to me. I cried. I could sense that she was not happy. We went to the train to see her off. On my way home when I was still crying, I looked down at my hand and the little diamond from my ring had been lost, tragedy upon tragedy. Then I found out that my aunt was going to the hospital to have an operation. They had to tell me since I was carrying on about the whole thing to such a degree.

I remember this rather calmed me down—because I realized this was something that she had to do—that she was not just leaving us. Somehow, I felt nothing but doom about this absence. Most unhappily, I was sitting on the floor trying to button my own shoes the second morning when my cousin Polly came in and told me Aunt Lena had died. This came as a climax to my feeling from the day she left.

The funeral was from our parlor. Death has never seemed to me to have been marked by any early fright because when I was lifted up to look into the casket, I remember seeing that little face looking so peaceful. There was not anything frightening about it. I remember wanting to see her. It was not forced upon me. I loved my aunt. She was so kind and loving, and the only incident that was not the most gentle was the incident of the little lie. But I'm sure that came about from her love of me and not wanting me to lie. There was no violent scene about it. Just an administering of justice. But she has become a symbol of the hardship and painful, long-suffering of many of the women of her time. So if women today seem to be useless and spoiled, it must be an accumulated credit that they have been given by their pioneering, self-sacrificing mothers and grandmothers.

It seems to me I did a great deal of crying in those days, but also, they were happy days. Contented days. I was not lonely. Now my friend had gone, and there was another adjustment to be made.

It was Sunday—everybody was dressed up, including me. I was told my father was coming for me. I loved my father, though I did not see much of him. I was looking for him. The back gate opened, and there he was. Looking very different from other men. He was dressed in extremely well-pressed clothes. He wore a large, fine Panama hat.

He always had fine eyes, and they shone more than ever this day because they were serious. I remember being allowed to rush out to meet him. He was always businesslike. But kind. Never had much time. Things moved fast. All three dolls and my belongings had been packed in a straw telescope basket, and the whole family saw us off on the train that very night. My Papa had come to take us away to Los Angeles.

Only one year had passed since we had left our mother. Now we were on our way to a new world. A train was a new experience. A bit frightening at night. I was unhappy and cried. My dad was clumsy about getting me undressed. I can imagine what an ordeal it must have been for him. I insisted upon sleeping with him in the berth. I guess I was just scared. It must have taken a night and a day on the train in those days to go from San Francisco to Los Angeles. At any rate, I know when we arrived, it was at night, and I insisted again that I sleep with my father, but when I woke up in the morning, I woke up alone. I remember this little girl getting up and wandering about looking for her papa and found him in bed with a strange woman! That was a shock!!

I was told that the strange woman was my stepmother. Not a very good introduction to my stepmother. Hard on her and hard on me. It was as simple and natural as that, but to me, most unnatural to find my father had disappeared, and now a strange woman was sort of forced into my consciousness as a stepmother. She tried to be nice, but we knew my father was going to go to work, and both my brother and I insisted upon going with him—we did not want to be left with this strange woman. In desperation, my father took us with him.

All seemed to be fairly calm downtown with him until the woman who was now known as my stepmother arrived on the scene and literally dragged me away from my father. In retrospect, it is understandable. My father's business was a restaurant in back of a saloon and in connection with a theater. The Grand Opera House. One of the oldest theaters in Los Angeles, located at First and Main Streets. I screamed and yelled my lungs out, threw myself down on the sidewalk, and was dragged bodily through the streets and up a long flight of stairs to a hairdressing parlor.

There were two very nice women, sisters. They proceeded to placate me—they finally calmed me down by making designs with hairpins—ordering an ice cream soda to be brought up to me and constantly reasoning with me. I finally calmed down. But this introduction to my stepmother was the beginning of what was always a strained relationship full of misunderstandings and oppositions.

I do remember before I left that I, too, had my hair dressed by one of the very pleasant ladies, and I thought I looked rather nice. They did it so carefully without pulling it. It was softly curled and trimmed and a round comb was placed on my head like a little crown, and the hair was softly held away from my face. I thought I looked rather pretty for the first time. I guess the hairdresser had diverted my misery with flattery, and it must have worked. Also, my stepmother complimented me on my lovely hair. As I look back on this incident, I must have been a pretty tousled-looking little girl by the time I was dragged into the hairdressers. Also, I doubt that my hair had been combed since I had left, except as my father might have struggled with it. I'm sure I wouldn't have let my stepmother touch me.

My brother had stayed with my father. He probably had his own problems in making the adjustment, but I was too full of my own miseries to know what was happening to him. Only after I had matured a bit did I develop a real sympathy for all concerned. It must have been just as difficult for Dad and for Mabel, my stepmother. But somebody should have some wisdom about those things. I often wonder how long it will take for man to have any wisdom at all.

The next I knew, we were to be boarded out. Living in a boarding house was a special kind of experience for children.

Part III

In one year, my brother David and I had been transplanted twice—cut off from our mother and father—then from a loving aunt and uncle—taken to an unknown land, Los Angeles, introduced to a stepmother—and now taken to call on some strange people: Mrs. Dunlap, her two daughters, one a nurse named Emma and Jeanette, who was pretty and cashiered at Jevne's Candy Store. There was Fred, a son, about my brother's age, and a young man boarder, a plasterer by trade. He was rather handsome in a slick way, greased hair and very sure of himself. Mrs. Dunlap seemed kind enough, but there was something about her that was strange: her hair sat on her head like a cloche cap, rather too reddish-brown and always shiny and too perfectly wavy.

We sat in the parlor—a few words were exchanged with us, then Emma, the nurse, came in to look us over, and Fred, the tow-headed, rather disheveled boy, came in barefooted, and he was introduced. My brother and I were always dressed very well, and I noticed these people looked different. Mrs. Dunlap and my father exchanged a few words that sealed the bargain that Mrs. Dunlap would take us on, and we left.

The next day, we were given all the things we had wanted. My brother had a new bicycle and a gun and I a new tricycle and a new French doll with a lot of luxurious clothes in a little trunk—and a table and chairs. This seemed to represent a home of my own to me, which I could make for myself. It was white with blue flowers painted on it. My stepmother was the instrument of this generosity, and I realized then how very giving she was, but somehow there was no harmony in our natures.

We arrived at Mrs. Dunlap's bag and baggage. Me with my little telescope basket full of dolls and clothes. I was to room with the younger daughter, who was nice and was away most of the day and into the night. I rarely saw her. We started to school and soon played with the neighborhood children. This life had very little personal affection in it, just the business of living. People came and went—there were outside people who came in to dinner. On Sunday, I remember I always got the neck of the chicken. For many years after, I thought that was the part I liked best because I hadn't been given the other white meat.

This was a boarding house. There were many little inharmonies. I saw Mrs. Dunlap whack her son with a butcher knife. I suppose she was careful and just happened to have it in her hand, but she was always taking a slap at him. My brother made his own friends, and I tagged along. There were often words about us being gone so long or being late or staying away too long. I would want something, and he would stand up for me to get it. No one dared correct us too drastically because when my father left us, he had taken us aside and told us not to let anyone raise a hand to us—if so, "You tell me," he admonished my brother and told him to take care of his little sister. So he did as best he knew. I tagged along wherever he went—chasing after a gang of little boys or playing baseball. I was never comfortable in the house alone. The people were strange to me. The sleek man was too affectionate. The older daughter, engaged to him, was not friendly. He was always showing off his strength. When I would run from him, he would catch me by the waist of my dress and pick me up at arm's length and hang me over the banister while I screamed. Between that and forcing kisses on me, I was not happy.

Every afternoon, there was a time that Mrs. Dunlap disappeared into her room and locked the door—though I called and knocked, she would not answer until she was ready to see me. Up to that hour, she wore a boudoir cap, and I didn't think it was very pretty; the ruffle flopping around her face bothered me. One day when I was looking for her, I tried her door and it was not locked—the door opened wide, and to my surprise, there she sat directly facing me and completely bald! She was dressing her wig on a wooden head. Just one frightening flash picture, and I slammed the door and scampered away. Now a definite barrier existed between me and Mrs. Dunlap. This, I had to keep a secret; it was too odd to tell to anyone, not even my brother. It was her secret and I had stumbled onto it, and somehow, I knew I must keep it to myself.

On a rainy day not long after, I wanted my table and chairs up in my own room. I carried them from the basement, where I had been told I should keep them. Mrs. Dunlap didn't want them upstairs, so she carried them down again. I confided this injustice to my brother. I suppose I was crying because I couldn't have my own way. My brother took the incident into his own hands. He carried the table and chairs back upstairs to my room—got his gun and locked the door. We heard the voice of Mrs. Dunlap calling and saying, "Open that door! Open that door, or I'll break it down!" Then my brother called back, "If you do, I've got my gun, and I'll shoot you." The next day my father came, and we were packed up bag and baggage and taken away.

My brother was sent east to Cleveland, Ohio, to live with one of my mother's sisters, Aunt Annie. I was sent north to Oakland for a trial visit with my stepmother's mother.

A very sweet little woman whom I had never met before was to take me north on the train. She was the mother-in-law of my stepmother's brother, who was employed by my father. She seemed to have good sense about a child. She lived in a tiny apartment and gave over the entire day to entertaining me with making paper flowers. The next morning, we left on the train—sitting up all day—but she had a wonderful basket of food—all the things I liked, and she was so much fun.

I now have the deepest sympathy for my father and what he must have gone through—trying to find a place for his children. My stepmother never tried to force herself upon us. She gave us wonderful presents and was always with my father at his place of business. He owned the saloon and restaurant next to the Grand Opera House, one of the oldest theaters in Los Angeles, until it was torn down a few years ago. The actors and actresses were the main patrons of my dad's "café." While we boarded at Mrs. Dunlap's, Dad used to come every Saturday morning and take us downtown to be with him. My brother and I played hide and go seek in the theater, then went to the matinee. They were playing good old melodramas. I can't remember any of the subject matter, only the look of the people. It was a stock company. The villain, by the name of Lackaye—typical black, shiny hair and a black mustache. He used to come into my dad's restaurant, and I liked him best. He was always so much fun. Just the opposite from the parts he played, and he didn't have the mustache when I would see him after the theater.

Then there was the matinee idol, William Desmond. He was dashing and handsome. Came in followed by several women who[m] he had to dismiss one way or another because his wife, a very powerful woman, was always there waiting for him to come from the theater. These women used to wait at the stage door and follow him wherever he went. Very much like the movie fans of today, except that he could not step into a fast automobile and escape. The actor in those days was on foot mainly and therefore vulnerable. His wife, Lillian Desmond, was my mother's best friend and also the sister of Nance O'Neil, a famous actress of the day. All these theater people passed by pleasantly and patronizingly and were the bright spot of the week.

There were little incidents of my stepmother observing that our hands were dirty—nails not clean, hair unkempt, which made me uncomfortable. My dad, with his soft heart, only knew one way to treat a child—give them what they want. So we had candy and ice cream sodas and the food we wanted. The combination of emotional sensitivity and the sweets usually ended my day with my being sick to my stomach.

By the time I arrived in Oakland to live with "Mam" and having been happy on the trip, I was now an experienced person in making quick adjustments. I also was alone to make my way in this new trial. Everything went smoothly. Mrs. Holmes seemed to know how to how to receive a child. My own room was in readiness—little things were done for a child. I remember there was a tiny vase with a geranium in it. There was a place for all my things. She showed me around like a grown-up. There were lemonade and cookies that first afternoon.

I was introduced to a very nice boy who looked very handsome in a white sweater with a red stripe across the middle of it. He was about the age of my brother, and he asked me if I wouldn't like to see his domain. He had a little house of his own in the backyard. There was a skull and crossbones on the door and a big S.S. underneath, meaning Secret Service. There were pictures on the wall of ballplayers—I knew somehow this was an honor being bestowed upon me. I was told that no girl had entered this Secret Service room before but that I could be an honorary member. He showed me his bicycle and told me I could ride it if I wanted to. Everything was to my liking, and I reentered the house to ask if I could change my Sunday shoes to everyday shoes. I remember the comment made that it was wonderful how grown-up I was and that I was such an intelligent little girl to want to change my shoes. I think that gesture made everyone comfortable because they knew I had accepted my new home happily, and being good people, that was what they had not dared to hope—and made every effort to win the heart of a child. Mrs. Holmes, whom I later called "Mam" because this boy, Burt, called her that, was a real mother. She understood children. She adopted this boy after bringing up her own two children. This was the beginning of a rather involved array of relationships that later became always cumbersome when trying to explain who was who in my family.[7]

Now there was Tom, Mam's second husband. He was a Welshman, small, gnome-like, with a twinkle in his eye and a song in his heart. He came in toward the end of the first afternoon. I've always wondered if he stayed away and came in at the end to pick up the pieces if there were any knowing that a child should not have too many strangers to meet up with at one time. He and I struck up a friendship right off. He had the heart of a child and after dinner, the first night away, we two went hand-in-hand for a walk and to a candy shop. We bought licorice whips and jawbreaker jockey caps and peanuts. [He s]ang amusing little rhyming songs. He was a miner, and when the mines shut down periodically was the only time he was home. Fortunately for me, this was one of the times. I don't know how I got there, but when we arrived home, I was being ridden on his back piggyback. Everybody seemed to be so happy that I was happy.

Just before going to bed, Burt and I got into a hilarious game leaping off a couch onto many pillows that we had thrown onto the floor. When we were finally quieted down and told it was bedtime, I realized this activity was not to be repeated because Burt was admonished for starting the game. However, it was made clear that it was all right this time but not to be a usual habit. Life now was full of normal procedure. No hidden corners. All was open and healthy. Wrong things were never harshly corrected. School days started again. Neighbor children were invited in. Candy pulls were Saturday night celebrations. Books were brought from the library regularly, and Mam read them aloud to us. Many times, five or six neighbor children would come in, and we would all lie around on the floor in front of a warm coal fire burning brightly in an oval-topped fireplace in the dining room.

Going to the library on my bicycle returning a book and getting another became a regular routine. *The Wizard of Oz*, Louisa M. Alcott—one after another from *Little Women* to *Jo's Boys*. *Black Beauty*, the wonderful horse, and later, my own favorite private reading was the [Horatio] Alger boys' stories. This was my first introduction to books. The Alger stories had a picture on the cover of the books of a little boy with all of his belongings tied in a bandana handkerchief hung onto a stick over his shoulder—this somehow related itself to me. There was always the longing for my mother and an inner secret dream that I would leave home like the Alger boys and go looking for her someday when I grew up just a little bit more.

Apparently, there had been the warning that my mother would try to take us away. Even at my aunt's, there was a day the doorbell rang, and instead of opening the door, my aunt rushed to all of the windows and drew the blinds. Then I heard my mother's voice calling my name. Of course, I wanted to go to her, but I was held with a hand placed over my mouth as I tried to cry out to her. All around the outside of the house, I heard her voice calling me, but no sound was allowed to go out to her. She soon went away. There may have been a reason for not letting her see me, but it all seemed wrong and mysterious then, and no one ever said anything against her, and there were no explanations. So the mystery grew. Soon after, there were rumors that my mother had died. But in reality, she had not died until eight or ten years later. I discovered that by visiting her grave long after I had grown.[8]

For many years, I used to imagine that when I grew up, I would romantically find my mother very much like the storybook experiences of which I had been reading. She was always beautiful and like a storybook princess to me. Many of the early novels dramatized such situations. The play *Madame X* is a good example of the period.

Peculiarly, that child imagery became a melody that played a reprise. Many years later, after I had become a motion picture director, Ruth Chatterton was brought to Hollywood to play in *Madame X* with Lionel Barrymore, and Paramount Studios signed her to be starred. I made her first starring picture, called *Sarah and Son*. It was the story of a mother who had been separated from her baby son. After she had attained wealth in a career, she searched for her son and found him.

Pretty fundamental plot—it was an enormous success. By that time, I thought I was sophisticated and was afraid the story might be too "corny," but I knew the story down to the ground as far as emotional content, and with many early theatrical incidents, it evidently had a living quality that was unique and fresh. It is from such incidents that I have had the thought—that all we can ever do in our work is write our own biography. There we are—and our work is limited and enlarged according to how much we have been aware of our own biography and all its details and make some effort toward evaluating them, not always relative to ourselves but in relationship with the whole of life.

However, this inner longing for my mother was balanced by a very healthy, active life at Mam's, and I can't imagine a better person for me to have been with under the circumstances. It is interesting to note how easy we blend with one person and how difficult with another, her very own daughter. Everything went along smoothly and contentedly. Just once, when I was coming out of the door of a neighbor's house, I saw a very bleached blonde woman leaving our house. I didn't recognize who it was at first, but later realized it was my mother—just a glimpse of her after she had gone. I rushed into the house and asked if that was my mother! And was told it was Mother, demanding to see me. Evidently, the orders from my father were not to let her see me if she came, so she was sent away again. I was told that she left with the threat that she would get a lawyer. But I never saw or heard of my mother again until many years later, when I made inquiry and have gathered bits and pieces of a sad life.

I went to a fortune teller once for amusement and I suppose curiosity to find out if someone could tell me something I would believe about my life. She told me every detail of my early life and all about my mother. I was a bit amazed because by then, I didn't think anyone could know anything about my mother. Then she said, "I have watched your career constantly because I knew your mother."

It seems her mother and mine were friends, and it was to their home my mother went when she was first divorced. Of course, this woman was only a few years older than [me] and would have been a young girl then. She had great sympathy for my mother and, of course, told me another side of the story—how my dad had been taken away from my mother by this other woman, my stepmother. However, by now, I think I know all sides and see the inevitability of many things being just as they are.

It's a long road to wisdom.

Part IV

I found peace, at last, with Mam. I made my first girlfriend in spite of the fact that I always played with boys. She was Burt's best girl. She was enough older than I to know how to win my friendship at the same time I was living in the same house with the boy she admired. I now began to feel I belonged. Everyone was my friend, and I loved everyone. Life was pleasant. There were no more tears. Reports of contentment and good conduct must have gone out to my dad and stepmother. Letters were exchanged, and great five-pound boxes of candy and presents arrived periodically from the south. Mabel was very devoted to her mother, and my father's constant devotion to his children made for many indulgences in the luxuries of life.

The day I was about to start school again, Mam asked me if I had another name than Emma. "Oh, yes," I said, "my real name is Dorothy," but because my father's sister's name was Emma, he wanted me to be called that. He had a deep affection for his sister. In fact, all his life he took care of her. He never missed sending his mother part of his earnings, and when she died, he continued to send money to his sister. Until the day she died, he sent one hundred dollars every month and sometimes more. At any rate, my real name was Dorothy, and Mam thought that a much prettier name. I liked it better, too. Emma, the nurse at the Dunlaps, had turned me against the name, and I was glad to have it changed, though I corresponded with Aunt Emma and always signed "Emma." I didn't want to hurt her. She lived in Switzerland and constantly sent me religious postcards and spoke of God and Jesus. My father was not too sure he liked the changing of my name—I believe he was afraid his sister would be hurt. That beginning of subterfuge because of the fear of hurting someone became a subtle poison—which later had to be met head-on in my life. He continued to call me Emma until years later, and he called me Dot.

Stability began to grow, and courage. My stepmother came from pioneer stock. There was a grandmother, too, Mam's mother. She lived on the other side of the tracks. She had recently married a Portuguese street cleaner, to the family's consternation! I used to ride my bicycle over to see her. She was a real pioneer woman, stalwart and strong, built straight up and down, and stood straight as a column—I usually found her sitting on the back steps with a wheezy little black and tan dog and smoking a clay pipe. She used to tell me stories of crossing the plains. At sixteen, she rode a pony all the way from Pennsylvania to San Jose. They were Pennsylvania Dutch. Her grandfather was John Carroll, one of the signers of the Declaration of Independence.[9] Mam was the third white child born in San Jose. And Mabel, my stepmother, would ask for the wildest horses when going out for a drive. These were strong women. Mam's father had come to California in 1847. It took him six months to get here around Cape Horn in a sailing vessel bringing the lumber with him to build his house. These were brave people.

There was a dark alley between our house and the next-door neighbors' house and a large clump of dark bushes on both sides of the entrance to the alley. One night as I rode my bicycle by, I heard something in those bushes and saw them move. I raced to the back of the house—dropped my bicycle and flew upstairs and rushed into the house breathless, and exclaiming there was someone in the bushes as I passed. Calmly, Mam took me by the hand and led me to the spot to investigate. She pushed the bushes aside and there in the corner was a frightened kitten, meowing. She explained that he had probably been on the branches as I passed, and I had frightened him as much as he had frightened me. She seemed to impart to me in that experience that there were usually rational explanations for things that seemed frightening and, if we know what they are, many of the incidents will not be frightening. This idea of knowledge eliminating fear made a deep impression upon me.

If a report card had a low mark, she would say, "You did the best you knew how, didn't you? That's all you need to do. These marks don't matter—they will improve." With that faith in us, of course we tried to do the best we could. Mam was a woman with little or no formal education, but she read constantly, and every morning she read the newspaper from cover to cover. It was through this that I realized the "power of the press." If she read something in the paper, it was true. In later years, she would tell me what the paper had said I was going to do, and I would say, "No, Mam, I'm not going to do that, I'm doing this." She would come back with, "I guess they just haven't told you yet." This, of course, was during her later years. One's family of that other generation doesn't always comprehend that their children have attained a kind of authority of which they never dreamed. There were powers that they had been trained to think were beyond them.

These peaceful days were not to last long. One morning, I was awakened with a violent shaking of my bed, as though the giants of all stories had been let loose and were about to destroy humanity. The roar came from the bowels of the earth, and as far as I was concerned, the world was coming to an end! I had thought about such a thing happening, and here it was.

I rose from the couch where I had been sleeping, and just as I did, a tall glass bookcase was hurled down upon it—then bricks started to come crashing through the window. I looked out, and telegraph poles were swaying like trees, and a huge chimney built on the outside of the house across the street was thrown to the ground. I tried to get to my grandmother's door, but it was uphill. I couldn't make it—then suddenly, I was hurled through the door right into the middle of my grandmother's bed, screaming above the roar, "Mam, what is it?" "It's an earthquake!" she said, at the same time grabbing me and pulling me under the covers and piling pillows on top of me. All I was aware of after that was being rolled from side to side and almost smothering to death. It was only a matter of moments until it was over. I crawled out to see a house in shambles. But my grandmother calmly proceeded to put things in order and started making the familiar movements toward getting breakfast. Then we went out to investigate the damage about us. The old man who lived next door to us was on his front steps in his nightshirt with a vase of carnations in his hand. Great churches on the opposite corners of our block were half-demolished and their steeples tossed into the street. Immediately, news of the quake reached Los Angeles, and my dear vulnerable father came north by whatever vehicle he could command. Trains were not running into the city, and no one was allowed in or out except through the National Guard's okay. All men were commandeered to clear the street of brick and search for bodies. Two days after his arrival, he found us intact except for the chimney down—windows broken and the eaves torn off where our house bumped against the next about eight feet away.

The red glow from the burning city cast a fearful glow on everything, and the booming from whole blocks being dynamited in order to check the blaze was ominous. My father stayed a few days—making the decision that we should all be moved to Los Angeles as soon as he could find a house for us.

For weeks, the earth shook intermittently until our nerves were at the breaking point. We finally got to just sitting and waiting for the quakes to come.

Schools were condemned—soldiers everywhere, and constant lines of refugees passed our house, dragging their worldly goods in sheets and trunks and carts. Our house was filled with several of Mam's San Francisco friends who had been burned out. We set up kind of a canteen. We had water, which was rare, and we all helped to serve some food to people who were hungry. This went on for weeks, until finally, the earth subsided and the refugees were cared for, then the preparations for moving started.

A large house was bought on Wilshire Blvd. and Union Ave. It was just a residential street then, as far as MacArthur Park, then called Westlake Park. From the park on out to the beach were mustard fields. My brother Dave was brought from the east. Burt, Mam, Mam's mother, my stepmother, Dad, and Tom, who visited us periodically; all of us were to live under one roof. Four generations—four separate and distinct families all joined together. I managed to harmonize myself in the situation. But my brother had difficulty making his adjustment to so many people belonging to my stepmother's side of the family. He was never happy there and soon left home to board out near the college he attended. I went through grade school with one accomplishment. I was one of the best baseball players on the boys' team! I rarely played with girls. And girls did not play baseball at that time. How I know I was a good player was at recess or lunch hour or after school, the moment I would appear, I could hear the yells go up: "First Chooser! Second Chooser!" and then my name would be called next! I was a crack first baseman. They could burn the ball into me, and I never missed putting my man out on first. I could bat the ball out farther than most and run faster than any boy except one, Donald Lingle, who was my beau at the time. I rode his bicycle and wore his stickpin. These were the special insignia of a bond. Those were happy days of just pure healthy activity. I never even knew I had a face or a body. My mind was filled with the joyousness of competitive play. I was a reasonably good student—I jumped one grade, B seven, and for years have blamed my lack of knowledge of punctuation on the fact that it must have been missed then—I have no knowledge of having studied it.

The eighth grade was the year I seriously took up tennis. Most of the ball players turned to it also. We built our own court on a vacant lot and learned on the roughest and bumpiest ground. I continued to play with boys. The only girls I knew were friends of my brother or Burt's girlfriends. They were always about but looked upon me as a little girl and mothered me somewhat. At least that was my interest in them. They were not interesting to play with.

There were very few automobiles seen in those days, but down the street from us, there was an apartment house. It had just recently been built, and there was a very pretty lady that came from that apartment house every day and got into an electric automobile. I remember thinking then they were rather like a glass showcase. She was very blonde and very dressed up, and all the kids on the street thought she was very nice because she would smile so pleasantly at us, and we would pause in our games to let her go by. Sometimes she would give us candy as she passed returning home—they were big bags of it. We thought she was quite a wonderful lady. One day, she asked all of us if we would like to come up to her apartment and have ice cream and cake. (We used to call her "the pretty lady.") We all trailed up, a bit shy, as I remember, and a pretty grubby-looking troupe. We were standing about the dining room table, and she was telling a Japanese boy to get plates when suddenly, from a very low sweet voice giving directions—it rose into a harsh, hard shriek of words I had never heard before! The boy had left the electric coffee pot on and it was dry, and this was what had brought on the change of character. We were shocked!—and as I remember, we didn't even wait for ice cream—we all got out of there as fast as we could. We said very little to each other about it. I can remember the effect of disillusion on the part of all of us, and our only balance was regained when we immediately started into another game in the street. The pretty lady passed many times afterward, but there was always a shy response from us all. She no longer was the "pretty lady" as far as we were concerned. It was several years later that I realized she probably was a "kept lady." Certainly, she had all the traditional characteristics. Even to a very fluffy feather boa that she wore. And rather too much makeup for those times.

By the time I graduated from grade school, I'm sure my family had some concern as to what to do with me. I'm sure they decided I needed a little feminine polish because it was decided I should go to a girls' school. So, I was sent to the fashionable Westlake School for Girls. It was a very large house on Alvarado and Sixth Street. My first days have always made me think of Jack London's

White Fang. The white wolf that had such a difficult time adjusting himself to the world because he was different from the other wolves. I thought all the girls at school were such "sissies." I would stand at a distance and throw rocks while they greeted each other in the morning with such affection. Very soon came the day for the seniors to properly subordinate the freshmen. They dressed in long white robes, and we were called before a solemn ceremonial and were told what our conduct should be. I thought this was all pretty silly. They were just "other girls"—what they were doing dictating my conduct. Then we were told to kneel to them! That was too much for me. I stood alone as the others kneeled and gazed out the window. There was no attention paid to me. Soon everyone rose, and the meeting was dismissed.

A few weeks later, the seniors ganged up on me to haze me. They caught me alone, and the whole class was about to rush me off into a car and take me to one of their homes. What their plans were for me, I have no idea because that was a signal for me to let loose with all my boyish strength and "know-how." I went down in the skirmish grabbing legs and throwing girls down—punching and fighting to get free from them, when the principal appeared on the scene. Lifting me from the midst with torn clothes and a generally pretty disheveled appearance, I was told to report to the office for an explanation of this disgraceful and unladylike episode.

I told my side of the story—quietly and unemotionally, I remember. I think I enjoyed the skirmish. I think I was prepared to be rather happy if I was told I could not come back to school. However, I remember making a point of the fact of the injustice of thirty girls against one. That wasn't cricket, from my point of view. I had been used to very fair play with boys. Then I began asking questions. Why should I be asked to kneel to anyone, and why should I allow anyone to rush me off anywhere? I had never done anything to them. I remember the wry smile that played around the corner of that fine woman's mouth. And all she said was, "I shall see that it doesn't happen again. You may return to your classes." Nothing more was said. There were no further references to the incident—it had been completely dropped by everyone. I've often thought if nothing more were learned than that, much of the human relationship troubles would be eliminated. Everyone dramatizes things so much and builds small incidents into major differences. I later became friends with most of those young women. I played tennis on the team with the seniors and for three years held the school tennis championship cup—and won the girl's school championship pennant for Westlake.

There was always much discussion of preparation for college—what course to take—what college to go to. What career to aim for. I'm not sure how I arrived at the decision that I wanted to be a doctor. Possibly a combination of religious influence from my aunt. In reading the Bible, I was imbued with the idea of

Jesus healing the sick and raising the dead. I wanted to heal the sick and raise the dead.

I had made friends with a young married couple who lived across the street from us. He used to play "catch" with me in the evening. His wife was going to have a baby. They used to say they would be perfectly content if they had a little girl who would grow up to be just like me. They were a very loving couple and included me in their affection. I was with them constantly. Mam had her aged mother to care for, and my dad and stepmother were away all day and into the night. I was on my own to some degree. That baby coming was of paramount interest to all of us. Then one day—sadness—she lost her baby. There were weeks I saw those two people suffering. She was months getting well, and my dear friends were so deeply grieved that I was fired with the idea that there should be no such thing as pain—sadness—*death*. I would learn how to prevent this pain and sorrow. So my studies were directed toward that end—four years Latin—two years German—chemistry—biology and all the rest. No tennis my fourth year, just study—U.S.C. pre-med, two years.

War broke out! The First World War. I left school and joined an ambulance corps. The Drake Section Sanitaire. I was too young for the Red Cross—but the French government would take us at eighteen—at twenty-one, I could go overseas. I wanted to get over and drive right up to the frontline trenches. Adventure! Instead, I merely transported medical supplies to the base hospitals and delivered messages for the Intelligence Corps.

In one year, the war was over, and I was looking into space. I had had a taste of the outside world, and I didn't want to go back to school. My family was not very friendly about my ambulance corps duties. I think they would have preferred to have me stay home and help with the housework. I don't just know what was in their minds, but a tension and dissension began to grow. My stepmother didn't approve of my friends, and I stayed away more and more from home. Came in late at night and left in the morning. I went to parties with soldier boys, and I don't think they quite knew just what I was doing or who I was with. But I knew. Commander Starkweather and his wife were very fine people heading the Corps.[10]

I was having dinner with them—a farewell dinner. The war was over in eighteen months, and we were being disbanded. I passed the remark, "Well, where do we go from here?" I had had a taste of independence and being out in the world on my own. I didn't want to go back to school. The two of them started conferring as to what I should do. It was Mrs. Starkweather who made the remark: "Dorothy is a modern girl. She should be connected with modern things. I think she should be in the motion pictures." I have no idea why she associated me with the motion picture business unless it was a field she would like to have been in if she were younger and wanting activity. She was an artist and a writer. I saw some of her writing in rather obscure magazines.

Our Corps was smartly uniformed. Coats like the French Air Force, buttoning across to the shoulder. Short skirts and high leather riding boots. We made quite an impression with whomever we met.

I had met William de Mille, who was in the intelligence department for the studios during the war. Mrs. Starkweather made an appointment for me. He was a director along with his brother Cecil DeMille at the Paramount studios on Vine Street. Their original location. These two men had pioneered the beginning of the Paramount studio. It was then called Famous Players-Lasky Corp. William de Mille had organized many of the departments, including the scenario department.

I was shy about applying for work and would never have followed up the suggestion except that one day, Mrs. Starkweather drove me out and dropped me off at the studio, saying, "Go in and see Mr. de Mille; you have an appointment with him." Then she drove off, leaving me in the middle of the street, wishing I had never opened myself to this ordeal. But I went in. I was not in uniform and not nearly as attractive to Mr. de Mille. He commented on the fact that young ladies should always wear those uniforms. He then said, "Let me see your profile." "Oh, I don't want to be an actress!" I said. "What do you want to do?" he asked. Hesitantly, I grasped at a straw. "Well, maybe I could dress sets." That seemed easy enough to me, but he asked what the period of the furniture was that he had in his office. I did not know. "Franciscan," he told me rather sternly. I remember then having the impression he was like a professor in college. He also looked like the engravings of Shakespeare I had seen. I sat silent. He was quite formidable. Then with a drawl he said, "I think you'd better spend about a week looking around the lot. I'll arrange for you to observe all the departments and go on the sets and watch them shooting pictures."

I'd seen pictures being shot. D. W. Griffith, Mary Pickford, Mabel Normand, Mack Sennett, and all the rest of them used to eat at my dad's restaurant, and seeing actors was not particularly interesting to me. He then told me to come back in a week to see him. That last request was what made it imperative that I observe so I could at least make an intelligent report. I did just what he told me to do. In addition, I talked with his secretary and found out how she started. "Typing scripts," she told me, and now she was in the very important job of being William de Mille's private secretary. I was impressed with that.

I went into cutting rooms—projection rooms—and I visited Cecil DeMille's set. He was making a picture called *Male and Female*. There I saw the personification of directorial authority, and I remember thinking, "Well, if one were going to be in this business, the thing to be was the director. He was the one who told everyone what to do. He was the whole works!"

I returned to William de Mille's office at the end of the week, eager now to be connected with this very colorful activity. I opened the conversation after Mr. de Mille's questioning [me]. "Well?"

"I think I'd like to be in the picture business," I said.

"And where do you think you'd like to start?"

"At the bottom," I said.

"And where do you think the bottom is?" he said grimly.

"Typing scripts, I said.

"For that answer, I'll give you a job," Mr. de Mille [said and] took me right off to the stenographic department and introduced me to Miss Miller, a precise and rigid little English woman. She was told to give me the first opening in the department. Miss Miller took down my name, address, and telephone number. Today, I have been told that is the way one is sure they will never get the job. But I was too young to think anything but what people said they meant.

Days—weeks—a month passed, and one day I ran into one of my Westlake student friends on the street. To my surprise, she was working. "Where?" I asked. At a wholesale coffee house on the east side of Los Angeles down in the wholesale district. This seemed like [an] adventure to me, and I must have expressed a desire to work. I knew I had grown to be a problem to my family. I didn't want to stay home and learn to cook and do the things that all young women should know how to do. Also, there must have been a financial pinch after the war, and a very severe influenza epidemic had taken off many people. I was told one day that my allowance would have to be cut in half from sixty dollars a month to thirty. Thinking this had only to do with a disapproval of me, I rose to my most adolescent independence and announced to my father, "I don't want any money from you. I have friends. I'll manage somehow on my own." Of course, I contemplated leaving home, but I had no place to go. I saw only one way—"Go to work and be independent." [M]y friend expressed an enthusiastic assurance that she was sure there would be a job for me and that she would speak to the boss, who was one of the brothers of the Joannes Brothers Wholesale Coffee House. There were several openings, filing orders or working the switchboard. I was more than happy to accept. I went to work. I filed orders and ran the switchboard. For this, I was given the large sum of twelve dollars a week.

When I told my dad about my job, he seemed to be pleased. He would give me a dollar for every dollar I earned. From then on, my financial independence was assured. There were things about working that I had to get used to—I rather resented the brusque way salesmen came into the office and would speak to me. I'm afraid I felt a little superior to the people about me, but I tried not to show it. I was a working girl now. I liked the atmosphere of coming out at night with all the others after a day's work. There was something particularly interesting about the city downtown at night when everyone was on their way home and the streetlights were lit and it made me feel a part of a very vital life I had not experienced before, mixed with the feeling of independence.

Not three weeks had passed when I plugged into an outside call, and over the switchboard, the voice of Ruby Miller said, "There is an opening in our stenographic department typing scripts, would you like to have the job?" My next question was, "What is the salary?" "Fifteen dollars a week to begin with," she said. That was three dollars a week more than I was getting and that three dollars was the deciding factor. The motion picture studios held no attraction for me. I'd been brought up with actors all my life. In fact, I was just about to make a special place for myself, I thought. I had made a color sketch for a poster advertisement for the Joannes Bros. Coffee—and Mr. Joannes' wife, who was a painter, liked it and had asked to meet me. I was going to have dinner at their house. When I announced that I was leaving to accept a position at the Famous Players-Lasky Studio, the invitation was forgotten, and with courteous regret, I was allowed to leave as soon as I could train another girl to take my place.

I had one moment of regret that I was leaving, and that came when I said goodbye to Spencer, the accountant. He was known as a disgruntled little man. When I first met up with him, all I heard was complaints from him. Not anything directly, but just a general muttering all the time of things that were wrong in the office. He had been with the firm a long, long time, and no one paid much attention to him. His complaints didn't seem to count with anyone, but he was a fixture and a thorn to everyone. He looked undernourished, with narrow shoulders and a very shiny suit, worn thin, and had been cleaned and pressed too many times. His collar was a little too high in order to cover his thin neck but always immaculately clean.

His shirt was worn too many days and always looked mussed. I felt he had made a brave attempt to be as well-dressed as the others. One had the impression he had been at those accounts ever since the firm was established, and that date was obviously stamped on all correspondence. Est. 1886. Spencer learned that I was leaving from Mr. Joannes. He must have been told immediately after I announced my intention because I had planned to tell him myself. I had grown to have an affection for him—we had become friends. I made a point of winning his favor mainly because of my own sensitivity in being in the presence of anyone who would be unpleasant with me. It would have been impossible for me to work with him. I used to help him with his account filing after he had made his entries. This was not my job, but he seemed to be inundated constantly with work and things to be filed. No one seemed to like him. He was crisp and staccato—others thought him grouchy. I had the urge to help him, lighten his burden, and that seemed to soften his general conduct. There were rumors to the effect that at last, old Spencer had met up with someone who could gain his respect enough to make him human.

I had just arrived at my desk when I heard Spencer say, "That's the way with these society girls. They just begin to be of some value and then they up and leave!" I looked over at him, but he never raised his head from making his entries. I knew someone must have told him before I could. I tried to explain to him that I wasn't a society girl, but I did think I would never be very good at office work, and it would be just a matter of a short time until I would leave anyway. I explained how appreciative I was of his kindness to me and letting me learn so much—and he was the one real gentleman in the office. He never looked up at me the whole time. A day or so later was my last day, and he had not spoken to me. When it was time for me to say goodbye to everyone, he was the last one I went to. I put out my hand right under his nose and said, "I do want to say goodbye and thank you for your kindness to me." My hand was extended for a moment without response from him, and then suddenly he was on his feet, grumbled once, gave my hand one down shake and let it drop, then the saddest blue eyes I had ever seen look straight into mine for a moment only, and he sat down as abruptly as had risen and went back to his entries. There was nothing more I could say. I stood for a moment, then left. I had to stop thinking about him because he offered too many characters to me, and I would never know why he was as he was. But he was a gentle man—and the grumblings somehow were a cover that probably made it possible for him to go on.

With trepidation, I faced a new job the next day that I knew entailed typing. I had only typed college notes with two fingers on each hand. To this day, I type the same. But with a little more speed than I did that first day, and if I am careful, with a great deal more accuracy.

Fortunately for me, it was Miss Miller's day off. I was greeted by one of the other typists, Mike Leahy [i.e., Agnes Brand Leahy], a tall, freckle-faced girl with glasses. She was in charge. She directed me to a desk opposite hers in a small office. Miss Miller had left a pile of copy with my name on it. All I was supposed to do was to copy the handwritten pages for one of the scenario writers whose office was down the hall, but I was informed by Mike Leahy that the one thing Miss Miller was a stickler for was letter-perfect copy.

All day I struggled—hitting wrong letters—erasing—and hearing the rat-ti-tat-tat of the typewriter just across from me. Her pile was done hours before the end of the day, and I was left alone to hear my own repeater mind saying, "You aren't a typist—listen to how fast the other girls type—you'll never hold down this job. Why did you want to leave a job that you had learned to do so easily and come to this one that is something you don't know how to do? What are you thinking of? Better quit before you get fired. You couldn't stand to be fired. Better quit before you get fired."

I was in this state when Miss Leahy came in and informed me it was time to go home. I wasn't half through. I asked if it would be all right if I finished the work at home. Without revealing her superior wisdom about me, she said, "Oh, sure. Just be careful not to lose any of the original." And off she went, leaving me to my misery. I saw her beautiful, clean, expert typing laying [sic] on Miss Miller's desk before I left.

That night, I spent the whole night retyping everything I had done through the day and all the balance that had been given me to do. I hardly took time to eat dinner. Carefully, surely, and solidly I pounded the letters out one after the other. I proofread it carefully, made a few unseen corrections, and retyped a few pages. All was in readiness by the time eight o'clock arrived, and I had to leave to face another day of the same. However, the eagerness to make good somehow sustained me.

Miss Miller was at her desk when I arrived. I handed her my copy. A few pleasantries were passed. "How did I get along?" "Oh, fine," was my answer. "I'm awfully slow, though." She assured me I would pick up speed quickly each day. (It was a good thing for me the flu epidemic had made a shortage of typists or I never would have been retained, I'm sure.) Entering my office, I saw the usual pile laying [sic] on my desk. Miss Leahy was hard at it, dashing out copy—greeting me and inquiring after my welfare without pausing to look up. I had made up my mind I would do this day's work more carefully. At least I wouldn't have to do the pages over that I had done. Each one of us put our initials at the bottom of the page so it would be known whose work it was. Hours passed, and my pile showed little evidence of being half-finished, with Miss Leahy pick[ing] up all of her work and t[aking] it into Miss Miller for proofreading. She came back immediately, picked up half of what was left of mine, and said, "Miss Miller thinks your work was very well done for a first day."

It was then I confessed to Mike what I had done. How little of typing I'd ever done and how much I wanted to make good at this job. Did she think I would make it? "Oh, you'll be okay. Just keep at it. You can't help but gather speed. I'll just knock out these few pages for you, and nobody need ever know the difference." She did knock out those pages in no time at all and dropped them on my desk with my initials at the bottom. She took up some more, remaining, and soon I had finished my day's work! What a friend! And the kind of a girl I admire tremendously; "just a *grand* girl." I haven't met too many, but they are the shining lights on one's path.

This procedure continued until I could hold my own. Later, to my satisfaction, when work was slack, the four of us, who typed all the scenarios for the studio, used to race to see who could finish with letter-perfect copy. I was not the first—nor was I last. At the end of three months, a typist was either fired or received a raise of one dollar and a half. I got the raise. My salary would now be sixteen dollars and fifty cents a week.

Naturally, I began to hear of the big salaries people received as actors and directors, but I remember my thought was if I ever make as high as thirty dollars a week, that will be all I shall ever want. That will buy everything that I want. Of course, I was living at home and had no consciousness of what it meant to have to really pay for one's living needs. This was spending money for me, and besides, I had only been working altogether about four months, and I had not even needed to buy myself clothes.

I was kept pretty close to the typewriter those first few months, but there still remain a few outstanding impressions.

Things about me began to take on speed. Boys in uniform were returning to the studio from overseas. It was 1920. The four companies that made up the Lasky Studio now expanded to six. Mary Pickford and Douglas Fairbanks were leaving to start their own company, "The Big Four"—D. W. Griffith, Charles Chaplin, Mary Pickford, and Douglas Fairbanks. Mary Pickford's bungalow, the mark of "star of stars," stood empty. Not until Pola Negri came onto the lot was it occupied.

The Lasky Studio was located at Vine Street and Sunset. Huge pepper trees lined the oiled street. A narrow strip of sidewalk ran between the trees and a row of low, gray wooden buildings, the offices for executives, writers, directors, and business personnel. They were little wooden cubby holes, except for the four or five belonging to the DeMilles, Mr. Lasky, and Charles Eyton, studio manager. These were relatively more luxurious. Cecil DeMille's was the most pretentious. White bear rug and all. There was an opening in the buildings that led to "the lot" where the stages were located. There was a spring gate at that opening, which was guarded by an opening into the casting office. The assistant casting director stood there and saw that everyone going through was eligible to pass. There were no policemen in those days to keep you out. Everyone could go to the casting office window and make himself known.

"Famous Players-Lasky Corp." was the latest letterhead for correspondence. We could have for personal use the old letterhead Jesse Lasky Feature Play Co. That meant that Jesse Lasky, who was president, had negotiated a combine with Adolph Zukor, who owned theaters, and his company was known as Famous Players. This was the beginning of the growth of motion picture theaters and production in Hollywood.

Cecil DeMille presented a formidable and unique character to the studio. He would drive up in a gray Pierce Arrow Roadster with red leather seats. There was nothing like it about. He was at the wheel. Beside him was a uniformed Japanese chauffeur who jumped out, opened the door for him, and then followed just a few steps behind as DeMille strode through the gate, speaking to no one and dressed in a well-tailored gabardine Norfolk suit with leather puttees. It looked a little odd to me at that time, but now I realize it was showmanship. No one else dressed like that, but I soon learned they did wear puttees on location because there were many outdoor pictures, and they had to work in rough country.

Very few people had their own cars in those days. They lived near and walked. But my dad had given me a car the year before. We had cars from the time I entered high school through my persuasion. There were no "No Parking" signs, no need. One day I had parked my car just in front of the entrance when Mr. DeMille's Japanese chauffeur rushed up to me before I could get out and informed me I would have to move. That place belonged to Mr. DeMille. I looked about, and he was sitting in his car waiting. I realized by his expression that I had made an intolerable mistake. I noticed on the curb then, "Reserved for Mr. DeMille." That mark of distinction had grown in the studios. For the first time, I came up against class distinction, or as I prefer to call it, "power distinction." This was no problem for me. I don't believe I had any sense of inferiority or superiority. I was brought up to bow to certain customs, and there was always a sense of social sureness. I've always known no one was really so very superior and that there is a great deal of whistling in the dark when actions seem to have a false superiority.

As I look back, I think Cecil DeMille was having a great time for himself, dressing and acting a part he reveled in. He had attained to being a top movie director then, but he wasn't mature enough to wear the mantle with simplicity, and besides, he was and is a showman. I have heard since that before Cecil came to Hollywood to look the field over, he was an actor out of a job. He was going to join Teddy Roosevelt's Rough Riders in the border warfare. Jesse Lasky, his friend, was so concerned over what might happen to him that he, together with Sam Goldwyn, sent Cecil out to Hollywood to see what was going on. They had heard the motion pictures were beginning to take hold, and most of them were starting up in Hollywood. "Go out and look the place over and tell us what you think." Cecil did and sent back enthusiastic reports. Lasky raised some more money. Cecil rented a barn and started to make pictures. *The Squaw Man* with Dustin Farnum was the first. It was so successful he then started to make one by day and one by night. This was the beginning of a business in which I was to spend my life. Again I found myself strange, out of key with the people, having to make adjustments constantly. Not really at one with them but still in it.

I cannot cover the rest of my biography, but I shall try to set down the incident from which I have attempted to write a short story.

Notes

1. James Graham Fair made a fortune in silver mining in Virginia City, Nevada, and invested heavily in California railroads and San Francisco real estate.
2. Arzner was born on January 3, 1897.

3. According to the 1900 federal census, the Arzner family lived at 608 Franklin St. in San Francisco.
4. The song is "Then I'd Be Satisfied with Life," written by George M. Cohan in 1902.
5. According to various genealogical records, Arzner's uncle was Glasgow-born John Blair Young, and her aunt was Pauline "Lena" Ernstine Wilhelmine Werner, born in Mrotschen, Germany. Their three children were William Young, Pauline "Polly" Young, and John Young. The 1900 federal census lists their address as 1045 62nd St. in Oakland.
6. Arzner may have mixed up Shakespeare and Descartes on this point.
7. "Mam" was Elizabeth Holmes, who, with her husband Thomas Holmes, were the parents of Mabel Holmes Mills, Arzner's stepmother. "Burt" was Mabel Mills's adopted brother Burton Lund, who lived with the Holmes family at 537 Jones St. in Oakland and later with the extended Arzner family in Los Angeles.
8. Arzner's mother died on November 24, 1909.
9. Arzner likely meant John Carroll's cousin, Charles Carroll.
10. The commander of the Los Angeles emergency ambulance drivers' program was in fact Anna Starkweather (the "Mrs. Starkweather" noted in the text), not any male counterpart.

Index

Akins, Zoë, xx, xxix, xxx, xxxii, 33, 116, 130, 166
Alla Nazimova Company, xxvi, 5, 8, 19, 21, 22n1, 54, 84, 103, 127, 143
Anderson, Doris, xx
Anson, James "Yakima Jim," 111, 112
Arzner, David (brother), xxv, 171, 172, 174, 175, 177, 178, 181, 182, 183, 184, 190, 191
Arzner, Dorothy: on actors, 11–12, 13n1, 26, 36, 41, 42–43, 73, 80–81, 101, 117; on ambitious women, 40, 61; on analyzing story, 14, 19, 49, 54, 60; on audiences, 43, 51–52, 69; autobiography (unfinished), xiii, xiv, xvii, xxii, 169–200; on comedy, 20, 119; commercials, xxxii, xxxv, 134, 140, 162, 163, 166; and costumes, xvi, xx, 8, 19, 48, 51, 62n1, 67, 99, 129, 144; on critics, 119; on directing, 3, 17, 20, 21, 22, 23–24, 26, 30–31, 43–44, 53, 68, 70, 71, 79, 80, 106, 107–8, 119–20, 129, 157; directing style, 66–67, 115, 117; Directors Guild of America retrospective on, 136, 138–39; early years, 4–6, 7, 8, 9, 14–15, 17–18, 19, 24–25, 28–29, 40–41, 49–50, 53–54, 59–60, 74, 78, 81, 84, 85, 100–101, 116–17, 123, 139, 141–43; as editor (cutter), 8–9, 19–20, 25–26, 27n2, 29–30, 54, 60, 102, 104–6, 107–9, 114n4, 116, 124–35, 143, 145; on fashion, 63, 64, 65, 79, 83, 91; feminism in film, 136, 138; on filmmaking, 80, 86–87; on future of business, 41, 91; on gender roles in film, 160–61; on her own sexuality, 167–68; on her own success, 100; on Hollywood, 88, 92n1; as instructor, xvii–xviii, xxxv, 97–99, 139; on interviews, 96–97; on intuition, 92; on Katharine Hepburn, 121–22; on leaving film industry, 133–34, 135, 137; on marriage, 31, 61; on men and women, 32–33, 35, 43, 51, 85; on philosophy, 20, 39–40; on rehearsals, 100; as script continuity supervisor, xi, xxvi, xxxv, 22n1; on sets, 99; on sexism in Hollywood, 16, 26, 38, 39, 49, 58, 61, 68, 106, 127, 153, 161–62; on sound, 118–19, 153–55; on technology in film, 157; as typist, xi, xii, xiii, xx, xxvi, xxxv, 14, 18–19, 25, 28, 29, 36, 40, 48, 50, 53–54, 60, 74, 78, 81, 84, 85, 102–3, 117, 124, 141, 143, 162, 197, 198; on women directors, xviii–xix, 3, 4, 5, 15–16, 32, 33, 34–35, 38, 69, 70, 72, 82, 86, 167; as writer, xi, xiv, xxxv, 5, 9, 14, 20, 26, 37, 40, 46–47, 50, 61, 74, 81, 118, 126, 127, 131, 132, 133, 135, 138, 194

Works By: *Anybody's Woman*, xxix, xxxii, 37, 42–43, 44, 50, 91, 100, 116, 119, 129, 130, 162; *Behind the*

INDEX

Make-Up, xxviii, 128; *Blood and Sand*, xiv, xxvii, 8–9, 19, 22, 25, 27n2, 37, 54, 60, 106–7, 108–9, 116, 125, 143–44; *The Bride Wore Red (Once There Was a Lady)*, xxx, xxxiii, 83, 87, 90, 99, 132, 137; *Charming Sinners (The Constant Wife)*, xxviii, 128; *Christopher Strong*, xxix, xxxiii, 58, 80, 83, 89, 91, 119, 121, 130–31, 136, 138, 140, 165, 166; *The Covered Wagon*, xi, xxvii, xxxv, 9, 19, 22, 26, 30, 37, 54, 60, 104, 105, 108, 109–11, 112, 113n3, 116, 125–26, 143, 145–46, 149; *Craig's Wife*, xii, xvii, xx, xxx, 68, 69, 71, 73, 74, 75, 80, 83, 87, 90, 99, 100, 118, 131–32, 133, 136, 140, 146, 163; *Dance, Girl, Dance*, xxxi, xxxiii, 116, 133, 136, 140; *Fashions for Women*, xv, xix, xxvii, 3, 9, 16, 21, 26, 30, 37, 40, 50, 54–55, 61, 68, 73, 81, 83, 90, 97, 117–18, 127–28, 139, 152; *First Comes Courage*, xxi, xxxi, 128, 133, 137, 140, 158–59, 166; *Get Your Man*, xx, xxi, xxviii, 9, 17, 22, 34, 41, 71, 72n1, 90, 146–47, 156n11; *Glorifying the American Girl*, xx, xxviii, 154–55; *Honor Among Lovers*, xxix, 80, 128, 129; *The Last of Mrs. Cheyney*, 83; *Manhattan Cocktail*, xxviii, 17, 22, 34, 41, 91, 119, 156; *Merrily We Go to Hell*, xv, xvi, xxviii, xxix, 73, 80, 91, 118, 119, 128, 129, 130, 165; *Nana*, xxix, xxx, 57, 66–67, 80, 91, 92, 106, 116, 117, 119, 128, 131, 133; *Old Ironsides*, xi, xiv, xxvii, 5, 9, 19–20, 26, 30, 39, 54, 96, 116, 148, 152, 156nn6–7; *The Six Best Cellars*, 103, 143; *Stronger Than Death (The Secret Doctor of Gaya)*, xxvi, 22n1, 103, 127; *Ten Modern Commandments*, xxvii, 3, 9, 17, 22, 34, 41, 90; *The Wild Party*, xv, xvi, xxviii, xxxiii, 21, 22, 34, 41, 42, 44, 50, 73, 90, 91, 99, 116, 119, 128, 136, 139; *Working Girls*, xxix, 116, 118, 119, 130

Arzner, Janet "Jennie" Young (mother), xxv, 171, 172, 174, 175, 178, 180, 182, 186, 187

Arzner, Ludwig "Louis" (father), xiv, xvii, xxv, xxxiii, 4, 7, 17, 24, 54, 59, 62, 78, 79, 101, 116–17, 123, 137, 141, 142, 171, 175, 178, 180–81, 182, 183, 184, 188, 190

Ball, Lucille, 115, 116, 133, 136, 140
Bandaranaike, Sirimavo, 164
Banton, Travis, xx
Bell, Mildred, 143
Bill of Divorcement, A (Cukor), 57, 83
Boles, John, 68, 80, 147
Boleslawski, Richard, xxx, 83, 117
Bow, Clara, xv, xvi, xxvii, xxviii, 9, 17, 21, 28, 34, 37, 41, 42, 44, 50, 51–52, 71, 73, 89, 90, 99, 115, 116, 127, 128, 136, 139, 146–48, 153–54, 162
Boyd, William, 12
Bridges, Art, 149–50
Brook, Clive, 37, 42, 115, 116, 119
Brown, Clarence, 11
Brown, Karl, 110, 145
Brownlow, Kevin, v, xii, xiii, xiv, xv, xvi, xvii, xviii, xxi, xxii–xxiii, 96–113, 114n4, 116, 141–55
Bryant, Charles, 103
Burke, Billie, xxxii, 91, 130

Cagney, James, 72
Capra, Frank, xi, xvi, 117, 138
Carr, Harry, 148
Carroll, Nancy, 34, 37, 42, 90–91, 115, 119, 128
Chaplin, Charlie, xiv, 17, 59, 117, 137, 199
Chatterton, Ruth, xvi, xxix, xxx, 33, 34, 37, 41, 42–43, 44, 50, 58, 64, 65, 72, 73, 80, 91, 100, 115, 116, 128, 129, 162, 186

Chevalier, Maurice, xvi, 43
Clive, Colin, 122, 130
Cohn, Harry, xvi, xxi, xxx, 100, 118, 126, 132, 136, 137, 139, 140, 151, 152, 158–59, 164, 165
Columbia Pictures, xvi, xxvi, xxx, xxxi, 83, 118, 126–27, 132, 133, 140, 159, 160, 165
Coppola, Francis Ford, xxxiii, 97, 136, 139
Crawford, Joan, xxx, xxxii, 81, 83, 90, 99, 115, 132, 134, 140, 159, 163, 165, 166
Crisp, Donald, xx, xxvi, 103, 104, 105, 107, 108, 127, 143
Cruze, James, xiv, xv, xx, xxvii, xxviii, xxxv, 5, 6, 7, 8–9, 17, 19–20, 22, 26, 30, 40, 54, 59–60, 84, 104, 108, 109, 110, 111, 112, 113, 116, 117, 125–26, 127, 144, 145, 148–49, 150–51, 156n5

Daniels, Bebe, 104, 108, 125
Davis, Bette, 160–61
de Mille, William, xiv, xx, xxvi, 5, 8, 18, 27n1, 38n1, 40, 54, 60, 78, 81, 84, 85, 101, 103, 117, 124, 141, 142, 143, 194, 195
de Purucker, Gottfried, 35n1
de Rosa, Helen, 112
Decatur, Stephen, 148
DeMille, Cecil B., xi, 5, 25, 27n1, 37, 38, 101, 124, 127, 142, 194, 199, 200
Dietrich, Marlene, xvi, 81, 129, 161
Doherty, Ethel, xx

Famous Players-Lasky, xi, xii, xiii, xxvi, xxvii, xxviii, xxxv, 5, 60, 113, 124, 144–45, 156n5, 194, 196, 199. *See also* Paramount Pictures
Fischbeck, Harry, 115–16
Flesh and the Devil (Brown), 11
Forbes, Ralph, 12
Ford, John, 136

Four Sons (Ford), 12
Franck, Cesare, 88, 90
Frankau, Gilbert, xxix, 119, 121
Franklin, Sidney, 102

Gandhi, Indira, 164
Gangelin, Paul, xx, xxvii
Garbo, Greta, xvi, xxx, 62n1, 64, 81, 131, 135, 161
Geraghty, Tom, 4
Gill, David, 141
Girl Crazy (Sennett), 129
Girl from Trieste, The (Molnar), xxx, 9, 132, 137. *See also* Dorothy Arzner, Works By: *The Bride Wore Red* (*Once There Was a Lady*)
Gish, Dorothy, 4
Glyn, Elinor, xxvii, 148
Goldwyn, Samuel, 56, 57, 58, 62n1, 63–64, 66, 106, 117, 131, 133, 135, 139, 200
Grand Opera House, 101, 142, 181, 184
Griffith, D. W., xiv, 4, 7, 17, 115–16, 123, 141, 194, 199

Harriet Craig (Sherman), xx, 118, 163
Hart, William S., xiv, 4, 7, 17, 59, 117, 119
Hawley, Wanda, 108, 125
Hepburn, Katharine, xiv, xxix, 57–58, 64, 65, 71–72, 80, 83, 89, 91, 115, 119, 121–22, 128, 130, 135, 136, 137, 140, 165–66
Heron, Nan, xxvi, 103, 104, 143
Hobby, Oveta, xx
Hoffman Café (The Hoffman), xiv, xxv, 4, 7, 17, 59–60, 79, 116–17
Hopkins, Miriam, 64, 65

Ince, Thomas H., 4
International Festival of Women's Film, xxxiii, 117
Intolerance (Griffith), 141, 155

206　INDEX

Kahanamoku, Duke, 150, 156n7
Kaplan, Billy, 106
Kate: The Life of Katharine Hepburn (Higham), 121–22
Keays, Vernon, 113, 145
Keefe, Dan, 4
Kelly, George, xx, 68, 118, 132, 136, 140, 163
Kerrigan, Warren, 105, 112

Lackaye, Wilton, 142
Lasky, Jesse L., xv, xxx, xxxii, 3, 5, 9, 19, 21, 22, 60, 61, 118, 127, 148, 156n8, 199, 200
Lawrence, Viola, 133
Leahy, Agnes Brand "Mike," xx, 102–3, 198
Levy, Al, 79, 80
Lorenz, Edward, 93
Love, Bessie, 100, 113
Lubitsch, Ernst, xi, 99, 117
Lupino, Ida, 100, 166–67

Maedchen in Uniform (Sagan), 167
Magnascope, 151, 156n8
Male and Female (DeMille), 101, 142, 194
March, Fredric "Freddy," xvi, 41, 42, 72, 73, 80, 91, 115, 116, 119, 128, 129, 136, 139
Marion, Frances, 58
Mason Opera House, 101
Mayer, Louis B., xxi, 135, 137, 139, 161, 164, 167
Me: Stories of My Life (Hepburn), 121
Meeker, George, 12
Meir, Golda, 164
Miller, Ruby, 96, 102, 124, 196
Milton, Robert, xx, xxviii, xxxii, 128
Minter, Mary Miles, 108, 125
Montgomery, Robert, 83
Morgan, Marion, xi, xxi, xxvii, xxviii, xxxii, 62n3, 146, 169
Motion Picture Production Code, 158–60

Nagel, Conrad, 12
Naldi, Nita, 109, 125
Niblo, Fred, 109, 125, 127
Normand, Mabel, xiv, 4, 194

Oberon, Merle, 115, 128
O'Hara, Maureen, 115, 116, 133, 136, 140

Paramount Pictures, xi, xiii, xix, xx, xxviii, xxix, xxxiii, xxxv, 8, 9, 14–15, 21, 22, 25–26, 28, 29, 30, 34, 36, 37, 42, 49, 50, 54, 71, 73, 84, 101, 102, 103, 104, 109, 113, 116, 118, 124–25, 126, 127, 128, 129, 130, 136, 138, 139, 141, 142, 143, 144, 146, 149, 150, 151, 152, 153, 154, 156n9, 157, 161, 186, 193, 194
Pasadena Playhouse, xviii, xxxii, xxxv, 118, 133–34, 137, 140, 166
Pickford, Mary, xiv, xxviii, 123, 141, 153, 194, 199
Pommer, Erich, xxxi, 133

Radio Pictures Corporation, 57
Rainer, Luise, xxx, 83, 87, 99, 132
Ralston, Esther, xxvii, xxviii, 9, 16, 21, 26, 30, 34, 37, 40, 42, 50, 54, 61, 73, 81, 83, 90, 97, 115, 118, 127–28, 152, 154
Realart, xxvi, xxx, 27n2, 108–9, 116, 124–25, 139. *See also* Famous Players-Lasky; Paramount Pictures
Ripley, Arthur, 97–98
Rogers, Ginger, xxx, 73, 115, 129
Rork, Sam, 4
Russell, Rosalind, xvii, 68, 71, 73, 74, 80, 90, 100, 115, 118, 131, 136, 137, 140, 163

Sagan, Leontine, 167–68
Schulberg, B. P. (Ben), xv, 5, 16, 30, 54, 126, 127, 146, 151, 153
Selznick, David, xxix, 57, 130
Sennett, Mack, 4, 17, 59, 117, 123, 194

Shearer, Norma, 40
Slesinger, Tess, xx
Sondergaard, Gale, 92n1
Soren, David, xiii, xxii
Sorrows of Satan (Griffith), 115–16
Stallings, Laurence, xiv, xv, 5, 9, 20, 37, 148, 151
Starkweather, Anna, 27n1, 100, 101, 193–94, 201n10
Sten, Anna, 56–57, 62n1, 63–65, 66, 80, 91, 115, 117, 128, 131
Sturges, Preston, xx, xxxi
Symphony in D Minor (Franck), 88, 92

Talmage, Constance, 4
Talmage, Natalie, 4
Thalberg, Irving, xxx, 161
Toland, Gregg, xx, 92, 106, 116
Torrence, Ernie, 113
Tracy, Spencer, 166
Tuchock, Wanda, 131

University of California, Los Angeles (UCLA), xxxiii, xxxv, 93, 97, 113n1, 118, 134, 136, 137, 139, 140

University of Southern California (USC), xxvi, 101, 117, 142, 155n2

Valentino, Rudolph, xxvii, 8–9, 19, 22, 25, 37, 54, 60–61, 109, 116, 125, 143–44
Vidor, Charles, xxxi, 117, 159
Vitaphone, 156n10

Wanger, Walter, 126, 127, 151–52, 161–62
Washburn, Bryant, 103
Weber, Lois, xi, 14, 24, 36, 45, 58, 79, 100, 120, 203
Wellman, William, 118, 136
Westlake School for Girls, xxv, xxvi, 7, 18, 24, 36, 40, 102, 117, 191–92, 195
Whale, James, 159
White, Alice, 149
Wilker, Otto, 88
Williams, Frank, 114n5
Wise, Robert, 116, 136
Women's Army Auxiliary Corps, xx, xxivn18, xxxi, xxxv, 166

Zanuck, Daryl, 106, 153
Zukor, Adolph, 127, 153, 199

About the Editor

Martin F. Norden (1951–2023) taught film history and screenwriting as professor of communication at the University of Massachusetts Amherst. He has more than one hundred publications to his credit and presented his film research at dozens of professional conferences across North America and Europe. He served as a consultant on the documentary films *CinemAbility* and *Be Natural: The Untold Story of Alice Guy-Blaché*. He is editor of *Lois Weber: Interviews*, published by University Press of Mississippi.

www.ingramcontent.com/pod-product-compliance
Lightning Source LLC
Chambersburg PA
CBHW021837220426
43663CB00005B/283